Making Disciples

2nd Edition

Making Disciples

2nd Edition

EDITED BY

M. JANE CAREW

Our Sunday Visitor Publishing Division
Our Sunday Visitor, Inc.
Huntington, IN 46750

Nihil Obstat
Rev. Michael Heintz
Censor Librorum

Imprimatur
✠ John M. D'Arcy
Bishop of Fort Wayne-South Bend
April 11, 2005

The *Nihil Obstat* and *Imprimatur* are official declarations that a book or pamphlet is free of doctrinal or moral error. No implication is contained therein that those who have granted the *Nihil Obstat* and *Imprimatur* agree with the content, opinions, or statements expressed.

11 10 09 08 07 06   1 2 3 4 5 6 7 8 9

Our Sunday Visitor Publishing Division
Our Sunday Visitor, Inc.
200 Noll Plaza
Huntington, IN 46750

ISBN-13: 978-1-59276-138-8
ISBN-10: 1-59276-138-0 (Inventory No. X189)

Cover design by Troy Lefevra
Cover photo by Sharon Little (courtesy of *Today's Catholic*, Diocese of Fort Wayne-South Bend)
Interior design by Sherri L. Hoffman

PRINTED IN THE UNITED STATES OF AMERICA

Table of Contents

Foreword

The Rite of Christian Initiation of Adults and Church renewal

We live in a time when the Church is called to renewal. True renewal and reform within the Church always includes grasping afresh the Church's apostolic mission, internalizing it, and living it. Central to this mission is instruction in the faith. As part of this renewal, the Church has received a gift in the Rite of Christian Initiation of Adults.

This Rite, specifically geared toward those who have not been baptized, presents a liturgical structure, very ancient and yet new, through which these catechumens find themselves drawn to Christ and the Catholic Church. In a profound way, they experience the call of Christ present in the Church, and most especially in the Holy Liturgy.

Each Lent, in cathedrals throughout the land, bishops experience this renewal in a way that is most encouraging as they preside and preach at the Rite of Election. At this time, not only catechumens but also candidates, those already baptized but not yet in full communion with the Catholic Church, come forward. All begin their last steps toward baptism at the Easter Vigil, or toward full communion with the Church during Holy Week.

The importance of instruction

It has become increasingly clear to pastors, as already stated in the Rite itself, that these moments of great meaning for the community and for the individual soul, take on the fullness intended by the Holy Spirit only when the liturgical preparation, so beautiful and enriching in itself, is accompanied by a catechesis which is comprehensive and thorough.

People entering the Catholic Church, either through Baptism or the Profession of the Faith, are searching for Christ in the fullness of His revelation and truth. They have a right to such instruction; and those of us who are catechists and teachers of the faith have the obligation of giving it to them. In this, we are only following the practice of the Fathers of the Church who, we are told, presented a catechesis of three full years. St. Cyril of Jerusalem (+ c. 386), preaching in the middle of the fourth century, stated clearly to his listeners the importance of a kind of instruction which is thorough and systematic for those preparing for Baptism:

> **Be faithful in your attendance at the catechesis. Try not to be distracted during instruction (even if it seems lengthy). You are preparing yourself for a battle.... Study what you are taught and hold onto it forever. Do not confuse your baptismal preparation with ordinary sermons (as important as these are). But if the systematic instruction regarding the waters of new birth is neglected, when possibly can it be duplicated? ... Catechesis is like a building. Unless we methodically and carefully assemble the whole structure, we will have problems with both leakage and dry-rot. No, stones must be put one on top of the other sequentially, until the whole structure rises from the foundation: you are like stones of knowledge and you must be instructed in the doctrine of the living God, of the Judgment, of Christ, and of the Resurrection; these things are mentioned now in a kind of random way, but**

eventually the entire structure will fit together in a harmonious way. Unless you grasp the unity of the whole design, holding the parts together in your mind in an orderly way, your house will be a ruin, despite the best efforts of the builder.

— Cyril of Jerusalem, *Procatechesis* 10-11

Another great gift

Over 10 years ago, the Church experienced another gift with the publication of the *Catechism of the Catholic Church*. This compendium of Church teaching is, as Pope John Paul II has declared, "a sure norm for teaching the faith." These two documents taken together present to us an extraordinary opportunity. While respecting that part of the Rite of Christian Initiation of Adults, which is experiential and profoundly prayerful, we must also present to our inquiring catechumens and candidates a period of instruction which is comprehensive and rich, and which is faithful to the *Catechism of the Catholic Church*.

In this text, Sister Jane Carew, director of the Office of Catechesis of the Diocese of Fort Wayne-South Bend, respecting both the *Catechism* and the Rite of Christian Initiation of Adults, has done a great service for parishes and pastors.

If properly used by catechists, this will respond to the question of many pastors. Are our catechumens and candidates being properly instructed before they come to the Rite of Election?

The Catholic Church has the great tradition of respecting faith and reason. Priests from Africa tell me that in the churches of Africa they still follow the three-year period of instruction and teaching so common in the early Church, where the great Fathers and Bishops of the East and West were often the teachers.

This document provides a period of instruction over twelve months. Many working in this ministry of preparation of adults for entrance into the Catholic Church consider this to be the minimum.

It can be asserted that in this document, *Making Disciples, 2nd Edition*, we have the best text available in our country. It draws together and respects both the Rite of Christian Initiation and the *Catechism of the Catholic Church*. It responds to the great need that pastors and catechists have for a text which gives assurance, if followed carefully, that our people are sufficiently prepared for the great mystery they will be receiving at Easter.

I commend Sister Jane Carew and her staff for this great gift to our Church in this country.

✠ JOHN M. D'ARCY
Bishop of Fort Wayne-South Bend

Introduction

Many people who get involved in working with the RCIA in their parish find themselves being asked to do things they don't quite understand, without anyone explaining why they're doing them. Why are there all these ceremonies with their unfamiliar names? How do you prepare someone to be a Catholic — what do they need to know? Where did this RCIA come from, anyhow? How is it supposed to work?

It's much easier to do something if you understand *why* you're doing it. It's much easier to help people give their lives to God as members of the Catholic Church through the RCIA, if it's understood where the RCIA comes from, what its purpose is, and why it is set up the way it is. These introductory pages will provide basic answers to these questions, and explain how this collection of celebrations of the Word with catechesis for catechumens fits into the purpose and structure of the RCIA.

Where did the RCIA come from?

In the very first document promulgated by the Second Vatican Council, *The Constitution on the Sacred Liturgy* (1963), the Council Fathers called for the restoration of the catechumenate for adults (CSL 64). In the *Decree on the Missionary Activity of the Church* (1965), the bishops spelled out in greater detail what this catechumenate should look like:

> Those who, through the Church, have accepted from God a belief in Christ should be admitted to the catechumenate through liturgical rites. The catechumenate is not a mere expounding of doctrines and precepts, but a training period for the whole Christian life. It is an apprenticeship of appropriate length, during which disciples are joined to Christ their Teacher. Therefore, catechumens should be properly instructed in the mystery of salvation and in the practice of Gospel morality. By sacred rites which are to be held at successive intervals, they should be introduced into the life of faith, liturgy, and love which God's People lives. Then, when the sacraments of initiation have freed them from the power of darkness (cf. Col 1:13), having died with Christ, been buried with Him, and risen with Him (cf. Rom 6:4-11; Col 2:12-13; 1 Pt 3:21-22; Mk 16:16), they receive the Spirit (cf. 1 Thes 3:5-7; Acts 8:14-17) who makes them adopted sons, and celebrate the remembrance of the Lord's death and resurrection together with the whole People of God.
>
> It is the desire of this Council that the liturgy of the Lenten and Easter seasons be restored in such a way as to dispose the hearts of the catechumens to celebrate the paschal mystery at whose solemn ceremonies they are reborn to Christ through Baptism.
>
> But this Christian initiation through the catechumenate should be taken care of not only by catechists or priests, but by the entire community of the faithful, especially by the sponsors. Thus, right from the outset the catechumens will feel that they belong to the People of God. Since the life of the Church is an apostolic one, the catechumens should also learn to cooperate actively, by the witness of their lives and by the profession of their faith, in the spread of the Gospel and in the upbuilding of the Church (14).

NOTES...

In 1972, the *Rite of Christian Initiation of Adults* (RCIA) gave concrete form to the Council's call for the Church to restore the early Church's practice of preparing people for Baptism. But what exactly *was* the Council trying to restore? How *were* Christians prepared for Baptism in the early Church?

How were Christians prepared for Baptism in the early Church?

When Christianity first began to spread throughout the Greco-Roman world, the dominant culture of that world was often hostile to the new faith. For most of the first four centuries Christian worship was a crime punishable by death, and Christians who gathered to celebrate the Eucharist could pay for it with their lives. When people who had been raised with the values of that culture became convinced of the truth of the Christian Gospel and wanted to become Christians, they had to make a radical break with their culture. Their understanding of what life was for had to change, and their whole life-style had to change.

Those who wanted to become followers of Jesus Christ as part of the community of His followers, the Church, needed time to learn to live as His faithful disciples. They needed time not only to learn *what* His teachings were, but also to learn how to live according to His teachings in their daily lives, because they had to be able to change their behavior. And they needed time to learn how to hear God speak to them in prayer. Conversion to Jesus Christ and membership in His Body, the Church, required a whole new way of thinking and living.

The Church community knew that it was crucial for converts to be prepared carefully before they could be admitted to Baptism because, when they were baptized into Christ and became part of His Body, these converts would receive His own Spirit. Today we can be so used to repeating the theological truth that Christians receive the Holy Spirit at Baptism that we hardly stop to think about what an incredible thing we're saying. At Baptism, the Holy Spirit, the Third Person of the Blessed Trinity — comes to dwell in human beings.

For the adult converts baptized in the early Church, who could actually *experience* the Spirit coming to in dwell them, this made a tremendous difference. They described how, after Baptism, God's Spirit living in them changed the way they thought about things and changed what they desired. The Church community knew that people were not ready to receive Christ's Spirit at Baptism until they were capable of living in conscious obedience to His Spirit dwelling in them, so that they would not grieve the Spirit (cf. Eph 4:30), and would be able to be faithful to Christ in times of persecution.

In order to prepare converts to receive the Holy Spirit and to live faithful Christian lives by yielding to the power of the Spirit living in them, the early Church developed the *catechumenate.* The catechumenate was a period of training during which people (now known as *catechumens)* who wanted to give their lives to Christ as part of the Church learned how to live as members of the *faithful* (those already baptized).

Throughout their time as catechumens, converts were instructed in the teachings of Christ in the context of liturgical rites. Here, in a setting of communal worship, catechumens listened to proclamation of Scripture and preaching that flowed from that proclamation. This preaching proclaimed the mystery of Who God had revealed Himself to be through His actions in human history and sought to draw the catechumens into the mystery of God's relationship with the human race.

In this kind of teaching, which took place in the context of worship and prayer, the very nature of the teaching was affected because it was part of a celebration of worship. The teaching, or *catechesis,* actually became part of the act of worship, so that catechesis in the early Church was not at all like presenting information in a classroom lecture while those attending took notes. This liturgical catechesis accomplished two things simultaneously.

NOTES...

First, catechesis had to explain Who God is. But how can we know what God is like? How does God act in relationship with human beings? What can we expect from Him if we enter into relationship with Him? We can find answers to these questions by studying the encounters men and women have had with God that are recorded in Scripture. The first thing catechesis did, then, was to explain Who God has revealed Himself to be through His covenant with Israel, culminating in His definitive revelation in Jesus Christ, and what it is like to live in relationship with this God.

Catechists would tell the story of how God acted with Abraham and Sarah in calling them to faith, or how God worked in the life of David when He called him to repent. "If you respond to God's call to you the way they did," the teachers would assure their catechumens, "God will act in the same way with you." Catechists would describe to those seeking salvation how God has shown He is consistent in His desire to save. "He freed the children of Israel from slavery, He rescued Daniel from the lions — and so He will rescue you," the teachers would proclaim.

This catechesis also explained what it would mean for the converts to live their lives in relationship with the living Person of Jesus Christ, the Risen Lord Who pours out His Spirit of Sonship so that the baptized can live a completely new life of love and praise and obedience to the God they now know as Father. Catechesis described what a life directed by the indwelling Holy Spirit looks like, what it means to behave as Christ's disciples in daily life. Here, too, in explaining Christian moral teaching, catechists based their teaching on examples taken from Scripture.

The first thing that catechesis did, then, was to make clear who God had not revealed Himself to be and how men and women are called to respond. But second, even while this liturgical catechesis told the story of how God had acted to save, *simultaneously* it sought to draw the converts into that story, so that their lives would be the latest chapters in the story of how God calls and redeems a People. The catechesis of the early Church sought to be a vehicle through which the Holy Spirit could touch the hearts of listeners and convert them and draw them into relationship with God in Christ.

One way to get a sense of how liturgical catechesis worked in these two ways at once is to envision what happens when the tide comes in on a beach. The teaching about Who God has revealed Himself to be in His relationship with human beings was like powerful waves breaking over the listeners, surrounding them with the knowledge they needed to enter into a saving relationship with God in Christ. But the waves brought with them an undertow, as the catechists sought to be instruments through which God could work to draw the catechumens into this saving relationship as an experiential reality.

There are good examples of this kind of liturgical catechesis as it took place in fourth-century Jerusalem. Every morning during Lent, converts preparing for Baptism at Easter came to church for catechesis. After prayer and exorcism, they would hear a reading from Scripture which was directly related to the topic to be presented that day. Then the Bishop of Jerusalem himself, Cyril, delivered the catechesis. In his first few catecheses Cyril gave clear explanations of sin, repentance, faith, and Baptism. In the remainder of his catecheses, he took the articles of the Creed and explained them one by one, using Scripture.

But Cyril's catecheses are not dry lectures on theological concepts. The bishop himself says that he has not come to offer abstract speculation, but to "make faith" in his listeners, as the Holy Spirit works through him. As Cyril tells the story of how from the beginning of the human race God has acted to bring salvation, he encourages his listeners to identify with those God has saved in Scripture. As the converts identify with those who have gone before them in salvation history, they themselves become part of it.

NOTES...

There is no separation here between conversion of heart and conversion of mind. Converts are being drawn to a deeper knowledge and a deeper love of God simultaneously, so that they will be able to surrender their lives to Him at Baptism. And this simultaneous conversion of mind and heart is being mediated through public rites of communal worship, not private, one-on-one sessions for instruction. Many members of the Church community were involved in helping the Church prepare converts for Baptism — by evangelizing, serving as sponsors or godparents, and teaching. The early Church understood that conversion to Christianity involves the whole Church community, and that since the place where the Church most fully realizes and expresses her identity is in worship, conversion is mediated through liturgical rites.

Through this kind of liturgical catechesis, converts were gradually prepared to surrender their lives to Christ in Baptism, where they would die and rise with Him and receive His Spirit. It was this kind of preparation for Baptism that formed saints, martyrs, and holy doctors in the early Church and helped enable Christianity to grow from the faith of a handful of Palestinian Jews to the official religion of the Roman Empire by the end of the fourth century.

This was the tradition that the bishops of Vatican II had in mind when they called for the restoration of the catechumenate and its rites. The reason that these rites needed to be restored was that over the centuries the practice of the Church had changed. As infant Baptism became the norm, liturgical catechesis for those preparing for Baptism gradually disappeared. Those who were baptized as infants were given various kinds of instruction as they grew. The catechesis of adults who had not been raised as Christians became mostly a matter of providing them with facts concerning Catholic doctrinal belief, and asking them to assent to it. By the generation before the Second Vatican Council, converts were usually instructed individually by a priest, and the rite of Baptism itself was performed more or less privately.

Why did the Church restore the catechumenate?

Why *did* Vatican II call for a return to the way the early Church prepared adult converts for Baptism? When the bishops first called for a restoration of the catechumenate in 1963, they seem to have had in mind primarily the needs of "mission countries." They were thinking about places where, just as in the early Church, Christianity is in conflict with the dominant culture. Perhaps practices such as voodoo or spiritism are common, or polygamy is the norm. Perhaps because of this conflict between Christianity and culture, converts are disowned by their families when they decide to become Christian, needing emotional and even material support.

Today, however, it is clear that the restoration of the richness of the early Christian rites of initiation is appropriate in other countries as well. In the West, it is no longer accurate to speak of the dominant culture as being Christian. Simply growing up in our society will not teach a person how to be a Christian, how to value what Christians value, as may have sometimes been possible in, for example, some areas of medieval Europe. When an adult in *any* country today decides to be baptized into the Catholic Church, it is not enough to give the convert a couple of pamphlets or classes and a quick baptismal ceremony and then expect that he or she will be able to live a Christian life. Converts do need information, but they also need formation. They need to learn how to know and love God, and how to live in loving and obedient relationship with Jesus Christ as part of His Body, the Church. And just as in the early centuries, that takes time.

When scholars compiled the RCIA their goal was to put together a modern equivalent of early Church practice, which would help people yield to the grace of conversion. It must never be forgotten that no human teacher can convert anyone. Only God can convert people, but in the experience of the Catholic community, God works in a special way to bring about conversion *through* ritual actions and the proclamation of Scripture when the Church is gathered for worship. That's the purpose behind the RCIA taking the form it does — to offer the Church a carefully-structured sequence of liturgical rites *through* which God can touch people and convert them to Himself, to living under the Lordship of Jesus Christ in the power of the Holy Spirit as members of the Catholic Church.

NOTES...

What is the structure of the RCIA?

What is this structure and how do the liturgical rites fit into it? It's important to remember that the RCIA is a *rite;* in other words, the liturgical form through which the Church celebrates the sacrament of Baptism for adults. In itself, the RCIA is not a program, or a course, or some kind of emotional process any more than any other sacramental rite is. The RCIA is made up of many liturgical services for specific occasions, which are also called rites, and which take place over a period of time during which converts increasingly surrender their lives to Christ. The Church understands that people experiencing conversion go through various stages in coming to Christ and that important moments in these stages need to be marked by liturgical celebrations. The RCIA is divided into four stages, and throughout these stages many people from the parish community are needed to help the converts, just as in the early Church. It is not possible to celebrate the RCIA in a parish without a large number of parishioners being involved.

The first stage of the RCIA is *Evangelization* (RCIA #36-40). During this stage men and women not raised as Christians come to believe that Jesus Christ is Lord, the Son of God Who gave His life to save them from their sins and from death. When converts come to the point that they believe in Christ, have a basic understanding of Catholic teaching, and want to give their lives to Christ as part of the Church, they are ready to be admitted into the catechumenate. This is celebrated at the *Rite of Acceptance into the Order of Catechumens* (RCIA #41-74).

This brings the converts into the second stage, the *Catechumenate* (RCIA #75-117), which the RCIA refers to as the "lengthy period of formation of the catechumens' minds and hearts" (RCIA #118). During this stage the catechumens are learning how to become part of the faithful, the baptized members of the Church. The catechumenate is centered around liturgies of the Word where catechumens are instructed (RCIA #81). Drawing on the experience of the early Church, the RCIA envisions catechesis as taking place in the context of prayer and communal worship. When the catechumens have learned enough about converting to be able to keep on converting for the rest of their lives, and their faith is mature enough for them to be members of the baptized faithful, they are chosen or "elected" to be baptized at Easter. This is celebrated in the *Rite of Election,* normally on the First Sunday of Lent. At the *Rite of Election* (RCIA #118-137), the catechumens, now called *Elect,* enter into the third stage.

The third stage of the RCIA, the period of *Purification and Enlightenment* (RCIA #138-184), normally takes place during Lent. By this time, the converts have a thorough knowledge of the faith and are living a Christian life. The time of *Purification and Enlightenment* is not for instruction in new material, but is like an intensive retreat during which converts can make a final, serious, spiritual preparation for Baptism. During this stage, two special kinds of liturgical rites, called *Scrutinies* and *Presentations,* are celebrated to help the converts. There are three *Scrutinies* (RCIA #141-156; 164-177), which are celebrated on the Third, Fourth, and Fifth Sundays of Lent. At these *Scrutinies,* the Elect are drawn through the liturgy into a deeper and deeper surrender of themselves to God in Christ, through

NOTES...

specific readings from Scripture, liturgical exorcisms, and the solemn intercession of the community. At the first *Presentation,* the Creed is formally presented to the Elect, who will memorize it and "give it back" at a later liturgical rite before they are baptized (RCIA #157-163; #193-196). At the second *Presentation,* the Elect receive the Lord's Prayer (RCIA #178-184).

After final preparation rites on Holy Saturday (RCIA #185-205), the Elect receive the sacraments of initiation (Baptism, Confirmation, and the Eucharist) at the Easter Vigil (RCIA #206-243). This brings them into the fourth and final stage of the RCIA, *Mystagogy* (RCIA #244-251). Now the converts are indwelt by the Holy Spirit, are members of the baptized faithful, and can receive the sacraments. During the stage of mystagogy, through worship, teaching, and various activities with other members of the parish community, those just baptized are helped to understand their new experience of God's presence in their lives, and to recognize and appropriate the many new graces God is giving them.

Through this structure of four stages with their liturgical rites, then, the RCIA helps adult converts to learn to live as Catholics, and enter into the conversion necessary for Baptism. But what makes this structure "work"?

How does the RCIA help people to convert?

The structure of the RCIA is centered around liturgical rites. This is because the central purpose of the RCIA is conversion — people giving their lives to God so that He can transform them by His love to be more and more like His Son, Jesus Christ. The place where human beings are most vulnerable to God, most receptive to Him, is when they are at worship. When men and women come before God and worship Him, they are most fully who they are created to be, so God has easiest access to them, to touch them, convert them, draw them to Himself in love.

Conversion means coming into a whole new way of living one's daily life. For people to learn to *act* differently, they need to learn to *think* differently, and that means learning to *perceive* differently. Such a deep change of heart and mind can only happen if *God* touches people, and people are most open to being touched by God when they are worshiping. So, through the liturgical rites of the RCIA described above, God works to convert people, to transform them.

How? God touches the converts through the prayers and the ritual actions (such as the signing of the senses with the Cross) — but, most especially, God works through the proclamation of the Word. Those who are preparing for Baptism are not able to receive the Eucharist, so God touches them, and changes the way they think and perceive, through the proclamation of the Word at the rites. The specific Scripture readings which are part of each liturgical rite have been very carefully chosen to help bring about conversion. In each rite the readings, the ritual actions, and the prayers work together as a vehicle for conversion, and they are inseparable from the faith-experience of the converts.

Because the RCIA is centered on liturgical rites celebrated by the parish community, it is clear that conversion to Christ in the Catholic Church is not private, individualistic, or subjective. It is not a matter of individuals trying to "psych up" their emotions so that they can feel like they love God. Conversion is surrendering oneself to the truth of Jesus Christ as sent by the Father to be Redeeming Lord. And since Christ lives in His Body, the Church, conversion to Christ means becoming part of His Body, His Church, becoming part of a new fabric of relationships, learning a new way of behaving toward other people.

The RCIA itself describes four main dimensions of conversion, which are clearly explained in #75. First, those preparing for Baptism are to be given doctrinal instruction which is "gradual and complete in its coverage, accommodated to the liturgical year," and

STRUCTURE OF THE RCIA

Evangelization (RCIA #36-40)

Rite of Acceptance into the Order of Catechumens (RCIA #41-74)

Catechumenate (RCIA #75-117)

Celebrations of the Word of God (RCIA #81-89)
Minor Exorcisms (RCIA #90-94)
Blessings (RCIA #95-97)

} Catecheses in this book are for use here (See #75:1. 3; #78; #81; #84.)

Rite of Election (First Sunday of Lent) (RCIA #118-137)

Purification and Enlightenment (Lent) (RCIA #138-184)

First Scrutiny (Third Sunday of Lent) (RCIA #141-156)
Presentation of the Creed (RCIA #157-163)
Second Scrutiny (Fourth Sunday of Lent) (RCIA #164-170)
Third Scrutiny (Fifth Sunday of Lent) (RCIA #171-177)
Presentation of the Lord's Prayer (RCIA #178-184)
Preparation Rites on Holy Saturday (RCIA #185-204)
Baptism, Confirmation, Eucharist (Easter Vigil) (RCIA #206-243)

Mystagogy (RCIA #244-251)

NOTES...

supported by liturgies of the Word. This instruction provides catechumens not only with intellectual concepts, but also with "a profound sense of the mystery of salvation in which they desire to participate." Second, the catechumens gradually learn the Christian way of living, both prayer and action, by association with the members of the parish community. The best way for converts to learn how to pray, fast, repent, celebrate, and serve their neighbors is by spending time with people who do these things naturally. The role of lay sponsors and catechists is crucial in this. Many members of the parish need to be involved in helping the catechumens learn Christian behavior and enabling them to be assimilated into the Christian community.

The third dimension of conversion is that, through liturgical rites, both through the Church community's public intercessory prayer for them and through the proclamation of the Word, the converts' participation in public worship draws them into a sacramental way of life. People learn the language of worship by speaking it, even as children learn to speak by repeating the words of their parents until the words are familiar. As the catechumens learn to repeat responses, when to stand or to kneel, they are gradually assimilated into the Church's life of worship and prayer. Fourth, the converts learn to participate in bearing witness to the Christian faith, both by the example of their lives and by actually evangelizing.

These four dimensions of conversion take place simultaneously. Through the liturgical rites which mark the four stages, the grace of God works to transform people and assimilate them into the Church community through their coming to share the community's beliefs, their way of thinking and living, and the Church's life of prayer and worship.

But what exactly are the converts taught to prepare them to live as Catholics? How does the RCIA draw on the wisdom of the early Church regarding catechesis? How does

NOTES...

it envision presenting what the Church believes as part of the whole experience of conversion?

How does catechetical instruction fit into the RCIA?

Much of what has been published about the RCIA describes how to celebrate the powerful liturgical rites which take place beginning when the converts are chosen for Baptism at the Rite of Election. These important rites enable the converts to assimilate what they have learned in the catechumenate on an even deeper level and to integrate it more and more with every part of their lives. But these rites (Scrutinies, Presentations, etc.) take place during the time of Purification and Enlightenment, which is like a final retreat deepening the Elect's spiritual preparation for Baptism. By this time the converts already know the teaching of the Church, or they wouldn't be able to be accepted for Easter Baptism.

What does the RCIA itself say about catechesis *before* the Rite of Election? How does the RCIA describe how converts are instructed about the truths of the faith during the catechumenate? Since it describes the catechumenate as "the lengthy period of formation of the catechumens' minds and hearts" (RCIA #118), clearly there must be conversion of mind as well as heart. The catechumens grow in knowledge of God and love of God simultaneously. Knowledge about God without love of God isn't real knowledge of God. At the same time, since people can't really love God if they don't have knowledge of Him, it is not possible for converts to give their lives to Jesus Christ in His Body, the Church, when they're baptized, if they don't know Who God in Christ is.

To ensure that the catechumens come to the knowledge of God necessary for Baptism, the RCIA calls for them to be instructed in all aspects of Catholic teaching. At the same time, the RCIA draws on the early Church tradition of presenting the teaching of the Church in the context of communal worship, since worship is a specially privileged setting for conversion. Catechesis is to be "gradual," "complete," and "solidly supported by celebrations of the word," providing both knowledge of "dogmas and precepts" and also "a profound sense of the mystery of salvation" in which the catechumens long to share (RCIA #75:1).

The RCIA calls for liturgies of the Word in connection with catechetical instruction (RCIA #81, 84) so that catechesis, as in the early Church, will occur "in a context of prayer" (RCIA #84). Further, "the instruction that the catechumens receive during this period should be of a kind that while presenting Catholic teaching in its entirety also enlightens faith, directs the heart toward God, fosters participation in the liturgy, inspires apostolic activity, and nurtures a life completely in accord with the spirit of Christ" (RCIA #78).

Given the experience of the early Church in helping people to convert, and given the way in which the RCIA seeks to restore that, what form of catechetical instruction can help enable converts to come to know God and surrender their lives to Him in keeping with the RCIA? How can catechists and sponsors develop catechesis which seeks transformation of both mind and heart, and which takes place in a communal and liturgical setting?

RCIA celebrations of the Word with catechesis

The liturgies of the Word with catechesis in this book present the teachings of the Church that catechumens should know and believe, in the context of community prayer and worship. Since the RCIA calls for presentation of Catholic teaching "in its entirety," the topics covered in these catecheses are derived from the main topics in the *Catechism of the Catholic Church.* The specific points covered under each topic have also been drawn from the *Catechism.*

NOTES...

In keeping with the experience of the early Church, catechesis is presented as flowing from the proclamation of the Word in Scripture. As the RCIA emphasizes, this teaching is presented in the context of communal worship. Each liturgy of the Word with catechesis has the following order. First, there is an opening song related to the topic to be presented. (If a particular group of catechumens has great difficulty singing, a relevant psalm could be recited instead.) Then the catechist invites all present to pray, and after a few minutes for all to turn to God in silent prayer, asking Him to open their hearts to hear His Word, the catechist focuses the community's prayer with a spoken formal prayer. After this, there is the proclamation of the Word from Scripture, which serves as a springboard to the catechesis. Then, and only then, when all are rooted in prayer and listening to the Word of God, is the teaching presented, flowing naturally from the proclamation of Scripture.

Inspired by early Church catechesis, this teaching is not intended to be like instruction in an academic classroom. It should be a living reflection on the Word of God which immerses the converts in revelation and seeks to draw them into relationship with the God who reveals Himself and actually communicates Himself through His Word. This catechesis seeks to present the truths of the faith, of God's love in Christ in the Church, in such a way that listeners are drawn into the mystery of salvation. It should inspire the catechumens who hear it to think, "I want that!"

Following the catechesis, there can be time for questions for clarification. This can be followed by spoken intercessory prayer, preparing the catechumens to enter into the worship life of the Church. This will help them to become aware of the needs of others in the parish community and beyond, and lead them into taking on the spiritual responsibility of praying for others' needs. It will also accustom them to praying aloud with others. Finally, the celebration of the Word can conclude with an appropriate song or psalm.

It must be emphasized that the catecheses in this book are intended for *catechumens,* for converts in the second stage of the RCIA, the catechumenate, who need instruction in the beliefs of the Catholic Church. These celebrations of the Word are in no way a substitute for the major liturgical rites (Election, etc.), which are crucial to the journey of conversion. In fact, the purpose of the catecheses given here is to prepare converts for those powerful rites they will later experience during the stage of Purification and Enlightenment, so that they will be as receptive as possible to the ways God will touch them at those rites and prepare them for Baptism.

Further, in order to be effective in helping bring about conversion, these catecheses must be presented in a parish where many members are involved in helping bring catechumens into the Church. The RCIA understands that teaching must be presented in the context of a community of faithful believers who live out what they teach, and of prayerful worship, in order for that teaching to become a living, experienced reality for those seeking to be members of the Church. The formation the catechumens will receive outside these celebrations of the Word — as they learn from the baptized how to live a life of service to others, personal holiness, how to study the Scriptures and hear God speaking through them, how to pray, etc. — is just as crucial a part of conversion as the formation they receive through these catecheses. Both are necessary in helping bring about the conversion needed for Baptism.

In recent years, many parishes implementing the RCIA have experienced a wonderful renewal in the way the parish helped adults to become part of the Catholic Church. The RCIA has brought a vital rediscovery of the power of God's Word in Scripture to speak to Christians in a personal way, of the key role played by members of the Church community, and by richly celebrated liturgical rites in preparing adults for Baptism.

NOTES...

How to Use Making Disciples, 2nd Edition

Making Disciples, 2nd Edition has been written for catechetical leaders and other catechists who are responsible for conveying the beliefs of Catholicism to those who come for entrance into the Church, either as catechumens or candidates, through the Rite of Christian Initiation of Adults.

This rite was canonically approved in the United States in November, 1986. At this time, the National Conference of Catholic Bishops stated that, "A thoroughly comprehensive catechesis on the truths of Catholic doctrine and moral life, aided by approved catechetical texts, is to be provided during the period of the catechumenate" (RCIA, Appendix III, #7). In support for this concern, *Making Disciples, 2nd Edition* provides forty-two catechetical sessions for a year-round catechumenate. The essential content is drawn from the *Catechism of the Catholic Church* and pertinent Church documents.

Making Disciples, 2nd Edition offers ample material for a comprehensive presentation of the faith as recommended in the *Rite*, #75, and "Appendix III," #7. The program uses a systematic and organic format rather than a lectionary-based approach. The Scripture readings are related to the topic to be presented.

The text assumes that this catechesis will integrate the policies and guidelines required by RCIA, namely:

- The catechumens or candidates embark on a journey of faith, preparing them for the sacraments of initiation. Catechumens are individuals who have never been baptized in any tradition and need basic evangelization and catechesis. Candidates are individuals seeking full communion with the Church and fall into one of two groups: 1) baptized Christians seeking full communion with the Church; and 2) Catholic people who have been baptized but who are not fully initiated, with little or no instruction in the Bible or general Christian teachings. It should be up to the pastor and the RCIA team to determine what catechesis each of these groups will need.
- The catechetical method is a dialogue of salvation that includes a proclamation of the Word of God and a positive response of faith by the catechumens and candidates.
- The parish community is involved in their journey in various ways, particularly at the rites and by prayer for their progress, acts of hospitality, and by the encouraging presence of the members of the leadership team.
- The content of the faith should be presented in an environment of love, religious hymnody, shared prayer, faith witness, and a maximum of involvement by the catechumens and candidates every step of the way. When the doctrinal content is integrated into this kind of process, there is a greater expectation that the catechumens and candidates will identify with the Church's Gospel teachings more effectively.
- The RCIA team needs to be conscious of the power of symbol and ritual as nonverbal ways to touch the heart and consciousness of the catechumens and candidates.

NOTES...

- The more these forty-two sessions help the catechumens and candidates and the catechists form a dynamic community of faith, hope, and love, the greater will be their enthusiasm for Christ and the Church, an energy which will increase their hunger for the sacraments of initiation and intensify their desire to serve the needs of love, justice, and mercy for others.

The experience of initiation through a comprehensive and systematic formation in the faith

A person seeking entrance into the Catholic Church has the *right* to be adequately informed of the essential truths of the faith. In his Apostolic Exhortation *Catechesi Tradendae* (On Catechesis in Our Time), Pope John Paul II states that "the person who becomes a disciple of Christ has the right to receive 'the word of faith' (Rm 10:8) not in mutilated, falsified or diminished form but whole and entire, in all its rigor and vigor..." (CT #30). The *Catechism of the Catholic Church* reaffirms that Christian doctrine should imparted in "'an organic and systematic way, with a view to initiating the hearers into the fullness of Christian life' (CT 18)" (CCC 5).

Continuing the clarification of a systematic catechesis, Pope John Paul II draws attention to some of the characteristics:

- "It must be a **systematic** catechesis, not improvised...."
- "It must deal with **essentials**, ..."
- "It must nevertheless be **sufficiently complete**, not stopping short at the initial proclamation of the Christian mystery such as we have in the *kerygma*, ..."
- "It must be an **integral Christian initiation**, open to all the other factors of Christian living...."

CT #21

Affirming the concerns of *Catechesi Tradendae*, the *General Directory for Catechesis*, issued in 1997 by the Congregation for the Clergy states that "this message by catechetics has a 'comprehensive hierarchical character' which constitutes a coherent and vital synthesis of the faith." The *General Directory* clarifies the nature of this by stating:

> "This is organized around the Most Holy Trinity, in a Christocentric perspective, because this is the 'source of all other mysteries of the faith, the light that enlightens them.' Starting with this point, the harmony of the overall message requires a 'hierarchy of truths,' insofar as the connection between each one of these and the foundation of the faith differs. Nevertheless, this hierarchy 'does not mean that some truths pertains to Faith itself less then others, but rather that some truths are based on others as of a higher priority and are illumined by them'."
>
> GDC #114

The *General Directory* goes on to highlight the aspects of the content of this hierarchical system.

A proper systematic catechesis must begin with God the Father revealing Himself.

- "The history of salvation, recounting the 'marvels of God,' what He had done, continues to do and will do in the future for us, is organized in reference to Jesus Christ, the 'center of salvation history.'"

- "The Apostles' Creed demonstrates how the Church has always desired to present the Christian mystery in a vital synthesis."
- "The sacraments, which like regenerating forces, spring from the paschal mystery of Jesus Christ, are also a whole"...with "the Eucharist presented as the 'sacrament of sacraments'."
- "The double commandment of love of God and neighbor is – in the moral message – a hierarchy of values which Jesus himself established..."
- "The Our Father gathers up the essence of the Gospel. It synthesizes and hierarchically structures the immense riches of prayer contained in Sacred Scripture and in all of the Church's life."

GDC #115

NOTES...

The plan put forth in *Making Disciples, 2nd Edition* is developed for the catechist. Respecting the concerns already cited from *Catechesi Tradendae* and the *General Directory for Catechesis*, it is recommended that Sessions One to Eighteen be presented consecutively. This lays the foundation beginning with God's revelation through His Covenant followed by the Creed, highlighting the teaching on the Trinity and a comprehensive development of the mystery of Christ.

Keeping in mind the recommendations of the United States Bishops in Appendix III #7 of the *Rite*, after the foundation of the Creed has been presented in the first phase of a year-round catechesis, Sessions Nineteen to Twenty-four are recommended to be presented to catechumens and candidates in an appropriate time frame. It is very important to note that moral teachings challenge the climate of contemporary culture. It is a matter of justice that those discerning entrance into the Church be given a proper understanding of the moral teachings and expectations of Catholicism in a timeframe that gives catechumens and candidates sufficient time for discernment.

The liturgical year helps to indicate appropriate times for certain sessions. A catechist may decide that the best time to teach the Last Things is during the month of November, the month dedicated to remembrance of the deceased. The session on Mary is timely early in Advent around the December 8 Feast of the Immaculate Conception.

Sessions Thirty-six to Forty-two are important topics related to the living out of Catholicism. Thus the approach of *Making Disciples, 2nd Edition* follows the directive of the *Rite of Christian Initiation* which states:

> A suitable catechesis is provided by priests or deacons, or by catechists and others of the faithful, planned to be gradual and complete in its coverage, accommodated to the liturgical year, and solidly supported by celebrations of the word. This catechesis leads the catechumens not only to an appropriate acquaintance with dogmas and precepts but also to a profound sense of the mystery of salvation in which they desire to participate.
>
> RCIA #75:1

In this model of using a systematic and comprehensive catechesis, the expectation is that sessions will be taught one evening each week. Each Sunday, the readings are recommended for the breaking open of the Word which accompany the catechumens' Sunday worship experience. Thus, the Sunday Scriptures provide spiritual enrichment.

NOTES...

Presentation of content

The RCIA catechist must become very familiar with the important information of the Introduction. Preparing to teach the content of each session, the catechist is to study and prayerfully reflect upon the topic in preparation for the presentation. Each session covers adequately the material essential to the topic. The catechist studies and prayerfully reflects upon the content of the session. He or she decides how to most effectively present it, keeping in mind effective adult learning principles.

A special component of *Making Disciples, 2nd Edition* is *Essentials of the Faith*. At the end of each session of *Making Disciples, 2nd Edition,* resources are listed. Each session identifies what chapter in *Essentials of the Faith* is of the same topic as the session. A very **effective learning strategy** is to have the catechumens and candidates read the chapter the week before the session is presented. For example, the week prior to the teaching of Session Four, The Mystery of God, the participant is directed to read Chapter Five of *Essentials of the Faith*. This method readies the catechumens and candidates to better understand the concepts and vocabulary of the RCIA catechist's presentation on "the Mystery of God."

Understanding adult catechesis

Making Disciples, 2nd Edition has been designed for an adult audience. Reflecting the insights of *Catechesi Tradendae,* the *National Directory for Catechesis* (2005) states that adult catechesis is the principal form of catechesis, because it is addressed to persons who have the greatest responsibilities and the capacity to live the Christian message in its fully developed form (CT #43).

The *National Directory for Catechesis* identifies three major goals of adult catechesis. They are:

1. It invites and enables adults to be engaged by a stance of "*conversion to the Lord.*" Transformation into Christ is gradual. God respects the nature of the human person. Faith formation, open to the activity of God's grace, takes time and commitment.
2. Adult catechesis assists people to make "a conscious and firm decision to live the gift and choice of faith through membership into the Christian community" (*Adult Catechesis in the Christian Community* #37). The parish is the ideal place to become active in worship and various activities of outreach. In and of itself the RCIA is an invigorating experience for all the parish community.
3. Adult catechesis helps all to be inspired to become disciples for others. This can happen locally as well as assisting the Church in her broader mission to evangelize and bring unity throughout the world.

The *National Directory for Catechesis* reaffirms tasks of Adult Catechesis as stated in the *General Directory for Catechesis.* They are:

- To promote formation and development of life in the Risen Christ through the sacraments, retreats, and spiritual direction
- To educate toward the correct evaluation of societal structures and changes in light of faith
- To clarify religious and moral questions
- To clarify the relationship between the Church and the world, especially in light of the Church's social doctrine

- To develop the rational foundations of the faith and demonstrate the compatibility of faith and reason
- To encourage adults to assume responsibility for the Church's mission and to be able to give Christian witness in society (GDC #175)

NOTES...

Catechesis for adults should foster discipleship. While forming the understanding with the content of the faith, the learning activities should be "cognitive, experiential, [and] behavioral" (GDC #35). Adults need to comprehend the truth and beauty of the faith as well as being able to recognize how it applies to Christian living.

Scripture and Tradition contain the major content for adult catechesis because they comprise "the supreme rule of faith" (DV #21). The *Catechism of the Catholic Church* is the normative reference resource for the catechesis of adults.

Adult catechesis provides for the development of the various yet distinct dimensions of the Catholic faith. The *General Directory for Catechesis* states: "The maturation of the Christian life requires that it be cultivated in all its dimensions: knowledge of the faith, liturgical life, moral formation, prayer, belonging to community, missionary spirit. When catechesis omits one of these elements, the Christian faith does not attain its full development" (GDC #87).

Catechetical methods for adults

In providing a necessary organic faith formation, the consciencious presentation of the fullness of Catholic doctrine must as well integrate the experience of how Catholicism is lived on a daily basis.

The *National Directory for Catechesis* gives principles which assist the use of effective methodogy for Adult Catechesis:

- Catechetical needs should be identified. With the help of leaders, ways to meet particular needs can be planned.
- Adult catechetical leaders should identify important characteristics of adult Catholics. A catechetical plan with related objectives is advised to be developed.
- Catechetical leaders should become familiar with effective methods, formats, and models. From these, teaching strategies can be developed by a "variety of forms: systematic and occasional, individual and community, organized and spontaneous (GDC #19).
- Talented catechists should be identified, given catechetical formation and training for teaching and teamwork.
- The experience of adults should be respected as well as personal skills used to meet the variety of needs.
- Adult catechesis respects the situational circumstances of the adults being catechized. This encompasses their race, culture, religious, social and economic circumstances as well as their experiences; educational, spiritual maturity and personal areas of struggle.
- The whole community should be involved as a supportive and welcoming environment (*Our Hearts Were Burning Within Us* #532).

A wonderful reflection on Adult Catechesis, *Our Hearts Were Burning Within Us*, encourages the use of special moments and events to complement the ongoing systematic and organic thrust of the catechetical endeavor. Some of these situations might be: adapting to the liturgical year, parental experiences, outreach that is local and far-reaching, critical

NOTES...

life events, such as a job-related experience, military service, and emigration. The affirmation of Sundays as a time of leisure; special holidays and travel; or any events which highlight life in the Church and society all bring the richness of life experience.

Just as educators distinguish between adult learning models and teaching methods for children and youth, more attention is being given to the variety of preferences individuals have in the learning experience. This is referred to as "multiple intelligence." An example might be that some learn better through visual experience. Others prefer hearing over seeing. Others experience learning through group discussion. The use of music and art enhances the experience for the learner who has a preference for intuitive learning. The use of the insights of multiple intelligence assists the learning experience.

Every parish community has its own experts in various professions. Drawing upon the expertise of teachers is a possibility for an RCIA catechist who wants to feel competent in his or her presentations. The integrity of the content must be maintained. Anything too gimmicky would be ineffective. Using good teaching methodology is an art to be explored as one tries to enhance this "dialogue of salvation."

Resources for the RCIA catechist

- *Making Disciples, 2nd Edition* is the primary resource and is available from Our Sunday Visitor.
- *Essentials of the Faith* is ideal as a companion for catechumens and candidates and is available from Our Sunday Visitor.
- *National Directory for Catechesis* (2005).
- *Nurturing Adult Faith: A manual for Parish Leaders* from the National Conference for Catechetical Leaders.
- *Our Hearts Were Burning Within Us: A Pastoral Plan for Adult Faith Formation in the United States* is a statement of the United States Catholic Bishops.
- *Separated Brethren, Revised,* by William J. Whalen, is a great resource. Candidates baptized in other denominations often have questions or concerns reflecting on their prior experience. *Separated Brethren, Revised* explains the many aspects of various non-Christian religions and Protestant denominations and provides very informative information which will benefit the RCIA team. This resource is available from Our Sunday Visitor.
- *Encyclopedia of Catholic Devotions and Practices,* by Ann Ball is available from Our Sunday Visitor.

Church Documents are available through the Vatican website. Documents written by the United States Conference of Catholic Bishops may also be accessed on the internet.

Session One

Our Desire and Capacity for God

LEARNING OBJECTIVE

To present the reality that each person is created to share in a relationship with God which brings true freedom and happiness. Only God can give us true fulfillment.

Hymn: "On Eagle's Wings"

Invitation to prayer — silent prayer

Oration:

Lord,
You inspire us to delight in praising you
because you made us for yourself
and our hearts are restless until they rest in you.
Fill us with your spirit of love
that we may thirst for you alone
as the fountain of wisdom
and seek you as the source of eternal love.

We ask this through our Lord Jesus Christ, your Son,
who lives and reigns with you and the Holy Spirit,
one God, for ever and ever.

Adapted from the Opening Prayer
Memorial of St. Augustine

Scripture reading: Psalm 42

As the deer longs for streams of water,
so my soul longs for you, O God.
My being thirsts for God, the living God.
When can I go and see the face of God?
My tears have been my food day and night,
as they ask daily, "Where is your God?"
Those times I recall
as I pour out my soul,
When I went in procession with the crowd,
I went with them to the house of God,
Amid loud cries of thanksgiving,
with the multitude keeping festival.
Why are you downcast, my soul;
why do you groan within me?

NOTES...

Wait for God, whom I shall praise again,
    my savior and my God.

My soul is downcast within me;
    therefore I will remember you
From the land of the Jordan and Hermon,
    from the land of Mount Mizar.
Here deep calls to deep in the roar of your torrents.
    All your waves and breakers sweep over me.
At dawn may the LORD bestow faithful love
    that I may sing praise through the night,
    praise to the God of my life.
I say to God, "My rock,
    why do you forget me?
Why must I go about mourning
    with the enemy oppressing me?"
It shatters my bones, when my adversaries reproach me.
    They say to me daily: "Where is your God?"
Why are you downcast, my soul,
    why do you groan within me?
Wait for God, whom I shall praise again,
    my savior and my God.

TEACHING TO BE PRESENTED

I. The natural desire for God.

A. God has created the human race with great dignity and the human person can truly say with St. Augustine that "'you have made us for yourself, and our heart is restless until it rests in you' (St. Augustine, *Conf.* 1, 1, 1: PL 32, 659-661)" (CCC 30).

1. God the Father created the human race to share His blessed life and is close to us at all times and in all places (CCC 1).
2. To live is to know and love God. Every act of perfect Christian virtue has no other origin and end other than charity (CCC 25).
3. The desire for God is written on every human heart and never ceases to draw us closer to Him. Only in God can we find the truth and happiness we constantly seek (CCC 27).

B. Each person has been created with the freedom to accept or reject the invitation to life with God (CCC 29).

1. *Free will* is *the capacity to make a reasonable choice.* It is a gift of God.
2. People can forget and reject God, but He still continues to call every person to seek Him (CCC 30).

II. The search for God.

A. The search for God requires the effort of the human intellect, a correct will, "an upright heart," and the witness of others who teach us to seek God (CCC 30).

1. The person who seeks God discovers certain ways of coming to know Him (CCC 31).
2. The human person's openness to truth and beauty, sense of moral goodness, freedom, voice of conscience, longings for the infinite, and for happiness provoke questions about God's existence (CCC 33).
3. The Catholic Church "teaches that God, the first principle and last end of all things, can be known with certainty from the created world by the natural light of human reason" (Vatican Council I, *Dei Filius* 2: DS 3004; cf. 3026; Vatican Council II, *Dei Verbum* 6) (CCC 36).
4. We have the ability to reason because we are created in God's image, without which we could not accept God's self-revelation.
5. The decision for God also means a decision for the freedom and the unconditional dignity of the human person (CCC 27).

B. We need God's revelation to enlighten us about what exceeds our understanding about religious and moral truths. The Church clarifies these truths with firm certitude because of the present condition of the human race (CCC 38).
   1. Only in Jesus Christ are the mystery of God and the mystery of the human person definitively disclosed. Jesus Christ reveals what it means to be fully human. When we learn about the life of Christ, we understand that only in giving ourselves to God and others do we truly find ourselves.
   2. Through Christ and in the Holy Spirit, the Father invites us to become His adopted sons and daughters and heirs to divine happiness (CCC 1).
   3. Faith in God demands that we accept ourselves and all others unconditionally because we have been unconditionally accepted (CCC 27). This is not easy. It requires conversion and is a very long road, but God will help us.
   4. Faith in God grounds the conviction of freedom's unconditional value. It obliges us to have unconditional respect for every person and to commit ourselves to a just order among people based on the principle of freedom.

NOTES...

FOCUS QUESTIONS

1. Have you experienced what Augustine describes as a "restless" heart?
2. Do you find that most people in society have a natural desire for God? How is that seen or not seen?
3. God has given us the freedom to choose the good. How is true self-fulfillment related to choosing the good?

Concluding prayers
Intercessions
Closing prayer
Hymn (optional)

NOTES...

RESOURCES

Catechism of the Catholic Church, 1-43
Confessions of St. Augustine
Dei verbum (Dogmatic Constitution on Divine Revelation), Vatican II
Gaudium et spes (Pastoral Constitution on the Church in the Modern World), Vatican II, 10, 11, 12-18, 22, 24-28
Essentials of the Faith, McBride, chap. 1

Session Two

Divine Revelation

The Initiative of God's Love

LEARNING OBJECTIVE

To provide an understanding of the covenant relationship which begins in Baptism. Having its roots in the Old Testament, this relationship takes into account God's initiative (revelation) and the response of the person (faith).

Hymn: "The King of Love My Shepherd Is"

Invitation to prayer — silent prayer

Oration:

Lord God,
in the new covenant
you shed light on the miracles you worked in ancient times:
the Red Sea is a symbol of our baptism,
and the nation you freed from slavery
is a sign of your Christian people.
May every nation
share the faith and privilege of Israel
and come to new birth in the Holy Spirit.

We ask this through Christ our Lord.

Prayer After the Third Reading
Easter Vigil

Scripture reading: Deuteronomy 26:16-19

"This day the LORD, your god, commands you to observe these statutes and decrees. Be careful, then, to observe them with all your heart and with all your soul. Today you are making this agreement with the LORD: he is to be your God and you are to walk in his ways and observe his statutes, commandments and decrees, and to hearken to his voice. And today the LORD is making this agreement with you: you are to be a people peculiarly his own, as he promised you; and provided you keep all his commandments, he will then raise you high in praise and renown and glory above all other nations he has made, and you will be a people sacred to the LORD, your God, as he promised."

NOTES...

TEACHING TO BE PRESENTED

I. The revelation of God.

A. Divine Revelation is an order of knowledge through which God has revealed and given Himself to us by making known "the mystery, his plan of loving goodness, formed from all eternity in Christ" on behalf of everyone (CCC 50).

1. God's gradual self-communication prepared humanity to accept "by stages the supernatural Revelation that is to culminate in the person and mission of the incarnate Word, Jesus Christ" (CCC 53).
2. God has fully revealed His plan by sending us His beloved Son, our Lord Jesus Christ, and His Spirit (CCC 50).
3. God's revelation enables us to respond to Him, and to know and love Him "far beyond [our] own natural capacity" (CCC 52).

B. Revelation in the Old Testament shows us the beautiful way through which God reveals Himself.

1. God's revelation began with creation and the manifestation of Himself to Adam and Eve (CCC 54).
2. God spoke to our first parents, inviting "them to intimate communion with himself and clothed them with resplendent grace and justice" (CCC 54).
3. The eventual sin of Adam and Eve did not thwart God's revelation. "'After the fall, [God] buoyed them up with the hope of salvation, by promising redemption' (DV 3; cf. Gn 3:15; Rom 2:6-7)" (CCC 55).
4. The covenant with Noah after the flood exemplified the divine economy towards people separated into their own lands, with their own languages and families (CCC 56).
   a. Covenant is a solemn promise or ritualized agreement.
   b. Economy is the theological term used to refer to God's activity in the world.
5. In order to gather the scattered human race, God called Abram and chose him to be the father of faith. Those descended from Abraham would be stewards of the promise made to the patriarchs, the people chosen to prepare for that day when God should gather all His children into the unity of the Church (CCC 59).
6. God continued to form "Israel as his people by freeing them from slavery in Egypt. He established with them the covenant of Mount Sinai" (cf. DV 3) (CCC 62).
7. Through the prophets God prepared the people to accept the salvation intended for all humanity (CCC 64).

C. Revelation in the New Testament — The New Covenant.

1. In Christ Jesus, God has fully revealed Himself. Because "the Christian economy, therefore, since it is the new and definitive Covenant, will never pass away; and no new public revelation is to be expected before the glorious manifestation of our Lord Jesus Christ" (DV 4; cf. 1 Tm 6:14; Ti 2:13) (CCC 66).
2. Christ commanded the apostles to preach the Gospel as the source of all saving truth and all moral discipline (CCC 75).

II. The threefold dimension of revelation — the deposit of faith.

A. The Holy Scriptures, both Old and New Testaments, contain God's Word and, because they are inspired, truly are His Word (CCC 135).

NOTES...

1. "God is the author of Sacred Scripture because he inspired its human authors; he acts in them and by means of them. He thus gives assurance that their writings teach without error his saving truth (cf. DV 11)" (CCC 136).
2. The Catholic Church accepts and honors as inspired the forty-six canonical books of the Old Testament and the twenty-seven canonical books of the New Testament (CCC 138).
3. "The unity of the two Testaments proceeds from the unity of God's plan and his Revelation. The Old Testament prepares for the New and the New Testament fulfills the Old; the two shed light on each other; both are true Word of God" (CCC 140).
4. Some denominations do not accept all seventy-three of these books as inspired. Compare the books in a King James Bible with the books in a Catholic Bible. There are thirty-nine books in the Old Testament in Protestant Bibles (and the Hebrew Scriptures); there are forty-six in Catholic, Eastern Orthodox, and Anglican. The additional seven books, called the Deuterocanonical, or "second canon," are: Sirach, Wisdom, Baruch, 1 and 2 Maccabees, Tobit, and Judith. Also included in this group are some additions to Esther and Daniel. These books were included in the Septuagint, the Greek translation of the Hebrew Scriptures (circa 250 B.C.). Our early Latin Bibles were a translation of the Septuagint. These seven books (and the additions) were accepted as inspired and included in our canon, but excluded from the Hebrew canon.
5. The Church has always honored the Sacred Scriptures and is nourished by them, as she has the very Body of the Lord. Both nourish and govern the whole Christian life (CCC 141).

B. Tradition is the living communication of the Word brought about by the Holy Spirit.

1. Through Tradition, "'the Church, in her doctrine, life, and worship perpetuates and transmits to every generation all that she herself is, all that she believes' (DV 8 § 1)" (CCC 78).
2. Tradition is a life force and draws from almost four-thousand years of faith experience.
3. In Catholicism, Tradition and sacred Scripture are bound closely together and communicate with each other. Both flow out of the same source, come together in a way to form a single reality, and tend toward the same goal (CCC 80).

C. Magisterium is the teaching authority of the Church expressed by the Pope and the bishops that are in union with him.

1. The Church's Magisterium is entrusted with the task of authentically interpreting God's Word, whether written or handed down orally. This teaching office exercises authority in the name of Jesus Christ to the bishops in communion with the successor of Peter, the bishop of Rome (CCC 85).
2. The Church's Magisterium exercises the authority it holds from Christ to the fullest extent when it defines dogmas.
   a. Dogmas are truths contained in divine Revelation that oblige "the Christian people to an irrevocable adherence of faith" (CCC 88). Belief in these truths is a requirement of our faith and God's help and grace is necessary for us to believe.
   b. "'The Sacred Scriptures contain the Word of God and, because they are inspired they are truly the Word of God' (DV 24)" (CCC 135).

NOTES...

3. Within the whole revelation of the Christian mystery there is a "'hierarchy' of truths" in the Catholic teaching (CCC 90). The Paschal Mystery and the revelation of God in Christ are the central core of Church doctrine. All Church teachings are to be embraced because they are interdependent. However, certain doctrines are more intimately related to the centrality of Christ and His revelation of God's fullness.

III. The Church as servant of revelation.

A. Sacred Tradition, Sacred Scripture and the Church's Magisterium are so interconnected that none can stand without the others. "'Working together, each in its own way, under the action of the one Holy Spirit, they all contribute effectively to the salvation of souls' (DV 10 § 3)" (CCC 95).

B. So that the full, living Gospel should always be preserved in the Church, the apostles left bishops as their successors, giving them their own teaching authority (CCC 77).

C. All the faithful fully initiated into the Church have received the Holy Spirit, who instructs them and guides them into all truth. They share in the understanding and handing on of revealed truth (CCC 91).

1. "Throughout the ages, there have been so-called 'private' revelations, some of which have been recognized by the authority of the Church. They do not belong, however, to the deposit of faith. It is not their role to improve or complete Christ's definitive Revelation, but to help live more fully by it in a certain period of history" (CCC 67).
2. "Private" or personal revelation cannot contradict Christ's revelation in the teachings of the Church.

FOCUS QUESTIONS

1. How does God reveal Himself to you?
2. Which aspect of the deposit of faith (Scripture, Tradition, and Magisterium) do you feel is least appreciated? Why is it important to have all three?
3. What has the Bible meant in your life up until now?

Concluding prayers
Intercessions
Closing prayer
Hymn (optional)

RESOURCES

Catechism of the Catholic Church, 50-141
Dei verbum (Dogmatic Constitution on Divine Revelation), Vatican II
Essentials of the Faith, McBride, chaps. 2, 4

Session Three

The Life of Faith

Our Response to God's Invitation to Relationship

LEARNING OBJECTIVE

To further examine our covenant relationship with God and, in particular, how the person nourishes and fosters their response of faith.

Hymn: "Faith of Our Fathers"

Invitation to prayer — silent prayer

Oration:

God our Father,
we rejoice in the faith that draws us together,
aware that selfishness can drive us apart.
Let your encouragement be our constant strength.
Keep us one in the love that has sealed our lives,
help us to live as one family
the gospel we profess.
We ask this through Christ our Lord.

Alternate Opening Prayer
Eleventh Sunday in Ordinary Time

Scripture reading: Hebrews 11:1-3; 8-11

Faith is the realization of what is hoped for and evidence of things not seen. Because of it the ancients were well attested. By faith we understand that the universe was ordered by the word of God, so that what is visible came into being through the invisible....

By faith Abraham obeyed when he was called to go out to a place that he was to receive as an inheritance; he went out, not knowing where he was to go. By faith he sojourned in the promised land as in a foreign country, dwelling in tents with Isaac and Jacob, heirs of the same promise; for he was looking forward to the city with foundations, whose architect and maker is God. By faith he received power to generate, even though he was past the normal age — and Sarah herself was sterile — for he thought that the one who had made the promise was trustworthy.

TEACHING TO BE PRESENTED

I. **The nature of faith.**

A. Faith is the assent given in trust and obedience to truth.

NOTES...

1. By faith, humans submit themselves completely and give their assent of intellect and will to God who reveals Himself (CCC 143).
   a. Faith is first a personal commitment to God through Jesus Christ and in the Holy Spirit (CCC 150).
   b. Faith is secondly a free assent, a saying "yes" to the whole truth that God has revealed (CCC 150).
   c. Faith is a relationship — a loving yes to God who has first loved us. Faith is our response to God's love.
2. The obedience of faith (obedience meaning to "listen to") is free submission to God's spoken Word simply "because its truth is guaranteed by God, who is Truth itself" (CCC 144).

B. Faith is an act of the intellect.
1. Even though faith is possible only by grace it is an authentically human act. To trust in God and to believe the truths He has revealed does not contradict either human dignity or reason (CCC 154).
2. We believe because of the authority of God, who reveals and who can neither deceive nor be deceived. Therefore faith is certain. As Cardinal Newman stated, "'Ten thousand difficulties do not make one doubt' (John Henry Cardinal Newman, *Apologia pro vita sua* [London: Longman, 1878], 239)" (CCC 157).
   a. It is the nature of faith that, while it is *firm* because it comes from God's grace, it also contains an element of darkness and/or doubt.
   b. Faith is either growing or declining. It is our responsibility to cooperate with God in the growth of faith.
3. "'Faith *seeks understanding*' (St. Anselm, *Prosl. prooem.*: PL 153, 225A)" (CCC 158). "The grace of faith opens 'the eyes of your hearts' (Eph 1:18) to a lively understanding of the contents of Revelation" (CCC 158). Faith is our response to God's revelation.

II. The mystery of faith.

A. Faith is a gift of God.
1. "*Faith is a gift of God, a supernatural virtue infused by him*" (CCC 153). Faith exists with the help of grace. Grace is God's activity in our lives.
2. Faith is God's entire free gift. Faith must grow and be nurtured. We can lose this priceless gift through carelessness or sin. *(It is very important to get this across.)*
   a. Faith is under assault from without: sexual permissiveness in our society, secularism, violence in the world and in the media, etc.
   b. Faith is under assault from within ourselves. We will struggle with doubt and temptations until we see God face to face.

B. Faith is a loving relationship with God.
1. Faith is belief in God's love.
2. The two dimensions of the covenant with God are:
   a. God, as the initiator of the covenant, promises steadfast love and absolute fidelity.
   b. The human person responds to God through Jesus, all the time saying the "yes" of faith through the life of the Church.
3. Believing is an ecclesial act as well as personal (CCC 180-181). "The Church's faith precedes, engenders, supports, and nourishes our faith. The Church is the mother of all believers" (CCC 181). As St. Cyprian has said, "'No one can

have God as Father who does not have the Church as Mother' (St. Cyprian, *De unit.* 6: PL 4, 519)" (CCC 181).

4. Faith in Jesus Christ is necessary for salvation since without faith it is impossible to please God (CCC 161).
   a. Every person who is "ignorant of the Gospel of Christ and of his Church, but seeks the truth and does the will of God in accordance with his understanding of it, can be saved" (CCC 1260).
   b. "It may be supposed that such persons would have *desired Baptism explicitly* if they had known its necessity" (CCC 1260).
5. Believing is a free and conscious human act, corresponding to the dignity of the human person. No one can be forced to embrace the faith unwillingly (CCC 1260).
6. Faith enables us to enjoy on earth the very life of God. It is in a sense "eternity already begun." Faith on earth leads to vision in the life to come. Faith in this life is the beginning of vision in the next life.

C. Mary is the perfect model of faith.
   1. Mary, the virgin Mother, is most perfectly the model of obedient faith (CCC 144). "It is for this faith that all generations have called Mary blessed" (cf. Lk 1:48) (CCC 148).
   2. Mary's "yes" to the message of the angel gives us inspiration to say "yes" (CCC 494).
   3. Mary's faith never wavered. She never doubted that God would fulfill His word. The Church honors in Mary the supreme fulfillment of faith (CCC 148-149). At the Visitation, Elizabeth said, "'Blessed is she who believed that there would be a fulfillment of what was spoken to her from the Lord' (Lk 1:45)" (CCC 148).

NOTES...

FOCUS QUESTIONS

1. "Ten thousand difficulties do not make one doubt." Have you experienced what Cardinal John Henry Newman describes as certain faith? How do you deal with doubts?
2. What can be done to keep faith active and growing?
3. Do you find any difficulty with the Church's emphasis on Mary?

Concluding prayers
Intercessions
Closing prayer
Hymn (optional)

RESOURCES

Catechism of the Catholic Church, 26-184, 1260
Dei verbum (Dogmatic Constitution on Divine Revelation), Vatican II
Essentials of the Faith, McBride, chaps. 2-4

Session Four

The Mystery of God

LEARNING OBJECTIVE

To present the ways we have of coming to know God through His revelation.

Hymn: "Holy, Holy, Holy! Lord God Almighty"

Invitation to prayer — silent prayer

Oration:

Lord our God, Father of all,
you guard us under the shadow of your wings
and search into the depths of our hearts.

Remove the blindness that cannot know you
and relieve the fear that would hide us from your sight.

We ask this through Christ our Lord.

Alternate Opening Prayer
Twenty-ninth Sunday in Ordinary Time

Scripture reading: Exodus 3:1-14

Meanwhile Moses was tending the flock of his father-in-law Jethro, the priest of Midian. Leading the flock across the desert, he came to Horeb, the mountain of God. There an angel of the LORD appeared to him in fire flaming out of a bush. As he looked on, he was surprised to see that the bush, though on fire, was not consumed. So Moses decided, "I must go over to look at this remarkable sight, and see why the bush is not burned."

When the LORD saw him coming over to look at it more closely, God called out to him from the bush, "Moses! Moses!" He answered, "Here I am." God said, "Come no nearer! Remove the sandals from your feet, for the place where you stand is holy ground. I am the God of your father," he continued, "the God of Abraham, the God of Isaac, the God of Jacob." Moses hid his face, for he was afraid to look at God. But the LORD said, "I have witnessed the affliction of my people in Egypt and have heard their cry of complaint against their slave drivers, so I know well what they are suffering. Therefore I have come down to rescue them from the hands of the Egyptians and lead them out of that land into a good and spacious land, a land flowing with milk and honey, the country of the Canaanites, Hittites, Amorites, Perizzites, Hivites and Jebusites. So indeed the cry of the Israelites has reached me, and I have truly noted that the Egyptians are oppressing them. Come, now! I will send you to Pharaoh to lead my people, the Israelites, out of Egypt."

But Moses said to God, "Who am I that I should go to Pharaoh and lead the Israelites out of Egypt?" He answered, "I will be with you; and this shall be your proof that it is I who have sent you: when you bring my people out of Egypt, you will worship God on this very mountain." "But," said Moses to God, "when I go to the Israelites and say to them, 'The God of your fathers has sent me to you,' if they ask me, 'What is his name?' what am I to tell them?" God replied, "I am who am." Then he added, "This is what you shall tell the Israelites: I AM sent me to you."

NOTES...

TEACHING TO BE PRESENTED

I. In revealing Himself to Moses as "I am who am" God speaks of His uniqueness as being the One and only true God.

A. "'The Christian faith confesses that God is one in nature, substance, and essence' (*Roman Catechism*, I, 2, 2)" (CCC 200).

1. God said to His chosen people the Israelites that "'the LORD our God is one LORD' (Dt 6:4)" (CCC 201).
2. Following upon the statement of His being one Lord, God revealed that His people are to love Him "'with all your heart, and with all your soul, and with all your mind, and with all your strength' (Mk 12:29-30)" (CCC 202).
3. Through the teaching of His prophets God calls Israel and all people to turn to Him as the one, true God (CCC 201).

B. Jesus through His teaching affirms the oneness of God (CCC 202).

1. Distinctive to Christian faith is the confession that Jesus is Lord (CCC 202).
2. Jesus is one with the Father and the Holy Spirit, the Lord and giver of life (CCC 202).
3. In proclaiming three persons in one God the Lateran Council IV professed that "'there is only one true God, eternal, infinite (*immensus*) and unchangeable, incomprehensible, almighty, and ineffable' (Lateran Council IV: DS 800)" (CCC 202).

II. God reveals His name.

A. A name identifies and expresses a person's being, who he or she is. To give one's name is to "make oneself known to others" (CCC 203).

1. Progressively God revealed His name.
2. In the theophany of the burning bush, God said to Moses, "'I AM WHO I AM' (Ex 3:14)" (CCC 205). A theophany is a manifestation of God to the senses.
3. God's divine name is a mystery just as God Himself is (CCC 206).
4. Although God is hidden from our sight, He makes Himself close to His people (CCC 206).
5. In awe of God's divine presence Moses covers his face and removes his sandals. This recognition of God's greatness reveals the insignificance of humanity (CCC 208).

B. God is merciful and gracious.

1. Israel turns away from God by worshiping the golden calf.
2. Moses intercedes on behalf of the people and God agrees to walk in the midst of the Israelites' infidelity.
3. God reveals His steadfast love and absolute fidelity (CCC 210).

NOTES...

4. God's ultimate act of love is the fullness of revelation in and through His Son Jesus Christ (CCC 211).

C. God alone IS.
   1. As time progressed through the centuries, Israel's faith deepened and God's name became known: YHWH, "I AM WHO I AM."
      a. There are no other gods like the one true God, YHWH (CCC 212).
      b. In the one true God there is no change.
   2. "God is 'He who Is' from everlasting to everlasting, and as such remains ever faithful to himself and to his promises" (CCC 212).
      a. The one true God created heaven and earth.
      b. The one true God transcends the world and history.

III. God is truth and love.

A. The apostle John teaches that God is truth, for "'God is light and in him there is no darkness' (1 Jn 1:5)" (CCC 214).
   1. Throughout Scripture God's truth is proclaimed. "God's truth is his wisdom" (cf. Wis 13:1-9) (CCC 216).
   2. "God is also truthful when he reveals himself" (CCC 217). St. John teaches us that Jesus bore witness to the truth of God (cf. 1 Jn 5:20; Jn 17:3) (CCC 217).

B. God's love is steadfast and everlasting.
   1. God never tired of forgiving His chosen people Israel.
   2. Through the revelation of Tradition we are assured of God's loving mercy.
   3. "God so loved the world that he gave his only Son" (Jn 3:16) (cf. CCC 221).
   4. "God's very being is love" (CCC 221).

IV. Believing in the One God revealed through Jesus Christ has significant consequences for the entirety of life (CCC 222).

A. This belief means knowing and accepting the majesty and greatness of God (CCC 223).

B. This belief means living in gratitude (CCC 224).

C. This belief means knowing the dignity of each person created in God's image and likeness (CCC 225).

D. This belief means using created goods properly (CCC 226).

E. This belief means living in trust of God no matter what the circumstance (CCC 227).

F. "Faith in God leads us to turn to him alone as our first origin and our ultimate goal, and neither to prefer anything to him nor to substitute anything for him" (CCC 229).

V. God is personal.

A. God has made it quite clear that He cares about His people: He showed His mercy, fidelity and kindness as He led the Israelites out of slavery and into the promised land (Ps 105; 106).

B. God is one who acts. This shows clearly in the book of Exodus, where God acts on behalf of those He loves.

FOCUS QUESTIONS

1. Do you think most people believe in God?
2. Which attribute of God do you find most comforting and appealing?
3. What is there in the surrounding culture which prevents people from having a relationship with God?

Concluding prayers
Intercessions
Closing prayer
Hymn (optional)

RESOURCES

Catechism of the Catholic Church, 200-229
Essentials of the Faith, McBride, chap. 5

NOTES...

Session Five

The Mystery of the Trinity

LEARNING OBJECTIVE

To present the mystery of the Most Holy Trinity, which is the central mystery of the Christian faith and of Christian life.

Hymn: "Sing Praise to Our Creator"

Invitation to prayer — silent prayer

Oration:

Father,
you sent your Word to bring us truth
and your Spirit to make us holy.
Through them we come to know the mystery of your life.
Help us to worship you, one God in three Persons,
by proclaiming and living our faith in you.

Grant this through our Lord Jesus Christ, your Son,
who lives and reigns with you and the Holy Spirit,
one God, for ever and ever.

Opening Prayer
Trinity Sunday

Scripture reading: Matthew 28:16-20

The eleven disciples went to Galilee, to the mountain to which Jesus had ordered them. When they saw him, they worshiped, but they doubted. Then Jesus approached and said to them, "All power in heaven and on earth has been given to me. Go, therefore, and make disciples of all nations, baptizing them in the name of the Father, and of the Son, and of the holy Spirit, teaching them to observe all that I have commanded you. And behold, I am with you always, until the end of the age."

TEACHING TO BE PRESENTED

I. **God is triune from eternity. This is revealed in the Incarnation and the sending of the Holy Spirit. The missions of the Son and the Holy Spirit in the economy of salvation assist believers to grasp the mystery of the Trinity (CCC 236-237).**

   A. The Father is revealed by the Son. Jesus, the Son, reveals that God is Father — not simply as Creator of all, but Father in relation to His Son.

1. "God is Father because of the covenant and the gift of the law to Israel, 'his first-born son' (Ex 4:22)" (CCC 238).
2. God "is 'the Father of the poor,' of the orphaned and the widowed, who are under his loving protection" (cf. 2 Sm 7:14; Ps 68:6) (CCC 238).
3. By calling God "Father" the language of faith indicates:
   a. God is origin of all and transcendent authority (CCC 239).
   b. God is absolute "goodness and loving care for all his children" (CCC 239).
4. "God's parental tenderness can also be expressed by the image of motherhood (cf. Is 66:13; Ps 131:2), which emphasizes God's immanence, the intimacy between Creator and creature" (CCC 239).
5. However, God is neither male nor female — He is God. God transcends the human distinction between the sexes. God is, however, "their origin and standard (cf. Ps 27:10; Eph 3:14; Is 49:15): no one is father as God is Father" (CCC 239).
6. Jesus Christ has revealed that God is "eternally Father in relation to his only Son, who is eternally Son only in relation to his Father: 'No one knows the Son except the Father, and no one knows the Father except the Son and any one to whom the Son chooses to reveal him' (Mt 11:27)" (CCC 240).
7. The apostles confess Jesus to be the Word who was with God from the beginning. Jesus is "'the image of the invisible God' (Col 1:15); as the 'radiance of the glory of God and the very stamp of his nature' (Heb 1:3)" (CCC 241).
8. In the year 325 the first ecumenical council at Nicaea confessed "that the Son is 'consubstantial' with the Father, that is, one only God with him" (The English phrases "of one being" and "one in being" translate the Greek word *homoousios*, which was rendered in Latin by *consubstantialis*) (CCC 242).

B. The Father and the Son are revealed by the Holy Spirit.
1. The Holy Spirit reveals that God is Father and that Jesus is His Son when He is sent upon the apostles by the Father and the Son. The Holy Spirit is revealed as another divine person with Jesus and the Father (CCC 244).
2. At the second ecumenical council at Constantinople in 381 the Nicene Creed states, "'We believe in the Holy Spirit, the Lord and giver of life, who proceeds from the Father' (Nicene Creed; cf. DS 150)." Again this creed states, "'With the Father and the Son, he is worshipped and glorified' (Nicene Creed; cf. DS 150)" (CCC 245).

II. The formulation of belief in the Trinity is found in 2 Corinthians 13:13, "'The grace of the Lord Jesus Christ and the love of God and the fellowship of the Holy Spirit be with you all' (2 Cor 13:13; cf. 1 Cor 12:4-6; Eph 4:4-6)" (CCC 249).

A. The Church uses special terms to attempt to articulate the dogma of the Trinity.
1. "Substance," also called "nature" or "essence," "designate[s] the divine being in its unity" (CCC 252).
2. "Person" or "hypostasis" "designate the Father, Son, and Holy Spirit in the real distinction among them" (CCC 252).
3. The term "relation" designates "the fact that their distinction lies in the relationship of each to the others" (CCC 252).

B. The Trinity may be viewed from the perspective of the "economy of salvation" which pertains to the missions of the Son and the Holy Spirit as well as God's eternal inner life, which is described as the "immanent Trinity." Immanence means activity which is accomplished from within.

NOTES...

NOTES...

III. The Trinity is one.

A. There is one God in three persons, the "consubstantial Trinity" as confessed by the Council of Constantinople II in the year 553 (CCC 253).

B. Each person of the Trinity is God whole and entire. The divine persons do not share (CCC 253).

C. As in the words of the Council of Toledo XI in the year 675: "'The Father is that which the Son is, the Son that which the Father is, the Father and the Son that which the Holy Spirit is, i.e., by nature one God' (Council of Toledo XI [675]: DS 530:26)" (CCC 253).

D. In the year 1215 the Fourth Lateran Council confessed, "'Each of the persons is that supreme reality, viz., the divine substance, essence or nature' (Lateran Council IV [1215]: DS 804)" (CCC 253).

IV. The divine persons are really distinct from one another.

A. "'God is one but not solitary' (*Fides Damasi*: DS 71)" (CCC 254).

B. Father, Son, and Holy Spirit are "really distinct from one another" (CCC 254).

C. The Fourth Lateran Council proclaimed, "'It is the Father who generates, the Son who is begotten, and the Holy Spirit who proceeds' (Lateran Council IV [1215]: DS 804)" (CCC 254). "Begotten" means that what is brought forth is the same substance as the begetter.

D. "The divine Unity is Triune" (CCC 254).

V. "*The divine persons are relative to one another*" (CCC 255).

A. The true distinction of the Father, Son, and Holy Spirit from one another "resides solely in the relationships which relate them to one another" (CCC 255).

B. The Council of Florence in 1442 proclaimed: "'Everything (in them) is one where there is no opposition of relationship' (Council of Florence [1442]: DS 1330)" (CCC 255).

C. Again, the Council of Florence stated: "'Because of that unity the Father is wholly in the Son and wholly in the Holy Spirit; the Son is wholly in the Father and wholly in the Holy Spirit; the Holy Spirit is wholly in the Father and wholly in the Son' (Council of Florence [1442]: DS 1331)" (CCC 255).

VI. The mystery of the Trinity is profoundly summarized by St. Gregory of Nazianzus while given to the catechumens of Constantinople:

"'Above all guard for me this great deposit of faith for which I live and fight, which I want to take with me as a companion, and which makes me bear all evils and despise all pleasures: I mean the profession of faith in the Father and the Son and the Holy Spirit. I entrust it to you today. By it I am soon going to plunge you into water and raise you up from it. I give it to you as the companion and patron of your whole life. I give you but one divinity and power, existing one in three, and containing the three in a distinct way. Divinity without disparity of substance or nature, without superior degree that raises up or inferior degree that casts down … the infinite co-naturality of three infinites. Each person considered in himself is entirely God … the three considered together.... I have not even begun to think of unity when the Trinity bathes me in its splendor. I have not even begun to think of the Trinity when unity grasps me …' (St. Gregory of Nanzianzus, *Oratio* 40; 41: PG 36, 417)" (CCC 256).

VII. **It is through Baptism that we, as finite creatures, enter into the family of the infinite God and partake of His Trinitarian life (CCC 265).**

NOTES...

FOCUS QUESTIONS

1. Do you find yourself addressing one Person of the Trinity in prayer more than another? Which Person of the Blessed Trinity do you fail to incorporate into prayer?
2. Why do we begin our prayers as Catholics with the sign of the cross?
3. Can you describe the missions of the Son and the Holy Spirit?

Concluding prayers
Intercessions
Closing prayer
Hymn (optional)

RESOURCES

Catechism of the Catholic Church, 236-65
Essentials of the Faith, chaps. 6, 7

Session Six

The Mystery of Creation

LEARNING OBJECTIVE

To present the very foundations of all God's saving plans through a look at the origins of all things and their proper ends.

Hymn: "Praise to the Lord, the Almighty"

Invitation to prayer — silent prayer

Oration:

Almighty and eternal God,
you created all things in wonderful beauty and order.
Help us now to perceive
how still more wonderful is the new creation
by which in the fullness of time
you redeemed your people
through the sacrifice of our passover, Jesus Christ,
who lives and reigns for ever and ever.

Prayer After the First Reading
Easter Vigil

Scripture reading: Genesis 1:1-2:2

(Because this reading is so long, we do not print the entire passage here. Please reference it in your own Bible.)

TEACHING TO BE PRESENTED

I. **Two questions which have throughout history always risen in the hearts and minds of each generation are "Where do we come from?" and "What is our end?" (CCC 282).**
   A. The truth about creation was revealed by God to His people (CCC 286).
      1. Human reason can come to the knowledge of God because of His works (CCC 287).
      2. Beyond this natural knowledge, God progressively revealed to His people the mystery of creation (CCC 287).
      3. God revealed that He is the "One to whom belong all the peoples of the earth, and the whole earth itself; he is the One who alone 'made heaven and earth'" (cf. Is 43:1; Ps 115:15; 124:8; 134:3) (CCC 287).

B. The revelation of creation is inseparable from God's covenant with His people (CCC 288).
   1. Creation is revealed at God's initial "step toward this covenant, the first and universal witness to God's all-powerful love" (cf. Gn 15:5; Jer 33:19-26) (CCC 288).
   2. The truth of creation is expressed through the prophets, in the psalms and liturgy, and in the wisdom literature (CCC 288).

NOTES...

II. God is the Creator of angels and spiritual beings.

A. The angelic beings — the things "unseen."
   1. The belief in angels "is a truth of faith" (CCC 328). The term "angel" means "*servants* and messengers of God" (CCC 329). An angel is a pure spirit with an intellect and a will (CCC 330).
   2. Like all creation, the angels were created to give glory to God as their song to the shepherds describes (Lk 2:14) (CCC 333).
   3. We believe that the angels pray for us and act as true "friends" in heaven on our behalf.

B. The Scriptures give accounts of three archangels (Michael, Gabriel, and Raphael) and the presence of (guardian) angels (Ex 23:20-21) chosen by God to guard His people. These pure spirits are celebrated with specific feasts in the liturgical calendar.

III. God is the Creator of heaven and earth.

A. The first three chapters of Genesis remain the principal source for catechesis on mysteries of the "beginning" (CCC 293).
   1. Scripture and Tradition teach that "'the world was made for the glory of God' (*Dei Filius*, can. § 5: DS 3025)" (CCC 293).
   2. "God himself created the visible world in all its richness, diversity, and order" (CCC 337).
   3. Scripture presents the work of God symbolically as six days of divine work concluding with the seventh day, a day of rest.
   4. While the Bible itself does not teach evolution, neither does it say anything to oppose scientific theories concerning bodily evolution. Regarding the human person, if there was a long process of developing, it is only at the end of that process — when the human person is capable of reflective knowledge, responsible behavior, and relationships of love — that he or she comes to be "in the image of God," and to share in the like of grace by knowing and loving God.

B. The mystery of creation reveals much about God's attributes (CCC 299).
   1. God creates by wisdom and love.
   2. God creates everything out of nothing.
      a. The Nicene Creed reveals the teachings of the Church on God as the maker "of all that is seen and unseen."
      b. "No creature has the infinite power necessary to 'create'" (cf. DS 3624) (CCC 318).
   3. God creates an ordered and good world (CCC 299).
   4. God transcends creation yet is present to it (CCC 300).
   5. God upholds and sustains creation.
      a. "The universe was created 'in a state of journeying'" (CCC 302). Creation is ongoing.

NOTES...

b. "We call 'divine providence' the dispositions by which God guides his creation toward this perfection" (CCC 302).

IV. The human race occupies a unique place in creation, for we are created in the image of God (Gn 1:27) (CCC 355).

A. Bearers of God's image, individual humans possess the dignity of persons.
   1. We have intellect and free will.
   2. We are "capable of self-knowledge, of self-possession and of freely giving [ourselves] and entering into communion with other persons" (CCC 357).
   3. We are called, as persons, to a unique intimacy with God that no other creature can enter into. God calls us by grace to a covenant relationship with Him and we respond in faith and love (CCC 357).

B. In our nature, we unite the spiritual and material world.
   1. Human persons are "at once corporeal and spiritual.... 'Then the LORD God formed man of dust from the ground, and breathed into his nostrils the breath of life; and man became a living being' (Gn 2:7)" (CCC 362).
   2. The entire human unity of body and soul reflects God's image (CCC 362-64).
      a. The "soul" is the principle of life within us and makes us immortal. "The Church teaches that every spiritual soul is created immediately by God — it is not 'produced' by the parents" (cf. Pius XII, *Humani Generis*: DS 3896; Paul VI, CPG § 8; Lateran Council V [1513]: DS 1440) (CCC 366).
      b. "The human body shares in the dignity of 'the image of God'" and is therefore not to be despised or maltreated (CCC 364).

C. Human beings are created "male and female" (Gn 1:27).
   1. Men and women have been created with equal dignity to reflect the Creator's wisdom and goodness. "'Being man' or 'being woman' is a reality which is good and willed by God" (CCC 369).
   2. The coming together of man and woman in the Genesis creation account "'constitutes the first form of communion between persons' (GS 12 § 4)" (CCC 383).
   3. The Church has traditionally taught that there are two inseparable aspects of the nature and purpose of the coming together of man and woman.
      a. The union of man and woman — "the two of them become one body" (Gn 2:24).
      b. The procreative dimension — "be fertile and multiply" (Gn 1:28).

D. "In God's plan man and woman have the vocation of 'subduing' the earth (Gn 1:28) as stewards of God" (CCC 373).
   1. All of creation was brought into being for man, "but man in turn was created to serve and love God and to offer all creation back to him" (CCC 358).
   2. Work was not intended to be a burden, but was rather an opportunity for humanity to collaborate with God in perfecting creation (CCC 378).
   3. Mastery over the world is perfectly achieved in the mastery of self (CCC 377).

E. The first human persons were created in an "original 'state of holiness and justice' (cf. Council of Trent [1546]: DS 1511)" (CCC 375).
   1. God established us in His friendship — a divine intimacy that excluded human suffering and death (CCC 376).

2. "The inner harmony of the human person, the harmony between man and woman (cf. Gn 2:25), and finally the harmony between the first couple and all creation, comprised the state called 'original justice'" (CCC 376).
3. God's gift of original justice was forfeited by the sin of the first humans (CCC 379).

NOTES...

FOCUS QUESTIONS:

1. How does our society reflect, or fail to reflect, the goodness of creation?
2. How do you see the role of angels and guardian angels in your life?
3. Does our society live as if we are the "image of God'?" How do we live the role of stewardship that God has given us?

Concluding prayers
Intercessions
Closing prayer
Hymn (optional)

RESOURCES

Catechism of the Catholic Church, 279-384
The Bible
Humani generis (Concerning some false opinions threatening to undermine the foundations of Catholic doctrine), Pius XII
Humanae vitae (On the regulation of birth), Paul VI
Lumen gentium (Dogmatic Constitution on the Church), Vatican II
Essentials of the Faith, McBride, chaps. 8-9

Session Seven

The Mystery of Sin

LEARNING OBJECTIVE

To present the account of the fall of Adam and Eve and to describe how this sin has affected the whole human family.

Hymn: "Turn to Me"

Invitation to prayer — silent prayer

Oration:

Lord our God,
you formed man from the clay of the earth
and breathed into him the spirit of life,
but he turned from your face and sinned.

In this time of repentance
we call out for your mercy.
Bring us back to you
and to the life your Son won for us
by his death on the cross,
for he lives and reigns for ever and ever.

Alternate Opening Prayer
First Sunday of Lent

Scripture reading: Romans 5:12-21

Therefore, just as through one person sin entered the world, and through sin, death, and thus death came to all, inasmuch as all sinned — for up to the time of the law, sin was in the world, though sin is not accounted when there is no law. But death reigned from Adam to Moses, even over those who did not sin after the pattern of the trespass of Adam, who is the type of the one who was to come.

But the gift is not like the transgression. For if by that one person's transgression the many died, how much more did the grace of God and the gracious gift of the one person Jesus Christ overflow for the many. And the gift is not like the result of the one person's sinning. For after one sin there was the judgment that brought condemnation; but the gift, after many transgressions, brought acquittal. For if, by the transgression of one person, death came to reign through that one, how much more will those who receive the abundance of grace and of the gift of justification come to reign in life through the one person Jesus Christ. In conclusion, just as through one transgression condemnation came upon all, so through one righteous act acquittal and life came to all. For just as through the disobedience of one person the many were made sinners, so through the obedience of one the many will be made righteous. The law entered in so that transgression might increase but, where sin increased, grace overflowed all the more, so that, as sin reigned in death, grace also might reign through justification for eternal life through Jesus Christ our Lord.

NOTES...

TEACHING TO BE PRESENTED

I. **The reality of sin.**

A. Sin exists in the history of humanity (CCC 386).

1. Sin is that evil which can only be truly understood by first recognizing "*the profound relation of man to God*" (CCC 386).
2. Sin is humanity's rejection of an all loving God, opposition to Him, and the effects of this rejection on human life and history (CCC 386).

B. Divine Revelation clearly portrays the reality of sin; in particular, original sin (CCC 387).

1. Without revelation we are unable to clearly grasp the significance of sin (CCC 387).
2. "Only in the knowledge of God's plan for man can we grasp that sin is an abuse of the freedom that God gives to created persons so that they are capable of loving him and loving one another" (CCC 387).

II. **Revelation of sin in the Old Testament recognizes a universal need for salvation. In the New Testament Christ is the one sent to be the salvation for all.**

A. In light of the Genesis account, the Israelites tried to understand the wounded nature of the human condition.

B. It was only in the New Testament, after Christ's death and resurrection, that the depths of sin could be seen more clearly.

1. "We must know Christ as the source of grace in order to know Adam as the source of sin" (CCC 388).
2. It is the work of the Holy Spirit to enlighten minds and hearts to recognize Christ as the redeemer and at the same time perceive the darkness of sin (CCC 388).
3. "The doctrine of original sin is, so to speak, the 'reverse side' of the Good News that Jesus is the Savior of all men" (CCC 389).

C. "The Church, which has the mind of Christ (cf. 1 Cor 2:16), knows very well that we cannot tamper with the revelation of original sin without undermining the mystery of Christ" (CCC 389).

III. **Original sin is a part of humanity.**

A. Original sin is inherited.

1. Adam, the "first man," lost the original state of justice and holiness through original sin. All humanity is marked by this fault of our first parents and is also deprived of the grace of original holiness and justice (CCC 416).
2. In the descendants of Adam, original sin does not possess the character of personal fault. Because of this sin, our human nature is weakened in its powers,

NOTES...

subject to ignorance and suffering, and inclined to sin. Concupiscence is the inclination to sin (CCC 405-406).

3. Beginning with Cain's murder of his brother Abel (Gn 4:3-15), sin can be seen throughout the history of Israel (CCC 401). A veritable "invasion" of sin continues to inundate the world.
4. The ultimate effect of original sin is death. The liturgy of Ash Wednesday reminds us that humanity must

   "return to the ground,
      from which you were taken;
   For you are dirt,
      and to dirt you shall return" (Gn 3:19).

B. In Adam and Eve's disobedience, the harmony they experienced in original justice was destroyed (CCC 400).
   1. The loss of original justice shattered the soul's spiritual faculties over the body (CCC 400).
   2. The union of man and woman experiences tension. Lust and domination mark the struggle of male/female relations (CCC 400).
   3. Harmony with creation is also broken:
      a. Visible creation becomes "alien and hostile" to humanity (cf. Gn 3:17, 19) (CCC 400).
      b. "*Death makes its entrance into human history*" (cf. Rom 5:12) (CCC 400).

C. We are saved from the power of sin and death.
   1. "Christians believe that 'the world has been established and kept in being by the Creator's love; has fallen into slavery to sin but has been set free by Christ, crucified and risen to break the power of the evil one . . .' (GS 2 § 2)" (CCC 421).
   2. Christ's victory "over sin has given us greater blessings than those which sin had taken from us: 'where sin increased, grace abounded all the more' (Rom 5:20)" (CCC 420).
   3. Through Baptism we are immersed in Jesus' death and resurrection. Baptism, by imparting God's grace, erases original sin and all personal sin, although the consequences of sin will always remain in our human nature. The desire for the good calls us to a lifelong spiritual struggle.
   4. The Exsultet of the Easter Vigil makes reference to the fault of our first parents and proclaims: "O happy fault, O necessary sin of Adam, / which gained for us so great a Redeemer!" (cf. CCC 412).

IV. The book of Genesis, chapter three, reveals the reality figuratively, that at the beginning of history, man in some way seriously rejected God. Thus "the whole of human history is marked by the original fault freely committed by our first parents" (cf. Council of Trent: DS 1513; Pius XII: DS 3897; Paul VI: AAS 58 [1966], 654) (CCC 390).

A. The Scriptures speak of sin on the part of some of the angels who freely refused to serve God and His plan.
   1. "Satan" ("tempter") became the leader of the fallen angels. Jesus referred to him as "the father of lies" (Jn 8:44).
   2. Satan and other demons try to associate themselves with humanity in their revolt against God (CCC 414).

B. Original sin is a truth of our faith.

1. Humanity was created to live in friendship with God in free obedience to Him.
   a. The prohibition against eating of "the tree of knowledge of good and bad" (Gn 2:17) expresses this freedom of obedience.
   b. Creatures of God have limits that must be freely recognized and confidently respected. We are dependent on our Creator and subject to the laws of nature which He has established for the order of creation and the moral norms which govern our use of freedom (CCC 396).
2. The account of Genesis 3 affirms that the "fall" took place at the beginning of human history. Our first parents were deceived by Satan. They abused their freedom and sought to find their destiny apart from God (CCC 390).

NOTES...

FOCUS QUESTIONS

1. Where do you see evidence of original sin in our world and society?
2. Christ Jesus saves us from the power of sin. Do you think we had to sin to gain "so great a Redeemer"?
3. How are the contemporary struggles between men and women a reflection of the loss of original justice?

Concluding prayers
Intercessions
Closing prayer
Hymn (optional)

RESOURCES

Catechism of the Catholic Church, 386-421
The Bible, Genesis 3
Dives in misericordia (The Mercy of God), John Paul II, 8
Essentials of the Faith, McBride, chap. 10

Session Eight

Jesus Christ

The Fulfillment of God's Promise

LEARNING OBJECTIVE

To show the unfolding plan of God's love for His people and the preparations for the coming of Christ.

Hymn: "O Come, O Come, Emmanuel'

Invitation to prayer — silent prayer

Oration:

Father in heaven,
our hearts desire the warmth of your love
and our minds are searching for the light of your Word.

Increase our longing for Christ our Savior
and give us the strength to grow in love,
that the dawn of his coming
may find us rejoicing in his presence
and welcoming the light of his truth.

We ask this in the name of Jesus the Lord.

Alternate Opening Prayer
First Sunday of Advent

Scripture reading: Isaiah 7:10-14

Again the LORD spoke to Ahaz: Ask for a sign from the LORD, your God; let it be deep as the nether world, or high as the sky! But Ahaz answered, "I will not ask! I will not tempt the LORD!" Then he said: Listen, O house of David! Is it not enough for you to weary men, must you also weary my God? Therefore the Lord himself will give you this sign: the virgin shall be with child, and bear a son, and shall name him Immanuel.

TEACHING TO BE PRESENTED

I. **Salvation history.**

A. God chose to be part of the history of humanity from the very beginning. Salvation History is God's saving activity for His people.

NOTES...

1. Genesis 3:15, "called the *Protoevangelium* ('first gospel'): the first announcement of the Messiah and Redeemer, of a battle between the serpent and the Woman, and of the final victory of a descendant of hers" (CCC 410).

   "I will put enmity between you and the woman,
   and between your offspring and hers;
   He will strike at your head,
   while you strike at his heel" (Gn 3:15).

2. Many of the Church Fathers see Mary, the "new Eve," as the woman referred to in the *Protoevangelium* (CCC 411).
3. Even though sin often filled the hearts of His people, God desired to protect and save them. Although Adam and Eve were forced to leave the garden of paradise because of their sin (cf. Gn 3:23-24) and were banished to the land of the nomads, He had no desire for them to suffer.
4. God felt closely bound to His people by a covenant that was not to be broken. God's covenant of love can be seen through the:
   a. Covenant with Noah (cf. Gn 9:8-17);
   b. Covenant with Abraham, (Isaac, Jacob, Twelve Tribes of Israel) (cf. Gn 15:17-18; 17:1-10);
   c. Exodus and Covenant with Moses (cf. Ex 19:4-6; 24:3-8);
   d. Davidic Kingdom: messianic expectation (cf. 2 Sam 7:8-29; 23:5);
   e. Exile and prophetic announcement of New Covenant (cf. Is 61:7-9; Jer 31:31-34; Ez 16:8, 60-63).
5. God's steadfast love and absolute fidelity saved the Israelites again and again from their sin.

B. The Old Covenant

1. As sin became more universal, Israel no longer was able to seek salvation except by invoking the name of the redeeming God (cf. Ps 79:9). The high priest invoked the name of the saving God once a year on the Day of Atonement and sprinkled the mercy seat in the Holy of Holies with the blood of sacrifice. A rich discussion on "mercy" and "covenant" is found in *Dives in misericordia,* n. 4.
2. The prophets announced that the covenant, concluded on the foundation of the Ten Commandments, had to give way to a new and everlasting covenant, to be written on the heart of every human person (cf. Jer 31; Ez 36-37). Only God could touch the hearts of His people. Only God could ultimately save His people from their sins.

II. Fulfillment of the promise: The Good News.

A. "'But when the time had fully come, God sent forth his Son, born of a woman, born under the law, to redeem those who were under the law, so that we might receive adoption as sons' (Gal 4:4-5)" (CCC 422).

B. In choosing a body for His Son, God wanted "the free cooperation of a creature" (CCC 488).

1. From all eternity God chose Mary, a young Jewish woman, a daughter of Israel (CCC 488).
2. She was "'a virgin betrothed to a man whose name was Joseph, of the house of David' (Lk 1:27)" (CCC 488).

NOTES...

C. "The Father of mercies willed that the incarnation should be preceded by the acceptance of her who was predestined to be the mother of His Son, so that just as a woman contributed to death, so also a woman should contribute to life" (LG 56; cf. LG 61).

D. God chose many women in the Old Covenant to accomplish His purposes (CCC 489).

   1. Eve is the mother of all the living. Even though she is disobedient, she does receive "the promise that she will be the mother of all the living" (cf. Gn 3:15, 20) (CCC 489).
   2. Sarah conceives a son in her old age (cf. Gn 18:10-14; 21:1-2) (CCC 489).
   3. God shows His fidelity to Hannah, Deborah, Ruth, Judith, and Esther, as well as many other women (CCC 489).

E. "Mary 'stands out among the poor and humble of the Lord'" and ends the long period of waiting as she becomes "the exalted Daughter of Sion, and the new plan of salvation is established" (LG 55) (CCC 489).

F. Jesus was born in Bethlehem at the time of King Herod the Great and Caesar Augustus, emperor (CCC 423).

   1. Jesus was a carpenter by trade (CCC 423).
   2. He "died crucified in Jerusalem under the procurator Pontius Pilate during the reign of the emperor Tiberius" (CCC 423).
   3. We believe and confess that this Jesus "is the eternal Son of God made man" (CCC 423).
   4. "He 'came from God' (Jn 13:3), 'descended from heaven' (Jn 3:13; 6:33), and 'came in the flesh' (1 Jn 4:2)" (CCC 423).

III. Who is Jesus Christ?

A. The name and principal christological titles of our Lord provide the summary and Christian belief in His identity and mission.

   1. The meaning of the name Jesus is "God saves." Born of the virgin Mary, Jesus "'will save his people from their sins' (Mt 1:21)" (CCC 452).
   2. The word "Christ" comes from the Greek translation of the Hebrew "Messiah," which means "Anointed One." "'God anointed Jesus of Nazareth with the Holy Spirit and with power' (Acts 10:38)" (CCC 453).
   3. The title "Son of God" identifies Jesus in His unique and eternal relationship to God His Father. He is the only Son of God the Father (cf. Jn 1:14, 18; 3:16, 18); Jesus is God Himself (cf. Jn 1:1) (CCC 454).
   4. When speaking of Jesus as "Lord," His divine sovereignty is addressed. "'No one can say, "Jesus is Lord" except by the Holy Spirit' (1 Cor 12:3)" (CCC 455).

IV. The season of Advent.

A. The beginning of the Church year celebrates four weeks of preparation for the coming of the Messiah. The term "Advent" means "coming." Predominant biblical figures in this liturgical season are Isaiah, John the Baptist, and Mary.

   1. Isaiah gives us a central prophecy concerning the birth of the Messiah (Is 7:14). The name "Emmanuel" or "God with us" is a common passage used in the course of the Advent season to express the joyful expectation of the coming of the Messiah. After the birth of Jesus, Matthew's Gospel directly quotes

NOTES...

this phrase to show the fulfillment of the Old Testament promise in Jesus (cf. Mt 1:23).

2. John the Baptist is the precursor of the Messiah (cf. Lk 1:16ff) who leads an austere life (cf. Mt 3:4), is a master teacher surrounded by his disciples (cf. in 1:35), and encourages people to fast, pray, and be sorry for their sins (cf. Mt 2:18; Lk 5:33). He humbled Himself to baptize Jesus and frequently described his submission to Christ throughout his ministry (CCC 523).
3. Mary is seen as the New Eve, the first to benefit from Jesus' victory over sin. Mary's "*fiat*" — be it done to me according to your word — is her "yes" in faith to God, and is the great model of faith for all generations. In faith and freedom, she entered into God's saving plan, accepting the role of Mother of the Savior.

B. The spirit of Advent should make us want to "prepare the way of the Lord" (Mk 1:3) so that we might better value the presence of the "Word became flesh" (Jn 1:14) who will save us from our sins (CCC 524).

FOCUS QUESTIONS

1. As you continue to grow in your relationship with Jesus Christ, how are you challenged to deeper conversion?
2. How does our longing for Christ Jesus during Advent compare to the People of the Old Covenant as they await the Messiah?
3. How can we be more like Mary or John the Baptist in our preparation for the Kingdom?

Concluding prayers
Intercessions
Closing prayer
Hymn (optional)

RESOURCES

Aperite portas Redemptori (Open the Doors to the Redeemer), John Paul II
Dives in misericordia (The Mercy of God), John Paul II
Lumen Gentium (Dogmatic Constitution on the Church), Vatican II
Redemptor hominis (Mother of the Redeemer), John Paul II
Essentials of the Faith, McBride, chap. 11

Session Nine

The Mystery of the Incarnation

LEARNING OBJECTIVE

To explain the centrality of the doctrine of the Incarnation and to show its impact on our understanding of redemption.

Hymn: "Let All Mortal Flesh Keep Silence"

Invitation to prayer — silent prayer

Oration:

The following prayer dates from the Middle Ages. It calls to mind the mystery of the Incarnation and was prayed three times a day (6 a.m., 12 noon, 6 p.m.) as the church bells would ring, to remind people to keep their day centered on Jesus.

The Angelus

The angel of the Lord declared unto Mary
and she conceived of the Holy Spirit.

Hail Mary, full of grace,
the Lord is with you.
Blessed are you among women
and blessed is the fruit of your womb, Jesus.
Holy Mary, mother of God,
pray for us sinners now
and at the hour of our death. Amen.

Behold the handmaid of the Lord.
Be it done unto me according to your word.

Hail Mary . . .

And the Word was made flesh
And dwelt among us.

Hail Mary . . .

Pray for us, O holy Mother of God,
That we may be made worthy of the promises of Christ.

Pour forth, we ask you, O Lord,
your grace into our hearts,
that we, to whom the Incarnation of Christ, your Son,
was made known by the message of an angel,
may by his passion and cross,
be brought to the glory of his resurrection
We ask this through the same Christ, our Lord.
Amen.

Scripture reading: John 1:1-14

In the beginning was the Word,
  and the Word was with God,
  and the Word was God.
He was in the beginning with God.
All things came to be through him,
  and without him nothing came to be.
What came to be through him was life,
  and this life was the light of the human race;
the light shines in the darkness,
  and the darkness has not overcome it.

A man named John was sent from God. He came for testimony, to testify to the light, so that all might believe through him. He was not the light, but came to testify to the light. The true light, which enlightens everyone, was coming into the world.

He was in the world,
  and the world came to be through him,
  but the world did not know him.
He came to what was his own,
  but his own people did not accept him.

But to those who did accept him he gave power to become children of God, to those who believe in his name, who were born not by natural generation nor by human choice nor by a man's decision but of God.

And the Word became flesh
  and made his dwelling among us,
  and we saw his glory,
  the glory as the Father's only Son,
  full of grace and truth.

NOTES...

NOTES...

TEACHING TO BE PRESENTED

I. "Belief in the true Incarnation of the Son of God is the distinctive sign of Christian faith" (CCC 463).

A. "The Church calls 'Incarnation' the fact that the Son of God assumed a human nature in order to accomplish our salvation in it" (CCC 461).

1. The term "Incarnation" may be broken down to its Latin root word *caro*, meaning "flesh." Incarnation is the "enfleshment" of God.
2. Jesus is the perfect expression of the Father. "He is the image of the invisible God" (Col 1:15).
3. Before the moment of the Incarnation, the Second Person of the Trinity is understood as the "Word" of God (cf. Jn 1:14). A "word" is an expression of someone or something.

B. "Jesus Christ is true God and true man" (CCC 464).

1. The Incarnation does not mean that Jesus Christ is a hybrid — part God and part man; neither does it mean the Jesus' humanity and divinity are jumbled and indiscriminate (CCC 464).
2. The Son of God became incarnate in Jesus Christ in a complete and total fashion. "He became truly man while remaining truly God" (CCC 464).

II. The christological hymns of the New Testament lay open the mystery of the Incarnation.

A. John 1:1-14

1. The Prologue of John's Gospel focuses upon the presence of the Word from the beginning of time (vs. 1).
2. The world was created through the mystery of the Word (vs. 3) and the Word "became flesh" and "made his dwelling" among us (vs. 14).
3. Herein lies the mystery of the Incarnation: The Word of God leapt down from heaven and was united to our humanity.

B. Philippians 2:6-11

1. This ancient hymn recorded by St. Paul reflects on the humility of Jesus — a model for all Christian service. Jesus "emptied himself" (vs. 7) to take on our human nature.
2. This passage helps elucidate the two natures of Jesus — divine and human. St. Paul uses the term "form" in reference to Jesus' two "natures" (vv. 6, 7).
3. The moment of the Incarnation was also the beginning of our Redemption. The hymn highlights this continuity and points to the early Church's faith in Jesus, who took on our human condition, accepted suffering and death, and is now Lord of all (vs. 11).

C. Colossians 1:15-20

1. The early Christians sang this hymn at Eucharistic celebrations. It expounds upon the mystery of the Incarnation and shows the supremacy of Christ to all creation.
2. The Liturgy of the Hours includes this hymn and the Philippians hymn cited above as New Testament canticles (songs). The Christians of today join with the Christians of the early centuries in singing and praying about what is central to our faith — namely, the union of two natures in Jesus Christ.

NOTES...

III. In opposition to false teaching concerning Christ, the ancient Church defended and clarified the truth of the Incarnation (CCC 464).

A. Some early Christian teachers denied Christ's true humanity, but orthodox teachers insisted that He truly came in the flesh and possessed a complete human nature, body and soul (CCC 465).

B. Others denied the full divinity of Christ (CCC 465).
   1. The Council of Nicaea (325) gathered to affirm that the Son of God is begotten of God from all eternity and is "one in being" with the Father.
   2. The council fathers at Nicaea composed a "creed" — a short summary of orthodox Christian beliefs. The Nicene Creed took a definitive shape at the first Council of Constantinople (381).
   3. Today we recite the Nicene Creed every Sunday and affirm with the apostles and early Christians the full truth about our Lord's Incarnation:
   We believe in one Lord, Jesus Christ, the only Son of God, eternally begotten of the Father, God from God, Light from Light, true God from true God, begotten, not made, one in Being with the Father. Through him all things were made.

C. Others denied the unity of Christ, supposing that the Son of God in heaven and Jesus on earth were two different subjects (CCC 466).
   1. The third ecumenical Council at Ephesus (431) rejected this "division" in Christ; it taught that "Christ's humanity has no other subject than the divine person of the Son of God, who assumed it and made it his own, from his conception" (CCC 466).
   2. Ephesus reinforced that "Mary truly became the Mother of God by the human conception of the Son of God in her womb" (CCC 466).

D. Still others denied Christ's full humanity: They taught that human nature was changed and ceased to exist once the divine person (the Son) assumed a human nature (CCC 467).
   1. The fourth ecumenical Council at Chalcedon (451) rejected this "confusion" of the two natures, teaching that in His human nature, Christ is "'like to us in all things except sin' (GS 22 § 2)" (CCC 467; 470).
   2. Although we cannot fully understand or imagine it, we believe that Christ possesses a human soul with its own intellect and will.
      a. As one who "emptied himself" (Phil 2:7), Christ knew with a human intellect, chose with a human will, and loved with a human heart.
      b. The Word incarnate was the subject of this knowing and choosing, living out His eternal Sonship under the conditions of our humanity, subject to weakness, temptation, physical and mental pain, and death (CCC 470).
   3. Chalcedon affirmed that Christ is one in being with the Father as to His divinity and one in being with us as to His humanity.
      a. One and the same subject or person, Christ, the Son of God, possesses two natures, divine and human, not confused but united (CCC 467, 481).
      b. Theology calls this union of the divine and human natures in the person of the Son the "hypostatic union."

E. Finally, some early Christians denied the unity of Christ.
   1. They taught that Christ's human nature is a personal subject distinct from the eternal Word.
   2. The fifth ecumenical Council of Constantinople (553) affirmed instead that Christ is only one personal subject, the divine person, "*one of the Holy Trinity*"

NOTES...

(Council of Constantinople II [553]: DS 432; cf. DS 424; Council of Ephesus, DS 255) (CCC 468).

IV. With the Nicene Creed, we confess that the Word became incarnate "'for us men and for our salvation'" (CCC 456).

A. The Incarnation of the Word brings about our salvation "*by reconciling us with God*" (CCC 457).

1. We see in the Incarnation the love of God, who "'loved us and sent his Son to be the expiation for our sins': 'the Father has sent his Son as the Savior of the world,' and 'he was revealed to take away sins'" (1 Jn 4:10; 4:14; 3:5) (CCC 457).
2. "We had lost the possession of the good; it was necessary for it to be given back to us," wrote St. Gregory of Nyssa. "Did [sin and weakness]," he asked, "not move God to descend to human nature and visit it, since humanity was in so miserable and unhappy a state?" (St. Gregory of Nyssa, *Orat. catech.* 15; PG 45, 48B) (CCC 457).

B. "The Word became flesh *so that thus we might know God's love*" (CCC 458).

1. "Jesus Christ is true God and true man, in the unity of his divine person; for this reason he is the one and only mediator between God and men" (CCC 480).
2. "'For God so loved the world that he gave his only Son, that whoever believes in him should not perish but have eternal life' (Jn 3:16)" (CCC 458).

C. The Incarnation of the divine Word in Christ makes Him "*our model of holiness*" (CCC 459).

1. Jesus taught His disciples that He was "'the way, and the truth, and the life; no one comes to the Father, but by me' (Jn 14:6)" (CCC 459).
2. "Jesus is the model for the Beatitudes and the norm of the new law: 'Love one another as I have loved you' (Jn 15:12). This love implies an effective offering of oneself, after his example (cf. Mk 8:34)" (CCC 459).

D. "The Word became flesh to make us '*partakers of the divine nature*' (2 Pt 1:4)" (CCC 460).

1. "For this is why the Word became man, and the Son of God became the Son of man: so that man, by entering into communion with the Word and thus receiving divine sonship, might become a son of God" (St. Irenaeus, *Adv. haeres.* 3, 19, 1: PG 7/1, 939) (CCC 460).
2. In a liturgical prayer still in use today during the preparation of the altar and the gifts, Pope St. Leo the Great (d. 461) expressed the connection between the Eucharist, the Incarnation, and our own transformation in Christ: "By the mystery of this water and wine may we come to share in the divinity of Christ, who humbled himself to share in our humanity."

FOCUS QUESTIONS

1. Why is it important that Jesus became fully human, like us in every way except sin? Why is it important that He is fully divine?
2. Despite the Church's definitive teaching, people continue to follow after false ideas concerning the Incarnation of the Word. What are some examples of this contemporary confusion and how do you think the Church would respond?
3. What do you think St. Athanasius meant when he wrote: "For the Son of God became man so that we might become God" (St. Athanasius, *De inc.*, 54, 3: PG 25, 192B) (CCC 460)?

Concluding prayers
Intercessions
Closing prayer
Hymn (optional)

RESOURCES

Catechism of the Catholic Church, 463-480
Cur Deus Homo (Why God Became Man), St. Anselm
Essentials of the Faith, McBride, chap. 12

NOTES...

Session Ten

Mary

The Virgin Mother of God

LEARNING OBJECTIVE

To present the Catholic belief on Mary with specific clarification as to why Mary receives such a significant place in the treasury of the Church.

Hymn: "Sing of Mary, Pure and Lowly"

Invitation to prayer — silent prayer

Oration:

Father,
the image of the Virgin is found in the Church.
Mary had a faith that your Spirit prepared
and a love that never knew sin,
for you kept her sinless from the first moment of her conception.
Trace in our actions the lines of her love,
in our hearts her readiness of faith.
Prepare once again a world for your Son
who lives and reigns with you and the Holy Spirit,
one God, for ever and ever.

Alternate Opening Prayer
Solemnity of the Immaculate Conception

Scripture reading: Luke 1:26-38

In the sixth month, the angel Gabriel was sent from God to a town of Galilee called Nazareth, to a virgin betrothed to a man named Joseph, of the house of David, and the virgin's name was Mary. And coming to her, he said, "Hail, favored one! The Lord is with you." But she was greatly troubled at what was said and pondered what sort of greeting this might be. Then the angel said to her, "Do not be afraid, Mary, for you have found favor with God. Behold, you will conceive in your womb and bear a son, and you shall name him Jesus. He will be great and will be called Son of the Most High, and the Lord God will give him the throne of David his father, and he will rule over the house of Jacob forever, and of his kingdom there will be no end." But Mary said to the angel, "How can this be, since I have no relations with a man?" And the angel said to her in reply, "The holy Spirit will come upon you, and the power of the Most High will overshadow you. Therefore the child to be born will be called holy, the Son of God. And behold, Elizabeth, your relative, has also conceived a son in her old age, and this is the sixth month for her who was called barren; for nothing will be impossible for God." Mary said, "Behold, I am the handmaid of the Lord. May it be done to me according to your word." Then the angel departed from her.

NOTES...

TEACHING TO BE PRESENTED

I. Mary's predestination and Immaculate Conception.

A. In His plan of salvation, God sent forth His only Son.
   1. Because His Son was to come on earth, God desired the free cooperation of a woman who would "prepare a body for him" (Heb 10:5) (CCC 488).
   2. "From all eternity God chose for the mother of his Son a daughter of Israel, a young Jewish woman of Nazareth in Galilee" (CCC 488).

B. "Throughout the Old Covenant the mission of many holy women *prepared* for that of Mary" (CCC 489).
   1. Mary was predestined to be the mother of God's only Son (CCC 488). Predestination means God's eternal design which brings about good in creation.
   2. The long period of waiting during the time of the Old Testament was over. The young virgin, Mary, who in faith also waited for a savior, received salvation from Him. As one of the poor and humble of the Lord, Mary became the exalted Daughter of Sion, "'and the new plan of salvation is established' (LG 55)" (CCC 489).

C. Mary's Immaculate Conception, celebrated on December 8, marks the conception of Mary.
   1. "'The most Blessed Virgin Mary was, from the first moment of her conception, by a singular grace and privilege of almighty God and by virtue of the merits of Jesus Christ, Savior of the human race, preserved immune from all stain of original sin' (Pius IX, *Ineffabilis Deus*, 1854: DS 2803)" (CCC 491).
   2. God blessed Mary more than any other human person (CCC 492). As prayed in the Hail Mary, she is full of grace. Grace is God's very own divine life in a person.
   3. Mary is the new Eve. God in His mercy willed that Mary's *fiat*, her submission to whatever God had in mind for her, would contribute to the coming of life. Eve, in her disobedience, shared in the coming of death in the beginnings of God's revelation to His people. In contrast, Mary gave her obedient consent to God's will. With God, dependent on Him and by God's grace, she serves the mystery of redemption (CCC 494). *Fiat* is a Latin word meaning "let it be done." At her Annunciation, Mary proclaimed submission to whatever God had in mind for her.
   4. That Mary is full of grace determines the extraordinary greatness and beauty of her whole being. The dogma of the Immaculate Conception, proclaimed by Pope Pius IX in 1854, calls us to see her magnificence in the order of grace. She was born without sin and by God's special grace remained without sin her entire life (CCC 491).

NOTES...

II. The Gospels call Mary the "mother of Jesus."

A. Mary's motherhood is divine. She conceived Jesus by the power of the Holy Spirit. The Father's only Son became flesh in the womb of Mary. While she was still carrying Jesus in her womb, Elizabeth at the Visitation acclaimed her as "the mother of my Lord" (Lk 1:43). At the Council of Ephesus in 431, Mary was proclaimed "Mother of God" (*Theotokos*) (CCC 495).

B. The Church proclaims Mary's virginal motherhood.
   1. Jesus was conceived solely by the power of the Holy Spirit in her womb. The Council of the Lateran in 649 professed that Jesus was conceived without human seed (CCC 496).
   2. The early Church Fathers see in the virginal conception the truth that Jesus, the Son of God, came in a humanity like our own (CCC 496).
   3. The Church understands the virginal conception of Jesus as a "divine work" that is beyond human comprehension and possibility (CCC 497). Thus is fulfilled the promise given through the prophet Isaiah: "The virgin shall be with child, and bear a son" (Is 7:14).

C. Mary is proclaimed by the Church as "*Aeiparthenos,* the 'Ever-virgin' (cf. LG 52)" (CCC 499).
   1. Christ's birth "'did not diminish his mother's virginal integrity but sanctified it' (LG 57)" (CCC 499).
   2. The Church confesses that Mary remained a virgin (CCC 499).

D. Mary's virginal motherhood is part of God's saving plan of salvation.
   1. "Mary's virginity manifests God's absolute initiative in the Incarnation" (CCC 503).
   2. As to His divinity Jesus is "'naturally Son of the Father as to his divinity and naturally son of his mother as to his humanity, but properly Son of the Father in both natures' (Council of Friuli [796]: DS 619; cf. Lk 2:48-49)" (CCC 503).
   3. Jesus, conceived by the Holy Spirit in the womb of the Virgin Mary is the New Adam who brings about the new Creation (CCC 504).
   4. By His virginal conception, Jesus brings about "*the new birth* of children adopted in the Holy Spirit through faith." The acceptance of life as divine and of God "is virginal because it is entirely the Spirit's gift to man. The spousal character of the human vocation in relation to God (cf. 2 Cor 11:2) is fulfilled perfectly in Mary's virginal motherhood" (CCC 505).
   5. Mary's virginity "is *the sign of her faith* 'unadulterated by any doubt,' and of her undivided gift of herself to God's will" (LG 63; cf. 1 Cor 7:34-35) (CCC 506).
   6. Mary, both virgin and mother, is the most perfect realization of the Church since, in receiving the Word of God in faith, the Church as well becomes herself a mother. We call the Church Holy Mother Church (CCC 507).

III. Mary is Mother of the Church. "Mary's role in the Church is inseparable from her union with Christ and flows directly from it" (CCC 964).

A. The Assumption, celebrated on August 15, marks the moment when Mary "'was taken up body and soul into heavenly glory, and exalted by the Lord as Queen over all things, so that she might be the more fully conformed to her Son, the Lord of lords and conqueror of sin and death' (LG 59; cf. Pius XII, *Munificentissimus Deus* [1950]: DS 3903; cf. Rv 19:16)" (CCC 966). This is the dogma of the Assumption of Mary proclaimed by Pope Pius XII in 1950.

NOTES...

1. The Assumption of the Blessed Virgin Mary is a singular participation in her Son's Resurrection and an anticipation of our own bodily resurrection.
2. "By her complete adherence to the Father's will, to his Son's redemptive work, and to every prompting of the Holy Spirit, the Virgin Mary is the Church's model of faith and charity" (CCC 967).
3. Mary is our Mother "'in the order of grace' (LG 61)" (CCC 968).
4. "'The Blessed Virgin is invoked in the Church under the titles of Advocate, Helper, Benefactress, and Mediatrix' (LG 62)" (CCC 969).
5. "The liturgical feasts dedicated to the Mother of God and Marian prayer, such as the rosary, an 'epitome of the whole Gospel,' expresses this devotion to the Virgin Mary" (cf. Paul VI, MC 42; SC 103) (CCC 971).
6. The Church's devotion to the Blessed Virgin Mary is at the very heart of her worship. The Church honors Mary with special devotion. This devotion differs from the adoration given to the three persons of the blessed Trinity (CCC 971).

B. The Church honors Mary with the prayer, "Hail Mary."

1. The angel greeted Mary at the Annunciation with the words "Hail Mary!"
2. ". . . full of grace, the Lord is with thee!" These again are from the angel's greeting. Mary is the place where the glory of the Lord dwells. She is wholly given over to Him who has come to dwell in her and whom she is about to give to the world.
3. "Blessed art thou among women and blessed is the fruit of thy womb, Jesus." After the angel's greeting we make Elizabeth's greeting our own. Mary is blessed among women, because she believed in the fulfillment of the Lord's word.
4. "Holy Mary, Mother of God. . ." Because she gives us Jesus, Mary is Mother of God and our Mother; we can entrust our cares and petitions to her.
5. "Pray for us sinners now, and at the hour of our death." We acknowledge ourselves as poor sinners. . . . As she was present to the death of her son, may she, as our mother, welcome us at the hour of our passing.

FOCUS QUESTIONS

1. What can you imitate in Mary's *fiat*?
2. How can you show your devotion to Mary?
3. Why do you think so many people misunderstand the Church's teaching on the role of Mary in salvation?

Concluding prayers
Intercessions
Closing prayer
Hymn (optional)

RESOURCES

Catechism of the Catholic Church, 488-507, 964-971
Lumen gentium (Dogmatic Constitution on the Church), Vatican II, chap. 8, art. 52-69

NOTES...

Marialis cultus (For the Right Ordering and Development of Devotion to the Blessed Virgin Mary), Paul VI
Redemptoris Mater (Mother of the Redeemer), John Paul II
Essentials of the Faith, McBride, chap. 13

Session Eleven

Jesus' Ministry

Teaching, Healing, Reconciling

LEARNING OBJECTIVE

To present the whole of Christ's public life as a continual lesson of selfless love for every human being, seen in the eyes of God as a person bearing great dignity.

Hymn: "The Cry of the Poor"

Invitation to prayer — silent prayer

Oration:

In faith and love we ask you, Father,
to watch over your family gathered here.
In your mercy and loving kindness
no thought of ours is left unguarded,
no tear unheeded, no joy unnoticed.

Through the prayer of Jesus
may the blessings promised to the poor in spirit
lead us to the treasures of your heavenly kingdom.

We ask this in the name of Jesus the Lord.

Alternate Opening Prayer
Fifth Sunday of Ordinary Time

Scripture reading: Luke 5:17-26

One day as Jesus was teaching, Pharisees and teachers of the law were sitting there who had come from every village of Galilee and Judea and Jerusalem, and the power of the Lord was with him for healing. And some men brought on a stretcher a man who was paralyzed; they were trying to bring him in and set [him] in his presence. But not finding a way to bring him in because of the crowd, they went up on the roof and lowered him on the stretcher through the tiles into the middle in front of Jesus. When he saw their faith, he said, "As for you, your sins are forgiven." Then the scribes and Pharisees began to ask themselves, "Who is this who speaks blasphemies? Who but God alone can forgive sins?" Jesus knew their thoughts and said to them in reply, "What are you thinking in your hearts? Which is easier, to say, 'Your sins are forgiven,' or to say, 'Rise and walk'? But that you may know that the Son of Man has authority on earth to forgive sins" — he said to the man who was paralyzed, "I say to you, rise, pick up

NOTES...

your stretcher, and go home." He stood up immediately before them, picked up what he had been lying on, and went home, glorifying God. Then astonishment seized them all and they glorified God, and, struck with awe, they said, "We have seen incredible things today."

TEACHING TO BE PRESENTED

I. The mysteries of Jesus' public life are His Baptism, temptations, and Transfiguration.

A. Jesus' public life is initiated with His Baptism by John the Baptist (CCC 535).
   1. Jesus' Baptism is His acceptance and beginning of the mission as God's suffering Servant. He allows Himself to be one among sinners. "The Spirit whom Jesus possessed in fullness from his conception comes to 'rest on him' (Jn 1:32-33; cf. Is 11:2)" (CCC 536).
   2. In His own Baptism, Jesus anticipates His death and resurrection. "The Christian must enter into this mystery of humble self-abasement and repentance, go down into the water with Jesus in order to rise with him, be reborn of water and the Spirit so as to become the Father's beloved son in the Son and 'walk in newness of life' (Rom 6:4)" (CCC 537).

B. Scripture accounts for us a time after His Baptism when He entered the desert for a period of solitude of forty days.
   1. In the desert Jesus fasts and prays. "At the end of this time Satan tempts him three times, seeking to compromise his filial attitude toward God" (CCC 538).
   2. In giving a meaning to this mysterious experience the Gospel writers see Jesus as "the new Adam who remained faithful just where the first Adam had given in to temptation" (CCC 539). "Jesus' victory over the tempter in the desert anticipates victory at the Passion, the supreme act of obedience of his filial love for the Father" (CCC 539).
   3. By enduring this test Jesus can sympathize with our human struggle. Jesus was tested in every way but did not sin. The Church unites herself to the mystery of Christ's experience in the desert by observing the solemn forty days of Lent (CCC 540).

C. The Transfiguration of Jesus
   1. After Peter confessed that Jesus is the Christ, Jesus began to try and help His disciples understand that suffering, death, and resurrection were awaiting Him. This was not accepted by Peter nor understood by the disciples (CCC 554).
   2. Jesus took Peter, James, and John with Him to a high mountain. "[Jesus'] face changed in appearance and his clothing became dazzling white. And behold, two men were conversing with him, Moses and Elijah, who appeared in glory and spoke of his exodus that he was going to accomplish in Jerusalem" (Lk 9:29-31). A cloud covers him and a voice from heaven says: "'This is my Son, my Chosen; listen to him!' (Lk 9:35)" (CCC 554).
   3. For a brief moment Jesus discloses His divinity. He also reveals that He will suffer in order to "'enter into his glory' (Lk 24:26)" (CCC 555).

4. Christ's Transfiguration was intended to strengthen the faith of the apostles as they journeyed towards Calvary. "Christ, Head of the Church, manifests what his Body contains and radiates in the sacraments: 'the hope of glory' (Col 1:27; cf. St. Leo the Great, *Sermo* 51, 3: PL 54, 310c)" (CCC 568).

NOTES...

II. Jesus came to proclaim the Good News.

A. "'The whole of Christ's life was a continual teaching: his silences, his miracles, his gestures, his prayer, his love for people, his special affection for the little and the poor' (John Paul II, CT 9)" (CCC 561).

1. Jesus teaches a moral requirement in the double commandment of love of God and love of neighbor (cf. Mk 12:30-31). He ties together two precepts of the Old Testament (cf. Dt 6:5; Lv 19:18, 34).
2. Matthew 25:31-46 gives us a profound teaching on our moral obligation to never overlook those who are in need. We must learn to treat others as we would treat Christ Himself. Jesus said, "Amen, I say to you, what you did not do for one of these least ones, you did not do for me" (Mt 25:45).
3. The radical choices which Jesus asked of His followers allowed them to see that His commandment of love was not only a commandment, but above all a gift. Every Christian is capable of living in the dimension of this gift, as Pope John Paul II so beautifully described in his admonition *To the Youth of the World* (1985). In this document and in *Veritatis Splendor* (1993), the Pope uses Jesus' discussion with the rich young man as an opportunity to show a mature outline of the Christian vocation.

B. Jesus proclaimed the good news of the kingdom of God. The people of the Old Testament longed for the Messiah, but Jesus did not bring the military might they expected, but mercy and love.

1. Jesus' proclamation bears the imprint of the language of the Old Testament, yet its central content is a unique proclamation that the Kingdom of God hoped for by the people of the Old Testament is here (cf. Mk 1:14-15) (CCC 541).
2. God's "kingdom belongs *to the poor and lowly*" (CCC 544). The Beatitudes (Mt 5:3-12) show that the message of Jesus is good news. He has reversed every earthly standard of value and looked at humanity in a completely realistic way.
3. The Beatitudes appeal to the heart of every human being to let themselves be grasped by God's mercy and love. Those who have nothing to expect from the world can expect all from God. Poverty and service in the cause of peace are requirements of the disciples of Jesus. The Beatitudes set standards for behavior in this world (CCC 1716-1724).
4. In the Sermon on the Mount, we see that "Jesus did not abolish the Law of Sinai, but rather fulfilled it (cf. Mt 5:17-19) with such perfection (cf. Jn 8:46) that he revealed its ultimate meaning (cf. Mt 5:33) . . ." (CCC 592).

III. Jesus' words and actions had power.

A. Jesus often taught by means of parables. Parables are stories of comparison used to teach a lesson. The parables used by Jesus serve as mirrors for humanity. They help people grasp the meaning of His teachings in a simple yet profound manner (Mk 4:33-34) (CCC 546).

1. The parable of the sower and the seed (cf. Mk 4:1-20) teaches that we must first accept the word of Jesus to enter the kingdom.

NOTES...

2. The parable of the Good Samaritan (cf. Lk 10:29-37) shows us the relationship that each of us must have towards our neighbor, and that every person we encounter is our neighbor. Our Lord teaches the true meaning of compassion based on love of all others, and not simply our friends and family. Jesus shows us that we must be sensitive to those who suffer and that we can only find ourselves through giving ourselves for the sake of others (GS 24). Pope John Paul II's encyclical *Salvifici Doloris,* n. 28-30, gives a beautiful explanation of this parable.
3. The parable of the Prodigal Son (cf. Lk 15:11-32) shows the deep meaning of the mercy of God and the "joy in heaven over one sinner who repents" (Lk 15:7). Pope John Paul II's encyclical *Dives in Misericordia,* n. 5-6, gives a description of the reality of conversion. Jesus invited sinners to the table of the kingdom: "I did not come to call the righteous but sinners" (Mk 2:17).
4. Other parables (cf. Mt 13:44-45; 22:1-14) invite people to the banquet of the kingdom and demand a radical choice. Words are not enough for the Christian. The believer is asked to make use of his or her talents.

B. Jesus was a witness to the power of God by means of miracles and signs.

1. Jesus' words were also accompanied by many "deeds, wonders, and signs" (Acts 2:22). His signs showed that the Father had sent Him and that He openly invites all people to believe in Him (cf. Jn 5:36; 10:25, 38). The miracles of Jesus strengthened people's faith. A look at Scriptures gives proof that Jesus freed certain people from the earthly evils of hunger, injustice, illness, and death (cf. Jn 6:5-15; Lk 19:8; Mk 1:30-45; 2:3-12; 3:1-6; 5:1-13, 25-34; 6:53-56) (CCC 547-48).
2. The cure of the man born blind (cf. Jn 9:1-41) is used in the Second Scrutiny for adults in their preparation for Baptism. This miracle helps the elect more deeply perceive a necessity for radical change in life and the sight which one receives in the waters of Baptism.
3. The raising of Lazarus (cf. Jn 11:1-44) is used in the Third Scrutiny. This miracle shows Jesus' power over death. Every person longs to be delivered from sin and saved from its present and future consequences.
4. "By freeing some individuals from the earthly evils of hunger, injustice, illness, and death (cf. Jn 6:5-15; Lk 19:8, Mt 11:5), Jesus performed messianic signs. Nevertheless he did not come to abolish all evils here below (cf. Lk 12:13-14; Jn 18:36), but to free men from the gravest slavery, sin, which thwarts them in their vocation as God's sons and causes all forms of human bondage (cf. Jn 8: 34-36)" (CCC 549).

FOCUS QUESTIONS

1. What would you say was Jesus' central message?
2. What is your favorite parable? What is it about its meaning that appeals to you?
3. Where do you see evidence of Jesus' healing today?

Concluding prayers
Intercessions
Closing prayer
Hymn (optional)

NOTES...

RESOURCES

Catechism of the Catholic Church, 535-561, 1716-1724
Catechesi tradendae (Catechhesis in Our Time), John Paul II
Dives in misericoidia (The Mercy of God), John Paul II
Gaudium et spes (Pastoral Constitution on the Church in the Modern World), Vatican II
Redemptionis donum (Apostolic Exhortation of His Holiness John Paul II to Men and Women Religious), John Paul II
Essentials of the Faith, McBride, chap. 14

Session Twelve

The Mystery of Redemption

LEARNING OBJECTIVE

To come to a deeper realization of Jesus' self-emptying love, which brought us to reconciliation with God and to recognize that happiness in our lives is a participation in the very Paschal Love of Christ.

Hymn: "O Sacred Head Surrounded"

Invitation to prayer — silent prayer

Oration:

Almighty, ever-living God,
you have given the human race Jesus Christ our Savior
as a model of humility.
He fulfilled your will
by becoming man and giving his life on the cross.
Help us to bear witness to you
by following his example of suffering
and make us worthy to share in his resurrection.

We ask this through our Lord Jesus Christ, your Son,
who lives and reigns with you and the Holy Spirit,
one God, for ever and ever.

Opening Prayer
Passion Sunday

Scripture reading: Philippians 2:6-11

[Christ Jesus], though he was in the form of God,
did not regard equality with God
something to be grasped.
Rather, he emptied himself,
taking the form of a slave,
coming in human likeness;
and found human in appearance,
he humbled himself,
becoming obedient to death,
even death on a cross.
Because of this, God greatly exalted him
and bestowed on him the name

> that is above every name,
> that at the name of Jesus
> every knee should bend,
> of those in heaven and on earth and under
> the earth,
> and every tongue confess that
> Jesus Christ is Lord,
> to the glory of God the Father.

NOTES...

TEACHING TO BE PRESENTED

I. Jesus' public ministry led to His crucifixion.

A. Jesus' Baptism marked His manifestation as the "Messiah of Israel and Son of God" (CCC 535).

B. Jesus' temptations in the wilderness likewise prefigured His passion — His battle with and victory over Satan (CCC 539).

C. By His proclamation of the Kingdom in word and signs, and by gathering the people around Him, Jesus anticipated the Paschal Mystery by which He would draw all to Himself (CCC 542).

D. Peter, by a revelation from the Father, confessed Jesus' messianic identity, after which Jesus announced His coming Passion (CCC 552).

E. Setting His face for Jerusalem, where the prophets were martyred, Jesus freely went to meet His violent end. "*Jesus' entry into Jerusalem* manifested the coming of the kingdom that the King-Messiah was going to accomplish by the Passover of his Death and Resurrection" (CCC 560). Each year on Palm Sunday, "the Church's liturgy solemnly opens Holy Week" (CCC 560) with the celebration of this event.

II. In God's plan, it was necessary that Jesus suffer.

A. The Paschal mystery of Christ's sufferings, death, and resurrection are at the very heart of the good news which the apostles and the Church are called to proclaim to all peoples (CCC 571).
   1. God fulfilled His saving plan once and for all in Christ.
   2. It was necessary that Jesus suffer in order to enter into His glory (CCC 572).

B. Jesus' sufferings took place in a historical concrete form.
   1. "He was 'rejected by the elders and the chief priests and the scribes' (Mk 8:31)" (CCC 572).
   2. He was then handed over "'to the Gentiles to be mocked and scourged and crucified' (Mt 20:19)" (CCC 572).

C. Some of Israel's religious leaders accused Jesus of violating the Mosaic Law — violations which were punishable by death.
   1. Jesus expelled demons.
   2. He forgave sins.
   3. He healed people on the Sabbath.
   4. His interpretation of the Law regarding purity caused reactions.
   5. He mingled with tax collectors and public sinners (CCC 574).

D. Jesus' words and deeds were a sign of contradiction.

NOTES...

1. Jesus' relations with the Pharisees were controversial. He affirmed some of their teaching and pious practices such as almsgiving, fasting, and prayer (CCC 575).
2. Their custom of calling God "Father" and their centrality of focus on love of God and neighbor were endorsed by Jesus (CCC 575).

E. Jesus seemed to oppose essential institutions of the Chosen People:
1. "— submission to the whole of the Law in its written commandments and, for the Pharisees, in the interpretation of oral tradition;
2. "— the centrality of the Temple at Jerusalem as the holy place where God's presence dwells in a special way;
3. "— faith in the one God whose glory no man can share" (CCC 576).

F. Jesus' major challenges to Israel centered around the Law, the Temple, and faith in one God.
1. Jesus came to fulfill the Law of Sinai (CCC 592). In perfecting the Law, Jesus interpreted it with divine authority, thus inciting the teaching authority of certain teachers of the Law (CCC 582).
2. Jesus was faithful to the Jewish feasts in the Temple. He loved this place of worship. He saw it as prefiguring His own mystery (CCC 593). When He saw the need of its cleansing and then announced the destruction of the Temple, Jesus was charged of being hostile to it (CCC 584-86).
3. Jesus challenged Israel's faith in One God and Savior. By acting with divine authority in calling sinners and forgiving sins, by laying claim to a unique role and relationship with God, and in demanding conversion, He was judged as a blasphemer (CCC 594).

III. Jesus' death by crucifixion.

A. The historical complexity of Jesus' trial and the responsibility for His death is very complex, as evidenced by the Gospels.
1. Christians cannot lay blame on the Jews in Jerusalem at the time; still less on the Jewish people as a whole.
2. The Church teaches the "sinners were the authors and the ministers of all the sufferings that the divine Redeemer endured" (Roman Catechism I, 5, 11).
3. Because the sins of people affect Christ Himself, the Church sees the culpability of Christians for the gravity of torments which were inflicted upon Christ. Unfortunately they have all too often projected the burden of this guilt on Jews alone (CCC 597-598).

B. Jesus' violent death was not a result of chance. Jesus' redemptive death is part of God's plan of salvation (CCC 599).
1. Jesus was handed over according to God's plan (CCC 599).
2. He died for our sins in accordance with the Scriptures, fulfilling Isaiah's prophecy regarding the suffering Servant, "Because of his affliction / he shall see the light in fullness of days; / Through his suffering, my servant shall justify many, / and their guilt he shall bear" (Is 53:11). St. Paul professes that "Christ died for our sins in accordance with the scriptures" (1 Cor 15:3) (cf. CCC 619).
3. The innocent One entered into solidarity with sinners out of love. By sending Jesus in the form of a slave, in the form of fallen humanity, and because of sin, God "'made him to be sin who knew no sin, so that in him we might become the righteousness of God' (2 Cor 5:21; cf. Phil 2:7; Rom 8:3)" (CCC 602).
4. God the Father took the initiative of universal redeeming love.

a. Prior to any merit on our part God manifested His love for us by sending His Son to be the expiation for our sins (CCC 604).

b. Our salvation flows from God's initiative of love for us, because "'he loved us and sent his Son to be the expiation for our sins' (1 Jn 4:10; 4:19)" (CCC 604). "God was reconciling the world to himself in Christ" (2 Cor 5:19).

NOTES...

IV. Christ offered Himself to His Father for our sins.

A. Christ's whole life is an offering to the Father. Christ desired to embrace His Father's will and plan inspired by Him, especially during His agony and passion (CCC 607).

B. He freely embraced the Father's redeeming love for all people and freely laid down His life for His friends (CCC 609).

C. He expressed this free offering of His life at the Last Supper when He instituted a memorial of His sacrifice: "'This is my body which is given for you.' 'This is my blood of the covenant, which is poured out for many for the forgiveness of sins' (Lk 22:19; Mt 26:28; cf. 1 Cor 5:7)" (CCC 610).

1. Jesus freely gave of Himself for the salvation of all (CCC 609).
2. "Beforehand, during the Last Supper, he both symbolized this offering and made it really present: 'This is my body which is given for you' (Lk 22:19)" (CCC 621).

D. He accepted the cup of suffering "from his Father's hands in his agony in the garden at Gethsemani (cf. Mt 26:42; Lk 22:20), making himself 'obedient unto death' (Phil 2:8)" (CCC 612).

E. Christ's death is the unique and definitive sacrifice: the "*Paschal sacrifice*" that accomplishes our redemption from sin and the "*sacrifice of the New Covenant*" that reconciles us to communion with God. It surpasses all other sacrifices (CCC 613).

F. Jesus, the New Adam, substituted His obedience for our disobedience; the suffering Servant (cf. Is 53:10-11), He bore our sins so that we might become righteous, atoning for our faults and making satisfaction to the Father for our sins (CCC 615).

G. It is love that gives Christ's sacrifice on the cross its redemptive value. "He knew and loved us all when he offered his life" (cf. Gal 2:20; Eph 5:2, 25) (CCC 616). Because He is the divine Son of God and Head of the human race, His sacrifice redeems all humanity; it is the source of salvation which merited our justification. Thus, we venerate the Cross of Christ (CCC 617).

H. Our participation in Christ's sacrifice: Jesus is the one Mediator between God and man, but He invites us to be partners in His paschal mystery by taking up our cross and following Him. We can associate ourselves with His redeeming sacrifice by offering our own sufferings in union with His. This path is open even to those who have not heard the Gospel.

NOTES...

FOCUS QUESTIONS

1. Have you ever had an experience of the Paschal mystery, life coming out of death?
2. Have you had an experience of the redemptive nature of suffering, where a painful experience turned out to be one of growth?
3. True fulfillment comes when a person can die to the self and be for others. Why does our culture have such difficulty with this reality of self transcendence?

Concluding prayers
Intercessions
Closing prayer
Hymn (optional)

RESOURCES

Catechism of the Catholic Church, 535-621
Redemptor hominis (The Redeemer of Man), John Paul II
Essentials of the Faith, McBride, chap. 15

Session Thirteen

The Mystery of the Resurrection, Ascension, and Lordship of Christ

LEARNING OBJECTIVE

To present the Risen Christ as the principle and source of our future resurrection and that He is with us always (Mt 28:20).

Hymn: "Crown Him with Many Crowns"

Invitation to prayer — silent prayer

Oration:

Father,
help us keep in mind that Christ our Savior
lives with you in glory
and promised to remain with us until the end of time.

We ask this through our Lord Jesus Christ, your Son,
who lives and reigns with you and the Holy Spirit,
one God, for ever and ever.

Opening Prayer
Seventh Sunday of Easter

Scripture reading: 1 Corinthians 15:20-28

But now Christ has been raised from the dead, the firstfruits of those who have fallen asleep. For since death came through a human being, the resurrection of the dead came also through a human being. For just as in Adam all die, so too in Christ shall all be brought to life, but each one in proper order: Christ the firstfruits; then, at his coming, those who belong to Christ; then comes the end, when he hands over the kingdom to his God and Father, when he has destroyed every sovereignty and every authority and power. For he must reign until he has put all his enemies under his feet. The last enemy to be destroyed is death, for "he subjected everything under his feet." But when it says that everything has been subjected, it is clear that it excludes the one who subjected everything to him. When everything is subjected to him, then the Son himself will [also] be subjected to the one who subjected everything to him, so that God may be all in all.

NOTES...

TEACHING TO BE PRESENTED

I. On the third day Christ rose from the dead.

A. The Creed and Exsultet celebrate the Resurrection.

1. The Apostles' Creed confesses in the same article Jesus' descent to the dead and His Resurrection from the dead on the third day, because in His Paschal mystery, He made life spring forth from death (CCC 636).
2. The Exsultet (Easter Proclamation) provides a beautiful reflection that may be studied to better understand the mystery of the Resurrection of Jesus and the service of light of the Easter Vigil Mass.

B. Christ's burial and descent into hell.

1. Baptism signifies the descent into the tomb, by those who die to sin with Christ in order to live a new life. Immersion is the original and full sign of Christ's descent (CCC 628).
2. The Creed says, "He descended into hell." This refers to Jesus going down into the realm of the dead *("Sheol"* in Hebrew, *"Hades"* in Greek) to rescue those holy souls who were deprived of the vision of God. This shows the ultimate phase of Jesus' messianic mission: the spread of His redemptive work to people of all times and places. Through His death and resurrection, all have been made sharers of the redemption (CCC 633).

II. The Resurrection of Christ.

A. The Resurrection culminates the truth of our faith. "'We bring you the good news that what God promised to the fathers, this day he has fulfilled to us their children by raising Jesus' (Acts 13:32-33). The Resurrection of Jesus is the crowning truth of our faith in Christ, a faith believed and lived as the central truth by the first Christian community; handed on as fundamental by Tradition; established by the documents of the New Testament; and preached as an essential part of the Paschal mystery along with the cross:

> Christ is risen from the dead!
> Dying, he conquered death;
> To the dead, he has given life (Byzantine Liturgy, Troparion of Easter)."
> (CCC 638)

B. Christ's Resurrection is a true event that had reported historical manifestations.

1. The finding of the empty tomb is the first element in the structure of the Easter events. When Peter and the disciple "whom Jesus loved" entered the empty tomb and found the head wrappings separated from the other pieces of the shroud, they perceived that the absence of Jesus' body could not have been a human work. They "saw and believed" (Jn 20:2, 8) (CCC 640).
2. The Church's faith is based on the witness of those to whom He appeared. "Mary Magdalene and the holy women...were the first to encounter the Risen One" (Mk 16:1; Lk 24:1; Jn 19:31, 42) (CCC 641). Peter also experienced the Risen One and the sharing of this experience strengthened the faith of those who came to believe (cf. Lk 22:31). The early community was able to proclaim: "'The Lord has risen indeed, and has appeared to Simon!' (Lk 24:34, 36)" (CCC 641).
3. The Resurrection appearances in the Gospels provide a rich understanding of the disciples' faith resulting from a direct experience with the Risen Jesus. The first words of the Risen Lord to His disciples were "Peace be with you" (Jn

20:21). His first action after the Resurrection was to breathe the Holy Spirit on His disciples and to institute the sacrament of Penance (cf. Jn 20:19-23). Thus, the immediate effect of the Paschal mystery is seen as the remission of sins.

The Risen Lord's encounter with the disciples at Emmaus (cf. Lk 24:13-35) demonstrates the joy in the hearts of His followers who listened to His teachings and welcomed Him to their table. This may be seen as a beautiful image of both the Liturgy of the Word and the Liturgy of the Eucharist. We even hear that one of the apostles, Thomas, experienced the test of doubt in the Resurrection (cf. Jn 20:24-29).

4. By means of touch and sharing in a meal (cf. Lk 24: 30, 39-40, 41-43; Jn 20:20, 27, 21:9, 13-15), Jesus proved to His followers that He was not a ghost, but that He was truly alive and bore the marks of His passion. His body now possessed new properties that were not limited by space and time. The Resurrection of Jesus was not a return to earthly life. In His risen body Jesus passed from the state of death to another life beyond time and space. No one can describe how the resurrection of Jesus physically came about (CCC 645).

C. The Resurrection of Christ transcends and surpasses any event that has ever occurred in history.
   1. Faith in the Resurrection is based on the historical testimony of the disciples who encountered the Risen One (CCC 656).
   2. This event of the Resurrection "is mysteriously transcendent insofar as it is the entry of Christ's humanity into the glory of God" (CCC 656).

III. The meaning of the Resurrection.

A. The Resurrection of Christ confirms His work and teaching. "All truths, even those most inaccessible to human reason, find their justification if Christ by his Resurrection has given the definitive proof of his divine authority, which he had promised" (CCC 651).

B. Christ's Resurrection fulfills the prophecies of the Old Testament and of Jesus Himself while on earth (CCC 652).

C. The Resurrection confirms the truth of Christ's divinity. "'When you have lifted up the Son of man, then you will know that I am he' (Jn 8:28)" (CCC 653). Christ's Resurrection is closely intertwined with His Incarnation, thus fulfilling God's eternal plan.

D. Christ's Resurrection opens a way to new life for us. The Paschal mystery:
   1. By Christ's death liberated us from sin (CCC 654).
   2. By His Resurrection opens for us a new life (CCC 654).
   3. "This new life is above all justification that reinstates us in God's grace" (CCC 654).
   4. Justification is both victory over death caused by sin and a new participation in the life of grace (CCC 654).

E. Christ's resurrection is the principle and source of our Resurrection. In Christ, Christians "'have tasted . . . the powers of the age to come' (Heb 6:5)" (CCC 655).

IV. The ascension of Christ.

A. Christ's ascension marks the entrance of His humanity into God's heavenly domain (CCC 665).

NOTES...

NOTES...

1. Christ's body was glorified at the moment of His Resurrection (CCC 659).
2. During the forty days after the Resurrection, while teaching the disciples about the Kingdom, "his glory remains veiled under the appearance of ordinary humanity" (cf. Acts 1:3; 10:41; Mk 16:12; Lk 24:15; Jn 20:14-15; 21:4) (CCC 659).
3. The ascension is Jesus' final apparition. The entry of "his humanity into divine glory, symbolized by the cloud and by heaven, where he is seated from that time forward at God's right hand" (cf. Acts 1:9; 2:33; 7:56; Lk 9:34-35; 24:51; Ex 13:22; Mk 16:19; Ps 110:1) (CCC 659).

B. The last words of Jesus before He ascended into heaven remind us of His abiding presence with His Church. "I am with you always" (Mt 28:20). Our Catholic faith reminds us that Jesus is truly present with us in the Holy Eucharist, the Sacred Scriptures, and the believing community. We have not been left as orphans (cf. Jn 14:18).

V. The glorification of Christ.

A. By professing that Jesus is now seated at the right hand of the Father, we understand the glory and honor which is proper to the Son of God. He existed before all ages, and is seated bodily in heaven after His Incarnation and glorification. His presence at the Father's right hand signals the inauguration of the Messiah's kingdom (cf. Dn 7:14). The kingdom of Jesus will have no end. He is our constant mediator, who assures us of the outpouring of the Holy Spirit (cf. Jn 16:5-16) (CCC 664).

B. Christ reigns over His Church. All things are to be recapitulated through Him (Eph 1:10). He is Lord (cf. Rom 14:9; Phil 2:11) (CCC 680).

C. Christ will come to judge the living and the dead at the end of time. We speak of this as the "Second Coming." His coming in glory at the end of time will be the ultimate triumph of good over evil. The study of the end of time is called eschatology. Clearly, the world as we know it is passing by (cf. 2 Pt 3:13). One day, the presence of the Risen Jesus will empower all things so that "God may be all in all" (1 Cor 15:28) (cf. CCC 674).

1. Many are frightened by a false interpretation of the Book of Revelation concerning the day of judgment and a reading of the signs of the times.
2. No one knows "the day nor the hour" (Mt 25:13). No one can make an accurate prediction of the end of the world.
3. When He comes again, Jesus will reveal the secret inclination of hearts and render to each person as he or she deserves (CCC 682).
4. Each person will either accept or refuse His grace (CCC 682).

FOCUS QUESTIONS

1. Do you see your faith in the Resurrection as Peter did, or is your faith more like that of Thomas?
2. What meaning does Christ's Ascension have for today's believers?
3. How have you imagined the day of judgment and the Second Coming?

Concluding prayers
Intercessions
Closing prayer
Hymn (optional)

RESOURCES

Catechism of the Catholic Church, 628-682
Redemptor hominis (The Redeemer of Man), John Paul II
Essentials of the Faith, McBride, chaps. 16-17

NOTES...

Session Fourteen

The Holy Spirit

LEARNING OBJECTIVE

To present the role of the Holy Spirit as the third person of the Blessed Trinity and the reality of His presence to the Church at all times.

Hymn: "Come, Holy Ghost"

Invitation to prayer — silent prayer

Oration:

Father of light, from whom every good gift comes,
send your Spirit into our lives
with the power of a mighty wind,
and by the flame of your wisdom
open the horizon of our minds.

Loosen our tongues to sing your praise
in words beyond the power of speech,
for without your Spirit
man could never raise his voice in words of peace
or announce the truth that Jesus is Lord,
who lives and reigns with you and the Holy Spirit,
one God, for ever and ever.

Alternate Opening Prayer
Pentecost Sunday

Scripture reading: John 20:19-23

On the evening of that first day of the week, when the doors were locked, where the disciples were, for fear of the Jews, Jesus came and stood in their midst and said to them, "Peace be with you." When he had said this, he showed them his hands and his side. The disciples rejoiced when they saw the Lord. [Jesus] said to them again, "Peace be with you. As the Father has sent me, so I send you." And when he had said this, he breathed on them and said to them, "Receive the holy Spirit. Whose sins you forgive are forgiven them, and whose sins you retain are retained."

TEACHING TO BE PRESENTED

NOTES...

I. The Holy Spirit, the third person of the blessed Trinity, sustains us.

A. "By virtue of our Baptism, the first sacrament of the faith, the Holy Spirit in the Church communicates to us, intimately and personally, the life that originates in the Father and is offered to us in the Son" (CCC 683).

1. "Through his grace, the Holy Spirit is the first to awaken faith in us and to communicate to us the new life, which is to 'know the Father and the one whom he has sent, Jesus Christ' (Jn 17:3)" (CCC 684).
2. "The Spirit who 'has spoken through the prophets' makes us hear the Father's Word, but we do not hear the Spirit himself. We know him only in the movement by which he reveals the Word to us and disposes us to welcome him in faith" (CCC 687).
3. "From the beginning until 'the fullness of time' (Gal 4:4), the joint mission of the Father's Word and Spirit remains *hidden,* but it is at work" (CCC 702).
4. "Whenever God sends his Son, he always sends his Spirit: their mission is conjoined and inseparable" (CCC 743).

B. We come to know the Holy Spirit most fully in the Church for He comes to us in many, diverse ways (CCC 688).

1. The Scriptures we read are inspired by the power of the Holy Spirit.
2. The Holy Spirit guides and inspires the Church's Magisterium in their effort to faithfully adhere to Tradition.
3. The Holy Spirit sustains us in the sacramental life of the Church.
4. The Holy Spirit is present in the charisms of the Church. Charisms are special gifts of the service given for the building up of the Body of Christ (CCC 799).
5. The Church is the temple of the Holy Spirit. "'What the soul is to the human body, the Holy Spirit is to the Body of Christ, which is the Church'" (St. Augustine, *Sermo* 267, 4: PL 38, 1231D) (CCC 797).

II. The Holy Spirit animates and inspires the faithful.

A. "The Holy Spirit, whom Christ the head pours out on his members, builds, animates, and sanctifies the Church. She is the sacrament of the Holy Trinity's communion with men" (CCC 747).

1. "The promise made to Abraham inaugurates the economy of salvation, at the culmination of which the Son himself will assume that 'image' (cf. Jn 1:14; Phil 2:7) and restore it in the Father's 'likeness' by giving it again its Glory, the Spirit who is 'the giver of life'" (CCC 705).
2. "In the fullness of time the Holy Spirit completes in Mary all the preparations for Christ's coming among the People of God. By the action of the Holy Spirit in her, the Father gives the world Emmanuel, 'God-with-us' (Mt 1:23)" (CCC 744).
3. "By his Death and his Resurrection, Jesus is constituted in glory as Lord and Christ (cf. Acts 2:36). From his fullness, he poured out the Holy Spirit on the apostles and the Church" (CCC 746).

B. On the day of Pentecost, when the seven weeks of Easter ended, Christ's Passover was fulfilled in the outpouring of the Holy Spirit. On that day the Holy Trinity was fully revealed (CCC 731-32).

1. "Confirmation is the special outpouring of the Holy Spirit as once granted to the apostles on the day of Pentecost" (CCC 1302).

NOTES...

2. "Confirmation brings an increase and deepening of baptismal grace ... — it increases the gifts of the Holy Spirit in us" (CCC 1303).

C. "The moral life of Christians is sustained by the gifts of the Holy Spirit. These are permanent dispositions which make man docile in following the promptings of the Holy Spirit" (CCC 1830).
   1. "The seven *gifts* of the Holy Spirit are wisdom, understanding, counsel, fortitude, knowledge, piety, and fear of the Lord. They belong in their fullness to Christ, Son of David (cf. Is 11:1-2). They complete and perfect the virtues of those who receive them" (CCC 1831).
   2. The Holy Spirit brings unity in diversity.

III. The Holy Spirit is symbolized and understood in varied ways.

A. The Holy Spirit has many titles (CCC 692-93).
   1. The Paraclete which means "he who is called to one's side" (CCC 692).
   2. Spirit of truth (Jn16:13).
   3. Spirit of the promise (Gal 3:14; Eph 1:13).
   4. Spirit of adoption (Rom 8:15; Gal 4:6).
   5. Spirit of Christ (Rom 8:9).
   6. Spirit of the Lord (2 Cor 3:17).
   7. Spirit of God (Rom 8:9, 14; 15:19; 1 Cor 6:11, 7:40).
   8. Spirit of glory (1 Pt 4:14).

B. The Holy Spirit is symbolized in many ways (CCC 694-701).
   1. Water
   2. Anointing
   3. Immersion.
   4. Fire.
   5. Cloud and light.
   6. The seal.
   7. The hand
   8. The finger.
   9. The dove.

FOCUS QUESTIONS

1. Have you known anyone who seemed truly "inspired" by the Holy Spirit?
2. How is the Holy Spirit the "fire of love"?
3. Which symbol of the Holy Spirit touches you most deeply? Which one best expresses your own experience of the Spirit?

Concluding prayers
Intercessions
Closing prayer
Hymn (optional)

RESOURCES

Catechism of the Catholic Church, 683-799, 1302-1303, 1830-31
Dominum et Vivificantem (The Holy Spirit in the Life of the Church and the World), John Paul II
Essentials of the Faith, McBride, chaps. 18-19

Session Fifteen

The Mystery of the Church

One and Holy

LEARNING OBJECTIVE

To teach that the Catholic Church is the sole Church of Christ in which, through the Creed, we profess to be one and holy.

Hymn: "O Christ the Great Foundation"

Invitation to prayer — silent prayer

Oration:

God our Father,
from living stones, your chosen people,
you built an eternal temple to your glory.
Increase the spiritual gifts you have given to your Church,
so that your faithful people may continue to grow
into the new and eternal Jerusalem.

We ask this through our Lord Jesus Christ, your Son,
who lives and reigns with you and the Holy Spirit,
one God, for ever and ever.

Opening Prayer
Mass for the Anniversary of the Dedication of a Church

Scripture reading: 1 Peter 2:1-17

Rid yourself of all malice and all deceit, insincerity, envy, and all slander; like newborn infants, long for pure spiritual milk so that through it you may grow into salvation, for you have tasted that the Lord is good. Come to him, a living stone, rejected by human beings but chosen and precious in the sight of God, and, like living stones, let yourselves be built into a spiritual house to be a holy priesthood to offer spiritual sacrifices acceptable to God through Jesus Christ. For it says in scripture:

"Behold, I am laying a stone in Zion,
a cornerstone, chosen and precious,
and whoever believes in it shall not be put to shame."

Therefore, its value is for you who have faith, but for those without faith:

"The stone which the builders rejected
has become the cornerstone,"

NOTES...

and

"A stone that will make people stumble,
and a rock that will make them fall."

They stumble by disobeying the word, as is their destiny.

But you are "a chosen race, a royal priesthood, a holy nation, a people of his own, so that you may announce the praises" of him who called you out of darkness into his wonderful light.

Once you were "no people"
but now you are God's people;
you "had not received mercy"
but now you have received mercy.

Beloved, I urge you as aliens and sojourners to keep away from worldly desires that wage war against the soul. Maintain good conduct among the Gentiles, so that if they speak of you as evildoers, they may observe your good works and glorify God on the day of visitation.

Be subject to every human institution for the Lord's sake, whether it be to the king as supreme or to governors as sent by him for the punishment of evildoers and the approval of those who do good. For it is the will of God that by doing good you may silence the ignorance of foolish people. Be free, yet without using freedom as a pretext for evil, but as slaves of God. Give honor to all, love the community, fear God, honor the king.

TEACHING TO BE PRESENTED

I. The Church is the Body of Christ — a mystical communion.

A. The Church is both a spiritual community endowed with heavenly riches and a visible, earthly society (CCC 771).
   1. "The Church is in history, but at the same time she transcends it." Only faith allows us to grasp the Church in both her visible and invisible dimensions (CCC 770).
   2. The Church's spiritual and earthly dimensions together constitute "'one complex reality which comes together from a human and a divine element' (LG 8)" (CCC 771).
   3. "'Christ ... established and ever sustains here on earth his holy Church . . . as a visible organization through which he communicates truth and grace to all men' (LG 8 § 1)" (CCC 771).
   4. "'[The Church's] structure is totally ordered to the holiness of Christ's members' (Pope John Paul II, MD 27)" (CCC 773).

B. The Church is the Body of Christ, the instrument of His saving plan.
   1. The Church exists primarily to bring about the inner communion of individual human persons with God (CCC 775).
      a. The word "communion" is from the Latin *communio,* meaning "shared unity" or "mutual participation."

b. "The Church is also the sacrament of the *unity of the human race*" since true social communion is only possible through union in God (CCC 775).

2. Through the power of the Holy Spirit, Christ "establishes the community of believers as his own Body" (CCC 805).
   a. "The comparison of the Church with the body casts light on the intimate bond between Christ and his Church. Not only is she gathered *around him*; she is united *in him*, in his body" (CCC 789).
   b. "Christ 'is the head of the body, the Church' (Col 1:18)" (CCC 792). The Church lives from, in, and for Christ; He lives with and in her (CCC 807).

C. The Body of Christ, the Church, is distinguished by four "marks."
1. The Church is one, holy, catholic, and apostolic.
   a. Inseparably linked, these four marks (or "characteristics") of the Church "indicate essential features of the Church and her mission" (CCC 811).
   b. The first Vatican Council recognized that the "'Church herself, with her marvelous propagation, eminent holiness, and inexhaustible fruitfulness in everything good, her catholic unity and invincible stability, is a great and perpetual motive of credibility and an irrefutable witness of her divine mission' (Vatican Council I, *Dei Filius* 3: DS 3013)" (CCC 812).
2. The Church's four marks are not her own possession, for it is Christ, "who, through the Holy Spirit, makes his Church one, holy, catholic, and apostolic, and it is he who calls her to realize each of these qualities" (CCC 811).
3. "Only faith can recognize that the Church possesses these properties from her divine source" (CCC 812).

NOTES...

II. The Church is one.

A. The "one-ness" of the Church has many dimensions.
1. "*The Church is one because of her source:* 'the highest exemplar and source of this mystery is the unity, in the Trinity of Persons, of one God, the Father and the Son in the Holy Spirit' (UR 2 § 5).... Unity is of the essence of the Church" (CCC 813).
2. *The Church is one because of her founder*, the Word made flesh, who reconciled all people to God by the cross, thus restoring the unity of all in one people and one body (CCC 813).
   a. "From the beginning, this one Church has been marked by a great *diversity* which comes from both the variety of God's gifts and the diversity of those who receive them" (CCC 814).
   b. The Holy Spirit brings unity in diversity.
3. "The Church is one *because of her 'soul'*: 'It is the Holy Spirit, dwelling in those who believe and pervading and ruling over the entire Church, who brings about that wonderful communion of the faithful and joins them together so intimately in Christ that he is the principle of the Church's unity' (UR 2 §2)" (CCC 813).
   a. "Within the unity of the People of God, a multiplicity of peoples and cultures is gathered together. Among the Church's members, there are different gifts, offices, conditions, and ways of life" (CCC 814).
   b. "'Holding a rightful place in the communion of the Church there are also particular Churches that retain their own traditions' (LG 13 § 2). The great richness of such diversity is not opposed to the Church's unity" (CCC 814).

NOTES...

c. The bond of unity is "above all, charity," which "'binds everything together in perfect harmony' (Col 3:14)" (CCC 815).

4. The visible bonds of unity of the pilgrim Church are the "profession of one faith received from the Apostles; common celebration of divine worship, especially of the sacraments; apostolic succession through the sacrament of Holy Orders, maintaining the fraternal concord of God's family" (cf. UR 2; LG 14; CIC, can. 205) (CCC 815).
   a. "'The sole Church of Christ [is that] which our Savior, after his Resurrection, entrusted to Peter's pastoral care, commissioning him and the other apostles to extend and rule it' (LG 8 § 2)" (CCC 816).
   b. "'This Church, constituted and organized as a society in the present world, subsists in *(subsistit in)* the Catholic Church, which is governed by the successor of Peter and by the bishops in communion with him' (LG 8 § 2)" (CCC 816).

B. There are wounds to unity in the Church and world.

1. It is sin and the burden of its consequences that constantly threaten the gift of unity (CCC 815).
   a. "The ruptures that wound the unity of Christ's Body — here we must distinguish heresy, apostasy, and schism (cf. CIC can. 751) — do not occur without human sin" (CCC 817).
   b. One cannot charge with the sin of separation, those who at present, are born into the communities (sects) that are the result of the separation (CCC 818).
2. Since the beginnings of the Church in antiquity, certain rifts have arisen. The Catholic Church is the only church which is not a sect — meaning the only one which has never broken away from the original vine of Christ. It rests truly with Christ from the very beginning (CCC 817).

C. The unity of all should be the concern of faithful and clergy. "'The reconciliation of all Christians in the unity of the one and only Church of Christ ... transcends human power and gifts.' That is why we place all our hope 'in the prayer of Christ for the Church, in the love of the Father for us, and in the power of the Holy Spirit' (UR 24 § 2)" (CCC 822).

1. As Vatican II redefines, "'It was to the apostolic college alone, of which Peter is the head, that we believe that our Lord entrusted all the blessings of the New Covenant, in order to establish on earth the one Body of Christ into which all those should be fully incorporated who belong in any way to the People of God' (UR 3 § 5)" (CCC 816).
2. "'All who have been justified by faith in Baptism are incorporated into Christ; they therefore have a right to be called Christians, and with good reason are accepted as brothers in the Lord by the children of the Catholic Church' (UR 3 § 1)" (CCC 818).
3. "Christ's Spirit uses these Churches and ecclesial communities as means of salvation, whose power derives from the fullness of grace and truth that Christ has entrusted to the Catholic Church. All these blessings come from Christ and lead to him (cf. UR 3) and are in themselves calls to 'Catholic unity' (cf. LG 8)" (CCC 819).
4. In order to work towards unity certain things are required (CCC 821).
   a. There should be an understanding of ecumenism. Ecumenism is the work and hope of Christian unity.
   b. The Church must understand that unity is what Jesus desired (cf. Jn 17).

c. The Church must work toward "*dialogue* among theologians and meetings among Christians of the different churches and communities (cf. UR 4; 9; 11); *collaboration* among Christians in various areas of service to mankind (cf. UR 12)" (CCC 821).

NOTES...

III. The Church is holy.

A. The Church is holy in essence.

1. The Church is holy because she is the Bride of Jesus Christ who is holy (CCC 823).
    a. "'He joined her to himself as his body and endowed her with the gift of the Holy Spirit for the glory of God' (LG 39; cf. Eph 5:25-26)" (CCC 823).
    b. "United with Christ, the Church is sanctified by him; through him and with him she becomes sanctifying" (CCC 824).
2. "It is in the Church that 'the fullness of the means of salvation' (UR 3 § 5) has been deposited. It is in her that 'by grace of God we acquire holiness' (LG 48)" (CCC 824).

B. The Church is holy because its members are capable of holiness.

1. "'The Church on earth is endowed already with a sanctity that is real though imperfect' (LG 48 § 3). In her members perfect holiness is something yet to be acquired" (CCC 825).
2. "Charity is the soul of the holiness to which all are called: it 'governs, shapes, and perfects all the means of sanctification' (LG 42)" (CCC 826).
3. "All members of the Church, including her ministers, must acknowledge that they are sinners (cf. 1 Jn 1:8-10). In everyone, the weeds of sin will still be mixed with the good wheat of the Gospel until the end of time (cf. Mt 13: 24-30)" (CCC 827).
4. By canonizing some of the faithful, by proclaiming the heroic virtue and fidelity to God's grace, the Church recognizes the power of the Spirit of holiness and sustains the hope of believers by proposing the saints to them as models and intercessors (CCC 828). Canonization is the process by which the Church declares a person a saint.
5. "'Holiness is the hidden source and infallible measure of her [the Church's] apostolic activity and missionary zeal' (CL 17, 3)" (CCC 828).
6. "'In the most Blessed Virgin the Church has already reached that perfection whereby she exists without spot or wrinkle, the faithful still strive to conquer sin and increase in holiness. And so they turn their eyes to Mary' (LG 65; cf. Eph 5:26-27)" who in the Church is already the "all-holy" (CCC 829).

FOCUS QUESTIONS

1. Explain why one finds Jesus through the life of the Church rather than through Jesus alone?
2. What does it mean to say that the Church is One?
3. Describe what it means to say that the Church is Holy.

NOTES...

Concluding prayers
Intercessions
Closing prayers
Hymn (optional)

RESOURCES

Catechism of the Catholic Church, 770-829
Christifideles laici (Lay Members of Christ's Faithful People), John Paul II
Codex Iuris Canonici (Code of Canon Law)
Lumen gentium, (Dogmatic Constitution on the Church), Vatican II
Mulieris dignitatem (On the Dignity and Vocation of Women), John Paul II
Unitatis redintegratio (Decree on Ecumenism), Vatican II

Session Sixteen

The Mystery of the Church

Catholic and Apostolic

LEARNING OBJECTIVE

To explain the meaning of Catholic, Apostolic, infallibility and the structure of the Church.

Hymn: "We Remember"

Invitation to prayer – silent prayer

Oration:

Lord,
you renew our life with this gift of redemption.
Through this help to eternal salvation
may the true faith continue to grow throughout the world.

We ask this in the name of Jesus the Lord.

Prayer After Communion
For the Spread of the Gospel

Scripture reading: Matthew 28:16-20

The eleven disciples went to Galilee, to the mountain to which Jesus had ordered them. When they saw him, they worshiped, but they doubted. Then Jesus approached and said to them, "All power in heaven and on earth has been given to me. Go, therefore, and make disciples of all nations, baptizing them in the name of the Father, and of the Son, and of the holy Spirit, teaching them to observe all that I have commanded you. And behold, I am with you always, until the end of the age."

TEACHING TO BE PRESENTED

I. **The Church is Catholic.**

A. Catholic means universal. This means she is "'universal,' in the sense of 'according to the totality' or 'in keeping with the whole'" (CCC 830). The word "Catholic" is found in the writings of Ignatius of Antioch who stated:

> Wherever the bishop appears, there let the people be; as wherever Jesus Christ is, there is the Catholic Church. It is not lawful to baptize or give Communion without the consent of the bishop. On the other

NOTES...

hand, whatever has his approval is pleasing to God. Thus, whatever you do will be safe and valid.

In the original Greek of this passage, the expression *katholike ekklesia* appears for the first time in Christian literature. Later, as in the *Catechesis of St. Cyril of Jerusalem*, *katholike* meant both "universal" and "orthodox." Here the word seems to mean only "universal." The etymology of the word *catholic* comes from two Greek words: *kata* meaning according to; and *olike* meaning the whole. The word has the connotation of integrity, and in this context, where the topic of schisms are addressed, Ignatius is concerned about people going by "according to the whole" teaching of the Apostles and not just bits and pieces or fragments of their teaching.

1. The Church was "catholic on the day of Pentecost (cf. AG 4) and will always be so until the day of the Parousia" (CCC 830).
2. "The Church is catholic because she has been sent out by Christ on a mission to the whole of the human race (cf. Mt 28:19)" calling all to belong to this new People of God (CCC 831).
3. The universal Church consists of dioceses who are a community under their local bishop ordained in apostolic succession. These particular churches (dioceses) "'are constituted after the model of the universal Church' (LG 23)" (CCC 833).

B. It is from God's love for all people "that the Church in every age receives both the obligation and the vigor of her missionary dynamism" (CCC 851).

1. "Outside the Church there is no salvation," formulated positively, "means that all salvation comes from Christ the Head through the Church which is his Body" (CCC 846).
2. As Vatican II states: "'Those who, through no fault of their own, do not know the Gospel of Christ or his Church, but who nevertheless seek God with a sincere heart, and, moved by grace, try in their actions to do his will as they know it through the dictates of their conscience — those too may achieve eternal salvation' (LG 16; cf. DS 3866-3872)" (CCC 847).
3. "The Lord's missionary mandate is ultimately grounded in the eternal love of the Most Holy Trinity: 'The Church on earth is by her nature missionary since, according to the plan of the Father, she has as her origin the mission of the Son and the Holy Spirit' (AG 2)" (CCC 850).

II. The Church is apostolic.

A. "The Church is apostolic because she is founded on the apostles, in three ways" (CCC 857):

1. Christ chose the apostles and sent them to proclaim the Gospel.
2. Since the time of Pentecost, the Holy Spirit has continually guided the apostles and their successors.
3. The deposit of faith has been passed on through apostolic succession.

B. "'The sole Church of Christ which in the Creed we profess to be one, holy, catholic, and apostolic, . . . subsists in the Catholic Church, which is governed by the successor of Peter and by the bishops in communion with him. Nevertheless, many elements of sanctification and of truth are found outside its visible confines' (LG 8)" (CCC 870).

1. Even though truth can be found outside the visible confines of the Church, the Church has been given a special gift known as infallibility. From Matthew

16:19 and the reference to the keys of the kingdom, the Church has come to understand the *charism* of Infallibility. The Pope when speaking *ex cathedra (from the chair)* can confirm the brethren on a doctrinal point concerning the faith or a moral teaching (CCC 881). This *charism* is also found in the "'body of bishops when, together with Peter's successor, they exercise the supreme Magisterium' (LG 25; cf. Vatican Council I: DS 3074" (CCC 891).

NOTES...

III. Infallibility (CCC 889-891, 2035, 2051).

A. The inability to err in teaching the truth. In theology, it refers to:
   1. The Church, in that she preserves and teaches the deposit of truth as revealed by Christ.
   2. The Roman Pontiff, when he teaches *ex cathedra* in matters of faith or morals, and indicates that the doctrine is to be believed by all the faithful.
   3. The College of Bishops, when speaking in union with the Pope in matters of faith and morals, agreeing that a doctrine must be held by the universal Church, and the doctrine is promulgated by the Pontiff.

IV. The basic visible structure of the Church.

A. The Parish is a geographical region whose care is entrusted to the pastor. Typically it is comprised of individuals and families registered at a local parish Church (CCC 2179).

B. The diocese, or "particular church" is again usually a geographical area where there are a grouping of parishes headed by a particular bishop, known as the ordinary (CCC 833).

C. The Magisterium, or teaching office of the Church, guides the people of God by unfailing adhering to the faith of the Church (CCC 889).

D. The Roman Curia – In exercising supreme, full, and immediate power in the universal Church, the Roman pontiff makes use of the departments of the Roman Curia which, therefore, perform their duties in his name and with his authority for the good of the *churches and in the service of the sacred pastors* (CD 9). The Curia are the respective offices, departments and congregations in Rome that support the various functions of the Church throughout the world.

E. The Pope is the first among equals and for the Roman Catholic Church has both Primacy of Honor and Primacy of Jurisdiction.
   1. The Pope can never create truth any more that the Church can create truth, but through the Holy Spirit is a faithful interpreter of putting into practice the truth as revealed to humanity through the Sacred Revelation (CCC 892).
   2. The Pope, united with the bishops have the role to govern the Church. The bishops are not "vicars of the Pope," but rather in union with the Pope they govern their respective churches or dioceses (CCC 895).

FOCUS QUESTIONS

1. Explain how the Church is both a spiritual community and an earthy society.
2. Describe the Church as Apostolic.
3. What does infallibility mean?

NOTES...

Concluding prayers
Intercessions
Closing prayers
Hymn (optional)

RESOURCES

Catechism of the Catholic Church, 830-896, 2035, 2051
Ad gentes divinitus (Decree on the Church's Missionary Activity), Vatican II
Christus dominus (Decree on the Pastoral Office of Bishops in the Church), Vatican II
Lumen gentium (Dogmatic Constitution on the Church), Vatican II
Unitatis redintegratio (Decree on Ecumenism), Vatican II
Essentials of the Faith, McBride, chaps. 20-23

Session Seventeen

The Call to Holiness

Communion of Saints

LEARNING OBJECTIVE

To recognize that Christ has proclaimed a universal call to holiness and to discover the authentic witness of the saints as models and intercessors.

Hymn: "For All the Saints"

Invitation to prayer — silent prayer

Oration:

God our Father,
source of all holiness,
the work of your hands is manifest in your saints,
the beauty of your truth is reflected in their faith.

May we who aspire to have part in their joy
be filled with the Spirit that blessed their lives,
so that having shared their faith on earth
we may also know their peace in your kingdom.

Grant this through Christ our Lord.

Alternate Opening Prayer
Solemnity of All Saints

Scripture reading: Revelation 7:2-4, 9-14

Then I saw another angel come up from the East, holding the seal of the living God. He cried out in a loud voice to the four angels who were given power to damage the land and the sea, "Do not damage the land or the sea or the trees until we put the seal on the foreheads of the servants of our God." I heard the number of those who had been marked with the seal, one hundred and forty-four thousand marked from every tribe of the Israelites....

After this I had a vision of great multitude, which no one could count, from every nation, race, people, and tongue. They stood before the throne and before the Lamb, wearing white robes and holding palm branches in their hands. They cried out in a loud voice:

NOTES...

> "Salvation comes from our God, who is
> seated on the throne,
> and from the Lamb."
>
> All the angels stood around the throne and around the elders and the four living creatures. They prostrated themselves before the throne, worshiped God, and exclaimed:
>
> "Amen. Blessing and glory, wisdom and
> thanksgiving,
> honor, power, and might
> to be our God forever and ever. Amen."
>
> Then one of the elders spoke up and said to me, "Who are these wearing white robes, and where did they come from?" I said to him, "My lord, you are the one who knows." He said to me, "These are the ones who have survived the time of great distress; they have washed their robes and made them white in the blood of the Lamb."

TEACHING TO BE PRESENTED

I. The Church is a communion of saints

- **A.** The Church is a "communion of saints." The term "saint" comes from the Latin word *"sanctus"* meaning "holy."
  1. The expression "communion of saints" refers first to the "holy things" *(sancta),* above all the Eucharist.
  2. It also refers to the communion of holy persons *(sancti)* in Christ who died for all, so that what each one does or suffers in and for Christ bears fruit for all. All who live a holy life share in the living communion of saints (CCC 948).
  3. There are three states of the communion of saints in the Church.
     - a. The members of the Church on earth.
     - b. Those who have died and are being purified.
     - c. Those who are in glory in heaven.
- **B.** "'All Christians in any state or walk of life are called to the fullness of Christian life and to the perfection of charity' (LG 40 § 2).... 'Be perfect, as your heavenly Father is perfect' (Mt 5:48)" (CCC 2013).
  1. The Christian should always desire a more intimate union with God. This spiritual progress is made possible through the sacraments, the holy mysteries, which draw each person into a closer union with Christ (CCC 2014).
  2. "The way of perfection passes by way of the Cross" (CCC 2015). Asceticism helps the Christian put the material world in its proper perspective. The lives of St. Francis of Assisi, St. John of the Cross, and St. Teresa of Jesus can help one discover the beautiful spiritual tradition of Christian asceticism. The Christian is called to renounce the things of this earth in order to share in the glory of the world that does not end (Col 3:1).
  3. Both the Sacred Scriptures (cf. Phil 3:20-21; Heb 11:13-16; 1 Pt 2:11-12) and the Second Vatican Council describe the life of the Christian as a pilgrimage. We are pilgrims on this earth who long to be at home with the Lord (cf. 2 Cor 5:6). As believers, we share a blessed hope that we will be gathered one day in

the holy city God wants us to share in (cf. Rv 21:1). God is glorified in His saints for their glory is the crowning of His gifts.

NOTES...

II. The examples of holy men and women inspires the Body of Christ.

A. The Church venerates, or honors, the saints. God alone is worshiped and adored.

1. In solemnly declaring the heroic virtues of the life of one who has died (process of beatification and canonization), the Church recognizes the power of the Holy Spirit to universally touch people of every race, language, and way of life. The lives of the saints sustain the hope of believers by looking to them as models and intercessors (CCC 828).
2. By saying that the saints make intercession for us, we believe that they, who are close to God in heaven, will plead before Him on our behalf. Thus, the Church declares that we have true friends in heaven. Hence, the Litany of the Saints petitions these holy men and women to beg the Lord on our behalf through the invocation "pray for us." (A litany is a prayer that includes a series of petitions.) Speaking out of concern for those left on this earth, St. Thérèse of the Child Jesus wrote, "I want to spend my heaven doing good on earth."
3. The saints contemplate God. They praise Him and care for those who are on this earth. The saints are our companions in prayer. We can and should ask them to intercede for us (CCC 2683). The name of a saint is given to a person at Baptism and Confirmation so that he or she might have a patron saint. Such a holy man or woman provides a model for charity and a true friend in heaven. Parishes, dioceses, and countries are given to the patronage of a particular saint.

B. The Church's calendar reflects the importance of saints.

1. A look at the rhythms of the sanctoral cycle will help to show the authentic witness of the lives of the saints in heaven. The sanctoral cycle *(sanctorale)* is the calendar of saints found in the missals of the Church and in the Liturgy of the Hours. A saint's feast day is celebrated on the day that he or she died (in other words, one's "birthday" into heaven). Catholics should read the lives of the saints to encourage them in the Christian life and to prove that it is possible to be holy.
2. The Scripture readings (Rv 7:2-4, 9-14; Ps 24; 1 Jn 3:1-3; Mt 5:1-12) and the Sacramentary prayers from the Solemnity of All Saints (November 1) provide an excellent catechesis on the call to be saints. More than just recognizing those men and women declared as saints (canonization), this feast celebrates the lives of all individuals from every time and place who now share the glory of heaven.
3. There does exist a certain hierarchy among the list of saints. This may be described while looking at the *sanctorale,* or "commons," in the back of the Sacramentary or the Liturgy of the Hours, or even glancing at the text of the Litany of the Saints.
   a. The greatest example of holiness and virtue is seen in the Virgin Mary. She is to be given the highest honor among the saints.
   b. St. Joseph (March 19), the foster father of Jesus, was placed at the head of the holy family of Nazareth, and as the husband of Mary and the patron saint of workers (May 1) is given special honor.
   c. St. John the Baptist is honored as the prophet who prepared the way for Christ. Jesus remarked that "among those born of women, no one is

NOTES...

greater than John" (Lk 7:28). His birth (June 24) and his martyrdom (August 29) are both celebrated in the liturgical year.

d. The apostles are honored with great devotion in the Tradition of the Church. The word apostle means "one sent" and their witness to the Risen Christ sent them to all parts of the earth to preach the Gospel (cf. Mt 28:19-20). St. Peter, the prince of the apostles, and St. Paul, the apostle to the Gentiles, are honored with a joint solemnity on June 29. The conversion of St. Paul is celebrated on January 25 and the Chair of St. Peter on February 22. The four evangelists (the evangelists are the ones to whom we attribute the Gospels: Matthew, Mark, Luke, and John), two of whom are also apostles (Matthew and John), have also been given the rank of a feast in the liturgical year.

III. The saints represent varied walks of life.

A. The memory of the martyrs, particularly the ancient martyrs of the Church, remains a living sign of the power given to a human being to "witness" to the life that Jesus asks us to live. Ancient martyrs such as St. Stephen (December 26) and St. Lawrence (August 10), and martyrs nearer to our own time, such as St. Isaac Jogues and Companions (October 19) and St. Maximilian Kolbe (August 14), prove that the Christian life was, and is, worth dying for. For centuries, the relics (relics are remains of a saint, or items touched by the saint) of the Christian martyrs were deposited in a consecrated altar to show that the suffering and death of a martyr is intimately connected with the sacrifice of Jesus on the Cross, and therefore, such sentiments are called to mind at every celebration of the Mass. In later years, the relics of many of the canonized saints came to be venerated.

B. Those honored as virgins have consecrated their lives for the sake of the kingdom of heaven. Tradition records the memory of many virgin/martyrs in the Roman Canon (i.e. saints Agatha, Lucy, Agnes, and Cecilia). Dedicated religious women (i.e. St. Clare, St. Thérèse of the Child Jesus) and lay women (i.e. St. Rose of Lima, Blessed Kateri Tekakwitha) further prove the all-embracing reach of the call to holiness.

C. Great men (such as St. Augustine, St. Gregory the Great, and St. Thomas Aquinas) and great women (such as St. Catherine of Siena and St. Teresa of Jesus) have been given the title "Doctor of the Church" to show the marvelous impact of one who truly is a "teacher" in the name of the Church.

D. Great pastors ("shepherds") of the Church, such as St. Pius X (pope), St. Francis de Sales (bishop), and St. John Vianney (priest), have been faithful stewards of the flock of Christ.

E. Other holy men and women have been honored throughout the centuries for their special heroic virtues. From lives that are mentioned in the New Testament (i.e. St. Mary Magdalene, St. Martha) to dedicated religious of our own era (i.e. St. Elizabeth Ann Seton, Blessed André Bessette), the Church promotes the fact that priests, religious, and lay people are living signs of Christ in people throughout the ages.

F. Many saints, because of a particular skill or virtue, are considered patrons in specific instances. St. Isidore the Farmer is the patron saint of rural life. St. Francis of Assisi is the patron saint of ecology. St. Luke is the patron saint of physicians. St. John Vianney is the patron saint of parish priests. St. Vincent de Paul is the patron saint of charitable works.

NOTES...

IV. Holiness and suffering.

A. Because of Christ's redemption, each person can live a life of hope of eternal life. The New Testament gives Christ's teaching of how to live the eight *beatitudes*. These "are addressed to people tried by various sufferings in their temporal life" (SD #16).

B. Suffering is part of the human condition and an opportunity for receiving God's grace. By joining one's sufferings to Christ, a person participates in His suffering. Thus, "It is precisely the Church, which ceaselessly draws on the infinite resources of the Redemption, introducing it into the life of humanity, *which is the dimension* in which the redemtive suffering of Christ can be constantly completed by the suffering of man" (SD #240).

FOCUS QUESTIONS

1. Do you pray for relatives who have died, or ask them to pray for you? Is the "communion of saints" a comfort to you?
2. Do you have a favorite saint? What is it about this saint that appeals to you?
3. How does suffering become redemptive in life?

Concluding prayers
Intercessions
Closing prayer
Hymn (optional)

RESOURCES

Catechism of the Catholic Church, 828, 948, 2013-2015, 2683
Lumen gentium (Dogmatic Constitution on the Church), Vatican II
Essentials of the Faith, McBride, chap. 24
Salvifici doloris (On the Christian Meaning of Human Suffering), John Paul II

Session Eighteen

The Last Things

LEARNING OBJECTIVE

To present the Catholic teaching on the ultimate destiny of the human person as they move through life towards death, the particular judgment, heaven, purgatory, hell, the last judgment, and the kingdom of God in its fullness.

Hymn: "Jerusalem, My Happy Home"

Invitation to prayer — silent prayer

Oration:

God our Father,
by raising Christ your Son
you conquered the power of death
and opened for us the way to eternal life.
Let our celebration today
raise us up and renew our lives
by the Spirit that is within us.

Grant this through our Lord Jesus Christ, your Son,
who lives and reigns with you and the Holy Spirit,
one God, for ever and ever.

Opening Prayer
Easter Sunday

Scripture reading: John 20:1-9

On the first day of the week, Mary of Magdala came to the tomb early in the morning, while it was still dark, and saw the stone removed from the tomb. So she ran and went to Simon Peter and to the other disciple whom Jesus loved, and told them, "They have taken the Lord from the tomb, and we don't know where they put him." So Peter and the other disciple went out and came to the tomb. They both ran, but the other disciple ran faster than Peter and arrived at the tomb first; he bent down and saw the burial cloths there, but did not go in. When Simon Peter arrived after him, he went into the tomb and saw the burial cloths there, and the cloth that had covered his head, not with the burial cloths but rolled up in a separate place. Then the other disciple also went in, the one who had arrived at the tomb first, and he saw and believed. For they did not yet understand the scripture that he had to rise from the dead.

TEACHING TO BE PRESENTED

NOTES...

I. From the very beginning of Christianity belief in death and resurrection of the body has been an essential teaching of Catholicism (CCC 991).

A. Hope in the bodily resurrection of the dead follows faith in God who is Creator of the whole person, body and soul (CCC 992).

1. God is the God of the living, not the God of the dead (CCC 993).
2. "Jesus links faith in the resurrection to his own person: 'I am the Resurrection and the life' (Jn 11:25)" (CCC 994).

B. Death is a reminder that we only have a limited time to live this life on earth (CCC 1013).

1. "*Death is the end of earthly life*" (CCC 1007).
2. The teaching of the Catholic Church states that death entered the world because of sin. Thus, it was contrary to God's original plan at the creation of man and woman (CCC 1008).
3. The obedience of Jesus Christ through the Paschal Mystery transformed the curse of death into a blessing (CCC 1009).

C. Through our Baptism eternal life begins in time. This participation of the heavenly life of the risen Christ remains "'hidden with Christ in God' (Col 3:3; cf. Phil 3:20)" (CCC 1003).

D. "Our participation in the Eucharist already gives us a foretaste of Christ's transfiguration of our bodies." In this reality we "'possess the hope of resurrection' (St. Irenaeus, *Adv. haeres.* 4, 18, 4-5: PG 7/1, 1028-1029)" (CCC 1000).

II. In death God calls all people to Himself (CCC 1011).

A. "By death the soul is separated from the body" (CCC 1016).

1. The human body decays and the soul goes to meet God.
2. The soul encounters God in the particular judgment. At this time our life is evaluated in relation to Christ.
3. The soul will receive in the particular judgment either entrance into blessedness (heaven); or a time of purification (purgatory); or everlasting damnation (hell) (CCC 1022).
   a. Heaven is for those who have been purified of self and are ready to be united with Christ forever, seeing Him face to face (CCC 1023).
   b. Purgatory is an experience of purification for those who die in God's friendship but still need to be readied for the holiness necessary for final union with God (CCC 1031). Purgatory is the ultimate purgation of the self needed in order to enter into divine union.
   c. Hell is the state of total self-exclusion from God. Because our hearts are created for God, this pain of eternal deprivation of His presence is excruciating.

B. Those who die in the state of mortal sin experience the punishment of eternal separation from God (CCC 1035).

1. "The teaching of the Church affirms the existence of hell and its eternity" (CCC 1035).
2. These teachings on hell remind us of our freedom and responsibility to choose the good and our future destiny (CCC 1036).
3. These teachings are a constant reminder of our need for conversion (CCC 1036).

NOTES...

III. The Last Judgment is the time at which Christ will come in all His glory to judge the living and the dead.

A. At the Last Judgment Christ will lay bare each persons relationship with God (CCC 1039).

1. The good each person has accomplished will be revealed (CCC 1039).
2. The evil or lack of good people have failed to do will be as well disclosed (CCC 1039).
3. On the day of the last judgment each person will appear in his or her own body (CCC 1059).

B. "At the end of time, the Kingdom of God will come in its fullness." Glorified in body and soul, the just will reign with Christ (CCC 1060).

1. The material universe will be itself transformed (CCC 1060).
2. God will be "'all in all' (1 Cor 15:28), in eternal life" (CCC 1060).

IV. No person knows the moment nor the hour when the Second Coming of Christ will occur.

A. "By virtue of the 'communion of saints,' the Church commends the dead to God's mercy and offers her prayers, especially the holy sacrifice of the Eucharist, on their behalf" (CCC 1055).

1. The Church prays that no person die separated from God (CCC 1058).
2. God desires all people to be saved (CCC 1058).

B. No person can save him- or herself. Each is saved in and through the grace of Christ.

1. We are commended to pray for ourselves at the hour of our death.
2. We are commended to pray for the souls in purgatory.

FOCUS QUESTIONS

1. Why do people in our culture reject heaven and hell?
2. How does the image of a glorified body for all eternity evoke in you a desire for conversion?
3. Why is it that we cannot save ourselves?

Concluding prayers
Intercessions
Closing prayer
Hymn (optional)

RESOURCES

Catechism of the Catholic Church, 988-1050
Gaudium et spes (Pastoral Constitution on the Church in the Modern World), Vatican II, 18 and 22
Essentials of the Faith, McBride, chaps. 27-29

Session Nineteen

Catholic Morality and the Dignity of the Human Person

LEARNING OBJECTIVE

To focus on the dignity of the human which is at the heart of Catholic moral teaching. In the Incarnation of Jesus, every human life finds the fullness of meaning.

Hymn: "Earthen Vessels"

Invitation to prayer — silent prayer

Oration:

God our Father,
your Word became man and was born of the Virgin Mary.
May we become more like Jesus Christ,
whom we acknowledge as our redeemer, God and man.

We ask this through our Lord Jesus Christ, your Son,
who lives and reigns with you and the Holy Spirit,
one God, forever and ever. Amen.

Opening Prayer
Solemnity of the Annunciation

Scripture reading: Genesis 2:4-7

At the time when the LORD God made the earth and the heavens — while as yet there was no field shrub on earth and no grass of the field had sprouted, for the LORD God had sent no rain upon the earth and there was no man to till the soil, but a stream was welling up out of the earth and was watering all the surface of the ground — the LORD God formed man out of the clay of the ground and blew into his nostrils the breath of life, and so man became a living being.

TEACHING TO BE PRESENTED

I. **The dignity of the human person.**
   A. Christian morality is based on the "Dignity of the Human Person."
      1. The divine image is present in every human being (cf. Gn 1:27). Every human being is created "good" prior to any covenanting with God. The soul is the principle of life in each human being, which makes him or her destined for

NOTES...

eternal happiness. The second story of creation (Gn 2:4-7) remarks that God formed man out of clay and breathed life into him. The words "spirit," "breath," and "life" often appear interchangeably in the Scriptures to show the creative force of God at work through the human gift of the soul (CCC 1702-1703).

2. Each human being has been given a will and an intellect. Through the gift of a free will, we are capable of choosing the good. By the gift of reason (intellect), human beings are capable of knowing the voice of God, and through the gift of actual grace, to choose the good and avoid evil. We are obliged to follow God's Law, which makes itself heard in conscience and is fulfilled in the love of God and neighbor. Moral living witnesses to the dignity of the person (CCC 1704-1706).
3. Each person is called to a "fullness of life" which is beyond the boundaries of life on earth. This participation in God's very own life in time reveals "the greatness and the inestimable value of human life" (EV 2). That each person is called to supernatural life, this in and of itself "highlights the relative character of each individual's earthly life" (EV 2).
4. Life presents difficulties and uncertainties. Even in the midst of these "every person sincerely open to truth and goodness can, by the light of reason and the hidden action of grace, come to recognize in the natural law written in the heart (cf. Rom 2:14-15) the sacred value of human life from its very beginfling until its end, and can affirm the right of every human being to have this primary good respected to the highest degree. Upon the recognition of this right every human community and political community itself are founded" (EV 2).

B. God's loving wisdom for the guidance of all things.
   1. God's eternal law is the divine regulation of creation, God's loving and wise plan for the guidance of all things to their proper fulfillments.
   2. Because God is only good, anything that conforms to God's eternal law of guidance to fulfillment may be called "good."
   3. Human beings are good when they freely choose to enter into a covenant with God by belonging to God and obeying His plan for them, to know Him, and to love Him and our neighbor. Such a covenant is only possible in and with Jesus Christ.
   4. The eternal law also reveals what evil is. Anything that is contrary to God's plan that is inscribed in creation, thereby breaking the covenant with Him, perverting things from their proper purposes, disturbing the communion between persons, and distorting the image of God is evil (VS 9-11).

C. Natural Law — human participation in God's eternal love.
   1. "The natural moral law expresses and lays down the purposes, rights and duties which are based upon the bodily and spiritual nature of the human person. Therefore this law cannot be thought of as simply a set of norms on the biological level; rather it must be defined as the rational order whereby man is called by the Creator to direct and regulate his life and actions and in particular to make use of his own body" (VS 50).
   2. Characteristics of the natural law:
      a. Universal — applies to each and every person because it is inscribed in each person's heart (cf. Rom 2:15).
      b. Objective — not subjective because it reflects the reality of the way God has revealed everything

NOTES...

   c. Permanent — can never be changed because human nature does not change.
   d. Expressed in specific, objective norms.
3. Natural law teaches the person to perfect him/herself by doing good and avoiding evil, being concerned for the transmission and preservation of life, refining and developing the riches of the material world, cultivating social life, seeking truth and contemplating beauty (VS 51).

D. The human person has freedom and responsibility.
1. An outstanding manifestation of the divine image is the gift of freedom. Men and women bear the power, through the gift of God's life to initiate and control their actions. "Freedom is the power, rooted in reason and will, to act or not to act, to do this or that, and so to perform deliberate actions on one's own responsibility" (CCC 1731). Through the gift of free will, one has the power to shape one's own life. Human freedom is a force for growth and maturity when it is based upon that which is true and good.
   a. "The more one does what is good, the freer one becomes. There is no true freedom except in the service of what is good and just" (CCC 1733).
   b. "If you remain in my word, you will truly be my disciples, and you will know the truth, and the truth will set you free" (Jn 8:31-32).
   c. There always lies the possibility of one to choose between good and evil. "This freedom characterizes properly human acts. It is the basis of praise or blame, merit or reproach" (CCC 1732).
   d. "The choice to disobey and do evil is an abuse of freedom and leads to 'the slavery of sin' (cf. Rom 6:17)" (CCC 1733).
   e. "Freedom is exercised in relationships between human beings" (CCC 1738). Every human being, created in God's image and likeness, has the right to be recognized as a free and responsible being. "All owe to each other this duty of respect. The *right to the exercise of freedom*, especially in moral and religious matters, is an inalienable requirement of the dignity of the human person" (CCC 1738). Civil authority must recognize and protect this right within the limits of the common good and public order.
2. With freedom comes responsibility. Freedom makes one responsible for his acts to the extent that they are voluntary (CCC 1745).
   a. "An action can be indirectly voluntary when it results from negligence regarding something one should have known or done." One would be held responsible when an accident occurs after one deliberately ignores a traffic law (CCC 1736).
   b. Responsibility for an action can be diminished by ignorance, fear, habit, and other psychological and social factors. The Old Testament has many references to prove that Adam and Eve (cf. Gn 3), Cain (cf. Gn 4:10), and David (cf. 2 Sm 12:7-15) were held responsible for their actions (CCC 1735).
   c. "An effect can be tolerated without being willed by its agent; for instance, a mother's exhaustion from tending her sick child.... For a bad effect to be imputable it must be foreseeable and the agent must have the possibility of avoiding it, as in the case of manslaughter caused by a drunken driver" (CCC 1737).
3. Progress in virtue, knowledge of the good, and self-discipline enhance the mastery of the will over its acts. The Christian who prays and struggles to live a

NOTES...

life of virtue becomes more docile to the prompting of God's grace and grows in inner freedom and confidence.

II. The Christian message concerning life.

A. Jesus Christ reveals through His person and actions "the complete truth concerning the value of human life" (EV 29). It is thus through Christ that humanity "receives in particular the capacity to 'accomplish' this truth perfectly (cf. Jn 3:21) that is to accept and fulfill completely the responsibility of loving and serving, of defending and promoting human life" (EV 29).

B. The Old Testament, especially the events of the Exodus, taught Israel how valued life is in God's eyes (EV 31).

1. The Exodus was "the centre of the Old Testament faith experience" (EV 31).
2. Israel came to experience God's power, realizing that their existence was not at the mercy of their oppressors but rather their life was, the object of God's gentle and intense love (EV 31).
3. For the Israelites, "freedom from slavery meant the gift of an identity, the recognition of an indestructible dignity and the beginning of a new history in which the discovery of God and discovery of self go hand in hand" (EV 31).

C. Jesus above all spoke to "the poor" through His preaching and actions. However, Jesus and the Church speak to all at their deepest level of existence. The heart of the Christian message is to present "the very meaning of every person's life in its moral and spiritual dimension" (EV 32).

1. Jesus' own life indicates a "singular 'dialectic' between the experience of the uncertainty of human life and the affirmation of its value" (EV 33).
2. Jesus was accepted by those who were at one with God. However, He also experienced the rejection and hostility of the world (EV 33).
3. The contradictions of life were fully accepted by Jesus nor was He afraid of the risks. Jesus suffered, died, and rose again. It was His self-oblation on the cross which became the source of "new life" for humankind. "Truly great must be the value of human life if the Son of God has taken it up and made it the instrument of the salvation of all humanity" (EV 33).

D. The love which we are called to in life is far more than self-expression, self-fulfillment, and/or entering into relationship with others. "Rather, it develops in a joyous awareness that life can become the 'place' where God manifests himself, where we meet him and enter into communion with him. The life which Jesus gives in no way lessens the value of our existence in time; it takes it and directs it to its final destiny: 'I am the resurrection and the life...whoever lives and believes in me shall never die' (Jn 11:25-26)" (EV 38).

E. It is the very sacredness of life which gives rise to its inviolability, written from the very beginning in each person's heart, his or her conscience. It is in the commandments that God, in the most profound depths of being protects human life. It is the intention of God that each and every person receive reverence and love (EV 40).

NOTES...

FOCUS QUESTIONS

1. How has society denied the dignity of the human person?
2. Why is society now so concerned with "virtue"?
3. How is freedom connected to responsibility? Do you think society has that understanding of freedom?

Concluding prayers
Intercessions
Closing prayer
Hymn (optional)

RESOURCES

Catechism of the Catholic Church, 1702-1737
Evangelium Vitae (The Gospel of Life), John Paul II
Veritatis splendor (The Splendor of Truth), John Paul II
Essentials of the Faith. McBride, chap. 42

Session Twenty

Living the Catholic Moral Life

LEARNING OBJECTIVE

To understand the process of conscience formation and to recognize the dignity that comes from choosing the good and living a life of virtue.

Hymn: "Grant to Us, O Lord, a Heart Renewed"

Invitation to prayer — silent prayer

Oration:

Father,
teach us to live good lives,
encourage us with your support
and bring us to eternal life.

We ask this through our Lord Jesus Christ, your Son,
who lives and reigns with you, and the Holy Spirit,
one God, for ever and ever.

Opening Prayer
Wednesday of the Second Week of Lent

Scripture reading: Psalm 1

Happy those who do not follow
the counsel of the wicked,
Nor go the way of sinners,
nor sit in company with scoffers.
Rather, the law of the LORD is their joy;
God's law they study day and night.
They are like a tree
planted near streams of water,
that yields its fruit in season;
Its leaves never wither;
whatever they do prospers.

But not the wicked!
They are like chaff driven by the wind.
Therefore the wicked will not survive judgment,
nor will sinners in the assembly of the just.
The LORD watches over the way of the just,
but the way of the wicked leads to ruin.

TEACHING TO BE PRESENTED

NOTES...

I. The evaluation of human acts.

A. The moral conscience.

1. "'Deep within his conscience man discovers a law which he has not laid upon himself but which he must obey. Its voice, ever calling him to love and to do what is good and to avoid evil, sounds in his heart at the right moment.... For man has in his heart a law inscribed by God.... His conscience is man's most secret core and his sanctuary. There he is alone with God whose voice echoes in his depths'(GS 16)" (CCC 1776).
2. The word "conscience" is derived from two Latin words meaning "with knowledge."
3. Conscience is a practical judgment by the use of reason that tells us in a concrete situation what our moral obligation is.
4. The fact that Adam and Eve tried to hide themselves from God (Gn 3:8) after they sinned shows that they "knew better than to do that." As children, our parents might have used those same words with us after we did something we knew was wrong.
5. During the moral decision-making process, one is not only in conversation with himself or herself, but is in dialogue with God.

B. Conscience formation.

1. "A well-formed conscience is upright and truthful. It formulates its judgments according to reason, in conformity with the true good willed by the wisdom of the Creator" (CCC 1783).
2. A Christian strives to form his or her conscience on the Word of God, for it must be assimilated in faith and prayer and put into practice (CCC 1785).
3. Conscience formation is a lifelong process; moral conscience is in need of continual conversion toward what is good and true.
4. Natural law, the Ten Commandments, the teachings of Christ, and the teachings of the Spirit-led Church (Magisterium) all contribute to the formation of a right conscience.
5. Parents stand responsible before God to see that their children have well-informed consciences.
6. A person who is considering joining the Catholic Church has the responsibility to know what the Church teaches beforehand to guarantee a conscience that is truly well informed.
7. A traditional Catholic practice is to frequently examine one's conscience to decide whether or not one is following the path to Truth. Some Scripture passages that are helpful are: Exodus 20:1-17 or Deuteronomy 5:6-21, Matthew 5:1-12, and Galatians 5:16-26.

C. Choosing in accord with conscience.

1. People have "the right to act in conscience and in freedom so as personally to make moral decisions" (CCC 1782).
2. "Conscience can make either a right judgment in accordance with reason and the divine law or ... an erroneous judgment that departs from them" (CCC 1786).
3. In making judgments, some rules apply in every case:
   a. "One may never do evil so that good may result from it" (CCC 1789).
   b. "The Golden Rule: 'Whatever you wish that men would do to you, do so to them' (Mt 7:12; cf. Lk 6:31; Tb 4:15)" (CCC 1789).

NOTES...

c. Charity above all else (CCC 1789).

<u>Note to catechists</u>: *The following points might help catechumens and candidates understand some of the types of consciences. It is included to help you give real examples rather than just information that must be learned to join the Church.*

4. A right conscience is well-formed and is in alignment with the Truth. We all strive to have a right conscience.
5. A certain conscience passes judgment on the good or evil of an act without fear of error. One has to follow a certain conscience. Note that a certain conscience can be wrong. Example: Did you ever answer a question on an exam and were one-hundred-percent sure that it was correct only to be shocked that the instructor marked it wrong? A certain conscience may be wrong because of ignorance — either invincible (cannot be changed) or vincible (capable of being changed).
   a. An invincibly erroneous conscience must be followed. The person is not responsible for the erroneous judgment and the evil committed by the person cannot be imputed to him or her. Nevertheless, the act is still objectively evil.
   b. A vincible erroneous conscience cannot be followed. Example: "I think artificial birth control is all right but I have some concerns and questions. I should check it out sometime, but not now." In this case the person is culpable if the action is followed.
6. A person cannot act with a doubtful conscience: "I'm not sure what is right." The doubt must be resolved. Some suggestions might be:
   a. Study the objective teaching
   b. Pray for guidance
   c. List the pros and cons for doing the act
   d. Check with a priest for counsel
7. A person with a lax conscience rationalizes his or her actions. Example: "I always mail in my church contributions — it doesn't matter that I don't regularly attend Sunday Mass." This type of conscience needs to be reeducated.
8. A person with a scrupulous conscience obsessively and compulsively sees sin where there is none. This type of person often needs professional help.

D. The morality of human acts
1. Freedom makes each one of us a moral subject. Human acts that are freely chosen in consequence of a judgment of conscience can be morally evaluated. "They are either good or evil" (CCC 1749).
2. The morality or immorality of human acts depend on three factors (CCC 1750):
   a. The act itself: The object chosen (the act) morally specifies the act of willing accordingly as it is judged good or evil (CCC 1751).
   b. The intention of the act: "The end is the first goal of the intention and indicates the purpose pursued in the action. The intention is a movement of the will toward the end: it is concerned with the goal of the activity" (CCC 1752). "'An evil action cannot be justified by reference to a good intention' (cf. St. Thomas Aquinas, *Dec. praec.* 6). The end does not justify the means" (CCC 1759).
   c. The *circumstances* surrounding the act: "The *circumstances*, including the consequences, are secondary elements of a moral act. They contribute to

increasing or diminishing the moral goodness or evil of human acts. . . . Circumstances of themselves cannot change the moral quality of acts themselves; they can make neither good nor right an action that is in itself evil" (CCC 1754).

3. "A morally good act requires the goodness of its object, of its end, and of its circumstances together" (CCC 1760).
4. In the *Veritatis Splendor* (Splendor of Truth), Pope John Paul II teaches: "The primary and decisive element for moral judgment is the object of the human act, which establishes whether it is *capable of being ordered to the good and to the ultimate end, which is God*" (VS 79).
5. The Church teaches that some acts are always intrinsically evil: "Whatever is hostile to life itself, such as any kind of homicide, genocide, abortion, euthanasia or voluntary suicide, or whatever is offensive to human dignity. . ." (GS 27).
   a. "If acts are intrinsically evil, a good intention or particular circumstances can diminish their evil, but they cannot remove it" (VS 81).
   b. An objectively evil act is not always sinful. To be so, it must be committed with full knowledge and complete consent.

E. The morality of the passions

1. "The term 'passions' refers to the affections or the feelings" (CCC 1771). "The passions are natural components of the human psyche" (CCC 1764).
2. "In themselves passions are neither good nor evil" (CCC 1767). In other words, we cannot be guilty of sin through our feelings. But insofar as they engage reason and will, there is moral good or evil in them.
3. "Emotions and feelings can be taken up in the virtues or perverted by the vices" (CCC 1774).
4. "Moral perfection consists in man's being moved to the good not by his will alone, but also by his sensitive appetite, as in the words of the psalm: 'My heart and flesh sing for joy to the living God' (Ps 84:2)" (CCC 1770).

II. Helps to living a moral life.

A. Virtues help us to live a moral life. The word "virtue" is derived from the Latin word *virtus* meaning "strength" or "courage."

1. To be a virtuous person means to possess the strength of great human power. "A virtue is an habitual and firm disposition to do the good. It allows the person not only to perform good acts, but to give the best of himself" (CCC 1803). "The goal of a virtuous life is to become like God" (St. Gregory of Nyssa, *De beatitudinibus*, 1: PG 44, 1200D) (CCC 1803).
2. The human virtues are disposition of the intellect and will "that govern our actions, order our passions, and guide our conduct according to reason and faith" (CCC 1804). They can be grouped around the four cardinal virtues: prudence, justice, fortitude, and temperance.
   a. "Prudence disposes the practical reason to discern, in every circumstance, our true good and to choose the right means for achieving it" (CCC 1835).
   b. "Justice consists in the firm and constant will to give God and neighbor their due." Justice deals with a right relationship that we should have with God and those around us (CCC 1836).

NOTES...

NOTES...

c. Fortitude comes from the Latin word *fortius*, which means "strength." This virtue "ensures firmness in difficulties and constancy in the pursuit of the good" (CCC 1837).
d. "Temperance moderates the attraction of the pleasures of the senses and provides balance in the use of created goods" (CCC 1838). "In the middle, lies all virtue" (St. Thomas Aquinas).

3. The above moral virtues grow through education, deliberate acts, and perseverance in struggle. Grace purifies and elevates them.
4. "There are three theological virtues: faith, hope, and charity [love]. They inform all the moral virtues and give life to them" (CCC 1841). "The theological virtues dispose Christians to live in a relationship with the Holy Trinity. They have God for their origin, their motive, and their object — God known by faith, God hoped in and loved for his own sake" (CCC 1840).
   a. "By faith, we believe in God and believe all that he has revealed to us and that Holy Church proposes for our belief" (CCC 1842). The traditional Act of Faith is:

      O my God, I firmly believe that You are one God in three Divine Persons, the Father, the Son, and the Holy Spirit. I believe in Jesus Christ, Your Son, who became man and died for our sins, and who will come to judge the living and the dead. I believe these and all truths which the Holy Catholic Church teaches, because You have revealed them, who can neither deceive nor be deceived. Amen.

   b. "By hope we desire, and with steadfast trust await from God, eternal life and the graces to merit it" (CCC 1843). The traditional Act of Hope is:

      O my God, trusting in Your infinite goodness and promises, I hope to obtain pardon of my sins, the help of Your grace, and life everlasting, through the merits of Jesus Christ, my Lord and Redeemer. Amen.

   c. "By charity, we love God above all things and our neighbor as ourselves for love of God. Charity, the form of all the virtues" is the greatest of virtues (CCC 1844). The traditional Act of Love is:

      O my God, I love You above all things, with my whole heart and soul, because You are all good and worthy of all my love. I love my neighbor as myself for love of You. I forgive all who have injured me, and I ask pardon of all whom I have injured. Amen.

B. The gifts and fruits of the Holy Spirit.

1. "The moral life of Christians is sustained by the gifts of the Holy Spirit. These are permanent dispositions which make man docile in following the prompting of the Holy Spirit" (CCC 1830).
2. The seven gifts of the Holy Spirit were originally outlined by the prophet Isaiah (Is 11:2-3). In the thirteenth century, St. Thomas Aquinas joined the gifts of the Holy Spirit with the Beatitudes to show how the wishes of Jesus are brought to life through the actions of the Holy Spirit.
3. To the Jewish people, the number "seven" was the symbol of perfection. The seven gifts of the Holy Spirit are:
   a. Wisdom — good judgment concerning the things we know from God.
   b. Understanding — deeper insight or awareness of the things that God has done for us.

c. Counsel — advice through the help of God in making decisions, especially on the practical order.
d. Fortitude — strength and courage from God to help us endure pain and misfortune. (This is the special gift that the martyrs have received.)
e. Knowledge — becoming familiar with God and with what He has taught us.
f. Piety — loyalty, devotion, and reverence of God and the people and things He has given us.
g. Fear of the Lord — a respectful sense of who God is. This gift helps to encourage one to make a good confession (CCC 1845).

4. The liturgical text for the Rite of Confirmation makes mention of the seven gifts of the Holy Spirit at the invocation of the Holy Spirit, prior to the anointing with Holy Chrism. Thus, one preparing to receive any of the Sacraments of Initiation should be well aware of the great gifts which they are about to receive.
5. The *fruits* of the Holy Spirit are supernatural works or perfections that are done with ease as signs of the Holy Spirit working within us. "The tradition of the Church lists twelve of them: 'charity, joy, peace, patience, kindness, goodness, generosity, gentleness, faithfulness, modesty, self-control, chastity' (Gal 5:22-23 [Vulg.])" (CCC 1832).

NOTES...

FOCUS QUESTIONS

1. Why is conscience formation a lifelong process?
2 Why doesn't the "end" justify the "means"?
3. Do you think most people strive to follow an informed conscience?

Concluding prayers
Intercessions
Closing prayer
Hymn (optional)

RESOURCES

Catechism of the Catholic Church, 1749-1845
Veritatis splendor (The Splendor of Truth), John Paul II
Essentials of the Faith, McBride, chap. 42

Session Twenty-one

The Ten Commandments

Introduction and Commandments I-III

LEARNING OBJECTIVE

To present the Commandments and their implications of belonging to God.

Hymn: "Praise God From Whom All Blessings Flow"

Invitation to prayer — silent prayer

Oration:

Father,
guide and protector of your people,
grant us an unfailing respect for your name,
and keep us always in your love.

Grant this through our Lord Jesus Christ, your Son,
who lives and reigns with you and the Holy Spirit,
one God, for ever and ever.

Opening Prayer
Twelfth Sunday in Ordinary Time

Scripture reading: Exodus 20:1-17

Then God delivered all these commandments:

"I, the LORD, am your God, who brought you out of the land of Egypt, that place of slavery. You shall not have other gods besides me. You shall not carve idols for yourselves in the shape of anything in the sky above or on the earth below or in the waters beneath the earth; you shall not bow down before them or worship them. For I, the LORD, your God, am a jealous God, inflicting punishment for their fathers' wickedness on the children of those who hate me, down to the third and fourth generation; but bestowing mercy down to the thousandth generation, on the children of those who love me and keep my commandments.

"You shall not take the name of the LORD, your God, in vain. For the LORD will not leave unpunished him who takes his name in vain.

"Remember to keep holy the sabbath day. Six days you may labor and do all your work, but the seventh day is the sabbath of the LORD, your God. No work may be done then either by you, or your son or daughter, or your male or female slave, or your beast, or by the alien who lives with you. In six days the LORD made the heavens and the earth, the sea and all that is in them; but on the seventh day he rested. That is why the LORD has blessed the sabbath day and made it holy.

"Honor your father and your mother, that you may have a long life in the land which the Lord, your God, is giving you.

"You shall not kill.

"You shall not commit adultery.

"You shall not steal.

"You shall not bear false witness against your neighbor.

"You shall not covet your neighbor's house. You shall not covet your neighbor's wife, nor his male or female slave, nor his ox or ass, nor anything else that belongs to him."

NOTES...

TEACHING TO BE PRESENTED

I. The Commandments in general.

A. The historical background of the Ten Commandments is most important to an understanding of their centrality.

1. Moses stood as the mediator between God and His people. "The Old Law is the first stage of revealed law. Its moral prescriptions are summed up in the Ten Commandments" (CCC 1980).
2. The Law of Moses contains many natural, or obvious, truths naturally accessible to reason. God has revealed them because people could not read them as they had been written in their own hearts (Jer 31:33) (CCC 1981).
3. "The Old Law is a preparation for the Gospel" (CCC 1982); "The New Law is a law of love, a law of grace, a law of freedom" (CCC 1985). "By his life and by his preaching Jesus attested to the permanent validity of the Decalogue" (CCC 2076). A young man asked Jesus, "Teacher, what good must I do to gain eternal life?" (Mt 19:16). Jesus answered, "If you wish to enter into life, keep the commandments" (Mt 19:17).
4. "Christ is the end of the law (cf. Rom 10:4); only he teaches and bestows the justice of God" (CCC 1977).
5. "According to Scripture the Law is a fatherly instruction by God" to help us lead a good life and avoid the way of evil (cf. Rom 7:12, 14, 16) (CCC 1975). "'Law is an ordinance of reason for the common good, promulgated by the one who is in charge of the community' (St. Thomas Aquinas, *STh* I-II, 90, 4)" (CCC 1976). By God giving the Law on Mount Sinai, and by Moses accepting the Law in the name of God's people, God was further demonstrating His right to hold the community of Israel as His own dear possession.
6. "The Decalogue contains a privileged expression of the natural law. It is made known to us by divine revelation and by human reason" (CCC 2080).

B. "The gift of the Decalogue is bestowed from within the covenant concluded by God with his people" (CCC 2077).

1. "God's commandments take on their true meaning in and through this covenant" (CCC 2077).
2. "In fidelity to Scripture and in conformity with Jesus' example, the tradition of the Church has always acknowledged the primordial importance and significance of the Decalogue" (CCC 2078).

NOTES...

3. "The Decalogue forms an organic unity in which each 'word' or 'commandment' refers to all the others taken together. To transgress one commandment is to infringe the whole Law (cf. Jas 2:10-11)" (CCC 2079).
4. "The Ten Commandments, in their fundamental content, state grave obligations. However, obedience to these precepts also implies obligations in matter which is, in itself, light" (CCC 2081).
5. "What God commands he makes possible by his grace" (CCC 2082). As it has often been said, God doesn't give us any more than we can handle.
6. The Ten Commandments state what is minimally required in the love of God and love of neighbor. The first three concern love of God, and the other seven, love of neighbor.

II. The First Commandment: "I, the LORD, am your God. . . . You shall not have other gods besides me" (Dt 5:6-7).

A. The first commandment asks us to believe in God, to hope in Him, and to love Him above all else (CCC 2134). Sins against the theological virtues include, incredulity, heresy, schism, despair, presumption, indifference, ingratitude, lukewarmness, spiritual sloth, atheism, agnosticism, and hatred of God.

B. Charity leads us to render to God what we as creatures owe Him in all justice. The virtue of religion disposes us to have this attitude. Adoring God, praying to Him, offering Him the worship that belongs to Him, fulfilling all of the vows and promises made to Him, fall under this virtue.

C. "The Lord, your God, shall you worship / and him alone shall you serve" (Mt 4:10). The duty to offer God authentic worship concerns human beings as individuals and as social beings. (CCC 2136) Thus, the Israelites were known as the People of God and we are rightfully called the community of the Church.

D. "Superstition is a departure from the worship that we give to the true God. It is manifested in idolatry, as well as in various forms of divination and magic" (CCC 2138). The veneration of sacred images is based on the Incarnation of the Word of God. It is not contrary to the first commandment (CCC 2141).

E. "Tempting God in words or deeds, sacrilege, and simony are sins of irreligion forbidden by the first commandment" (CCC 2139).

F. Atheism rejects or denies the existence of God (CCC 2140).

III. The Second Commandment: "You shall not take the name of the LORD, your God, in vain" (Ex 20:7; Dt 5:11).

A. "The second commandment enjoins respect for the Lord's name.
The name of the Lord is holy" (CCC 2161). It "forbids every improper use of God's name. Blasphemy is the use of the name of God, of Jesus Christ, of the Virgin Mary, and of the saints in an offensive way" (CCC 2162). Swearing is wrong. The Catholic Tradition has always maintained a respect for the Holy Names of Jesus and Mary. Some Catholics still bow their heads at the mention of the name of Jesus as a sign of respect.

B. "False oaths call on God to be witness to a lie. Perjury is a grave offence against the Lord who is always faithful to his promises" (CCC 2163).

IV. **The Third Commandment: "Remember to keep holy the sabbath day"** (Ex 20:8).

NOTES...

A. "The sabbath, which represented the completion of the first creation, has been replaced by Sunday which recalls the new creation inaugurated by the Resurrection of Christ" (CCC 2190). An understanding of the mystery of the Resurrection and the celebration of the Easter Vigil Mass should help to explain the beauty and centrality of the Sunday observance.

B. "'Sunday...is to be observed as the foremost holy day of obligation in the universal Church' (CIC, can. 1246 § 1). 'On Sundays and other holy days of obligation the faithful are bound to participate in the Mass' (CIC, can. 1247)" (CCC 2192). It is gravely wrong to miss Mass on Sundays or holy days.

C. Catholics are also bound to abstain from servile work on Sundays and holy days. Business and labor should not impede the worship of God and the joy which is proper to the Lord's Day. After the pattern of God Himself, the Christian should allow for a day of rest and leisure in order to cultivate friendships, family unity, and other social and cultural needs which humans find to be necessary as healthy, social beings (CCC 2193-2195).

FOCUS QUESTIONS

1. Catholics are obliged to attend Mass on Sundays. How does this relate to the First Commandment?
2. Why is perjury a grave offense?
3. How does the contemporary culture offend the Third Commandment?

Concluding prayers
Intercessions
Closing prayer
Hymn (optional)

RESOURCES

Catechism of the Catholic Church, 1949-1986, 2052-2195
Codes Iuris Canonici (Code of Canon Law)
Essentials of the Faith, chaps. 44-46

Session Twenty-two

The Ten Commandments

Commandments IV-X

LEARNING OBJECTIVE

To understand the charity involved towards our neighbor as proposed by God in the last seven Commandments.

Hymn: "You Are Near"

Invitation to prayer — silent prayer

Oration:

Lord,
fill our hearts with the spirit of your charity,
that we may please you by our thoughts,
and love you in our brothers and sisters.

We ask this through our Lord Jesus Christ, your Son,
who lives and reigns with you and the Holy Spirit,
one God, for ever and ever.

Opening Prayer
Mass for Charity

Scripture reading: Romans 12:1-2, 9-18

I urge you therefore, brothers, by the mercies of God, to offer your bodies as a living sacrifice, holy and pleasing to God, your spiritual worship. Do not conform yourselves to this age but be transformed by the renewal of your mind, that you may discern what is the will of God, what is good and pleasing and perfect....

Let love be sincere; hate what is evil, hold on to what is good; love one another with mutual affection; anticipate one another in showing honor. Do not grow slack in zeal, be fervent in spirit, serve the Lord. Rejoice in hope, endure in affliction, persevere in prayer. Contribute to the needs of the holy ones, exercise hospitality. Bless those who persecute [you], bless and do not curse them. Rejoice with those who rejoice, weep with those who weep. Have the same regard for one another; do not be haughty but associate with the lowly; do not be wise in your own estimation. Do not repay anyone evil for evil; be concerned for what is noble in the sight of all. If possible, on your part, live at peace with all.

TEACHING TO BE PRESENTED

NOTES...

I. The Fourth Commandment: "Honor your father and your mother" (Ex 20:12; Dt 5:16).

A. Honoring father and mother.

1. "According to the fourth commandment, God has willed that, after him, we should honor our parents and those whom he has vested with authority for our good" (CCC 2248).
2. Jesus gave His full respect, devotion, and obedience to Mary and Joseph. A look at the Gospel text of the finding of Jesus in the temple will help to explain this point (cf. Lk 2:41-52).
3. The annual Feast of the Holy Family, celebrated the Sunday after Christmas, gives biblical and devotional inspiration to the family, the basic unit of society. Of particular importance is the reading from the Book of Sirach (3:2-6, 12-14). This Scripture passage deals with the relationship between parents and children and the respect and care to be expected from children.
4. "Children owe their parents respect, gratitude, just obedience, and assistance. Filial respect fosters harmony in all of family life" (CCC 2251). One might make a special mention of the obligations necessary in caring for elderly parents or grandparents.
5. "Parents have the first responsibility for the education of their children in the faith, prayer, and all the virtues. They have the duty to provide as far as possible for the physical and spiritual needs of their children. Parents should respect and encourage their children's vocations. They should remember and teach that the first calling of the Christian is to follow Jesus" (CCC 2252-2253).

B. Honoring public authority.

1. "Public authority is obliged to respect the fundamental rights of the human person and the conditions for the exercise of his freedom" (CCC 2254).
2. It is the duty of citizens to work with civil authority for building up society in a spirit of truth, justice, solidarity, and freedom.
3. "Citizens are obliged in conscience not to follow the directives of civil authorities when they are contrary to the demands of the moral order [i.e. abortion, limiting the size of families through sterilization, deliberate impediments to help the poor]. 'We must obey God rather than men' (Acts 5:29)" (CCC 2256). "'Render therefore to Caesar the things that are Caesar's, and to God the things that are God's' (Mt 22:21)" (CCC 2242).
4. Every society's judgments and conduct reflect a vision of the human person and society. Societies easily become totalitarian without the light of the Gospel (CCC 2257).
5. As a nation, we have an obligation to welcome those who are in search of security and a better life. The care for aliens and refugees dates back to the Old Testament (cf. Dt 10:17-19; 24:17-22). Of particular note is the influx of Hispanic and Asian immigrants in the United States.
6. All human rights issues including the immoral acts of prejudice and discrimination should be an object of concern for each citizen. Social justice concerns (i.e. the need for almsgiving, the need for true evangelization, and mutual and loving concern for community needs through care of the poor and the sick) contribute to the common good and form a vital part in respect for all human beings created in God's image.

NOTES...

7. The love for our country comes from an understanding of this commandment. The defense of our country through the armed forces, respect for the president and other public officials, respect for the legal system of our government, respect for the flag, voting as citizens of the nation — are all signs of a deep understanding of the fourth commandment (CCC 2239-2240).

II. The Fifth Commandment: "You shall not kill" (Ex 20:13; Dt 5:17).

A. Respect for the human dignity of life.

1. "Every human life, from the moment of conception until death, is sacred because the human person has been willed for its own sake in the image and likeness of the living and holy God" (CCC 2319).
2. "The murder of a human being is gravely contrary to the dignity of the person and the holiness of the Creator" (CCC 2320).
3. "From its conception, the child has the right to life" (CCC 2322). "Because it should be treated as a person from conception, the embryo must be defended in its integrity, cared for, and healed like every other human being" (CCC 2323). "Direct abortion, that is, abortion willed as an end or as a means, is a 'criminal' practice (GS 27 § 3), gravely contrary to the moral law" (CCC 2322). "The Church imposes the canonical penalty of excommunication for this crime against human life" (CCC 2322). Care must always be shown that God and the Church continue to love the sinner but hate the sin. Abortion is not an unforgivable sin! One who has committed the sin of an abortion, and one who has assisted in this crime in any way, should be encouraged to make a good confession and seek counseling if necessary.
4. "Intentional euthanasia [mercy killing], whatever its forms or motives, is murder"(CCC 2324).
5. "Suicide is seriously contrary to justice, hope, and charity" (CCC 2325). An insightful discussion on what happens to the soul of someone who commits suicide might answer a lot of questions on this topic. Before the Second Vatican Council, a Catholic who committed suicide was forbidden a Funeral Mass and burial in blessed ground. An increased understanding of psychological problems has enlightened the Church's understanding of this point.
6. "Scandal is a grave offense when by deed or omission it deliberately leads others to sin gravely" (CCC 2326).

B. "Just war" principles.

1. Self-defense and the defense of one's country is a grave duty for whoever is responsible for the lives of others or the common good. St. Thomas Aquinas was fundamental in helping the Church to understand the theory of a "just war." In other words, war can be permitted to bring about justice and an end to oppression. The following "just war" principles can aid discussion. Violence may be used if:
   a. The cause is just (e.g. self-defense);
   b. Violence is the last resort;
   c. Innocent people, such as civilians, must not be harmed;
   d. The war must be declared by a legitimate authority;
   e. The war must be "winnable";
   f. The good must outweigh the evil.
2. This concept might be very difficult for some to understand. Jesus said: "Blessed are the peacemakers" (Mt 5:9). "The Church and human reason assert the permanent validity of the moral law during armed conflicts. Prac-

tices deliberately contrary to the law of nations and to its universal principles are crimes" (CCC 2328).

NOTES...

C. General issues of the Fifth Commandment.
   1. "Because of the evils and injustices that all war brings with it, we must do everything reasonably possible to avoid it. The Church prays: 'From famine, pestilence, and war, O Lord, deliver us'" (CCC 2327).
   2. Medical/moral issues such as human experimentation, test tube babies, surrogate motherhood, sterilization, and mutilations are contrary to the dignity of the person and to the moral law. God alone is the creator. Organ transplants and donating one's body to science are morally acceptable if those involved have given their informed consent.
   3. As life is enhanced and prolonged through modern medicine, the question of artificial means of life support often plays a role in people's lives. It is most acceptable to have a "living will," with the understanding that the patient will still receive ordinary means to maintain the dignity of life.
   4. We must respect our bodies as "temples of the Holy Spirit" (cf. 1 Cor 3:16). "The virtue of temperance disposes us to *avoid every kind of excess*: the abuse of food, alcohol, tobacco, or medicine." One may not endanger the life of others driving under the influence of drugs or alcohol or disobeying the speed limit (CCC 2290).

III. Sixth and Ninth Commandments: "You shall not covet your neighbor's wife" (Ex 20:17).

A. Both commandments are often grouped together because they deal with topics involving chastity and marital fidelity. The Sixth Commandment states, "You shall not commit adultery" (Ex 20:14; Dt 5:18).
   1. God gifted humanity with sexuality. This gift affects "all aspects of the human person in the unity of his body and soul. It especially concerns affectivity, the capacity to love and to procreate, and in a more general way the aptitude for forming bonds of communion with others" (CCC 2332).
   2. Chastity is the ability to successfully integrate the physical with the spiritual reality, of being truly human in relationship to another, as in the lifelong mutual gift of self to another through marriage (CCC 2337; 2349).
      a. Chastity is an integrity ensuring the unity of the person (CCC 2338).
      b. The development of chastity involves discipline and right choices. A person who can contain his or her passions finds peace. Domination by passion leads to unhappiness (CCC 2339).
      c. "Chastity is a moral virtue. It is also a gift from God . . ." (CCC 2345).
   3. Offenses against chastity involve lust, a disordered desire for sexual pleasure. Sexual pleasure is morally disordered in the eyes of the Church when isolated from its procreative and unitive purposes. Chastity means the integration of sexuality within the person. The Church's teaching finds masturbation, fornication, pornography, and homosexual practices contrary to the dignity of a life built on love. These issues should be dealt with in an atmosphere of respect, compassion, and sensitivity for the person. Condemnation does not bring about healing (CCC 2351, 2395, 2358).
   4. "Homosexuality refers to relations between men or between women who experience an exclusive or predominant sexual attraction toward persons of the same sex" (CCC 2357).
      a. Being homosexual is not morally wrong.

NOTES...

b. Homosexual acts are morally wrong and disordered.
c. "Homosexual persons are called to chastity" and with God's grace arrive at the fullness of Christian perfection (CCC 2359).

5. Conjugal fidelity is the lifelong commitment of a married man and woman in the total gift of self — one to the other, becoming one flesh.
   a. "Sexuality is a source of joy and pleasure" (CCC 2362).
   b. The intimate acts of love in marriage are "'noble and honorable' (GS 49 § 2) (CCC 2362).
   c. The fecundity of marriage is the fruit of marital love, a new life, a child (CCC 2366).
6. Adultery is marital infidelity. A married person who has sexual relations with another outside of the marriage bond commits adultery.
   a. "Adultery is an injustice" (CCC 2381).
   b. Adultery injures the covenant of the marital bond (CCC 2381).
   c. Adultery "undermines the institution of marriage" (CCC 2381).
   d. It compromises the "welfare of children who need their parents' stable union" (CCC 2381).
7. Divorce breaks the contract of marriage. It brings "grave harm to the deserted spouse, to children traumatized by the separation of their parents and often torn between them, and because of its contagious effect which makes it truly a plague on society" (CCC 2385).
8. Other offenses against marriage are polygamy, incest, free union, and trial marriages (CCC 2400).

B. The Ninth Commandment states, "You shall not covet your neighbor's wife" (Ex 20:17).

1. Because the human person is both "*spirit and body*" there is a tension and struggle. This is due as well to the fact that human nature has been affected by original sin (CCC 2516).
2. Purity of heart is the great challenge of the ninth commandment. Lust or carnal concupiscence are the great temptations (CCC 2517).
3. "The struggle against carnal covetousness entails purifying the heart and practicing temperance" (CCC 2517).
4. "Purification of the heart demands prayer, the practice of chastity, purity of intention and of vision" (CCC 2532).

IV. The Seventh Commandment: "You shall not steal" (Ex 20:15; Dt 5:19).

A. "The seventh commandment enjoins the practice of justice and charity in the administration of earthly goods and the fruits of men's labor" (CCC 2451).

B. "The goods of creation are destined for the entire human race. The right to private property does not abolish the universal destination of goods" (CCC 2452).

C. "The seventh commandment forbids theft" (CCC 2453). "Every manner of taking and using another's property unjustly is contrary to the seventh commandment. The injustice committed requires reparation" (CCC 2454).

D. In granting to humanity dominion over creation (cf. Gn 1:28-30), God willed a responsible stewardship. We have a moral obligation to respect the goodness that is present in all forms of life on this earth and a concern for generations to come after us (CCC 2456-2457).

E. "The moral law forbids acts which ... lead to the enslavement of human beings, or to their being bought, sold or exchanged like merchandise" (CCC 2455).

NOTES...

Communism, as well as some forms of socialism and capitalism, are ideologies that violate the moral law. (CCC 2425).

F. The value of labor stems from our dignity as humans to participate in the work of creation. Work united to Christ can be redemptive. Humanity is the author, center, and goal of all social and economic life (CCC 2460).

G. "A *just wage* is the legitimate fruit of work. To refuse or withhold it can be a grave injustice" (cf. Lv 19:13; Dt 24:14-15; Jas 5:4) (CCC 2434). "Recourse to a *strike* is morally legitimate when it cannot be avoided" (CCC 2435).

H. Paying taxes helps to ensure the economic life of the state. One is morally obliged to pay them.

I. "*Unemployment* almost always wounds the victim's dignity and threatens the equilibrium of his life" (CCC 2436). Society must provide jobs for citizens without unjust discrimination.

J. "Giving alms to the poor is a witness to fraternal charity" (CCC 2462). "How can we fail to hear Jesus: 'As you did it not to one of the least of these, you did it not to me' (Mt 25:45)?" (CCC 2463).

V. The Eighth Commandment: "You shall not bear false witness against your neighbor" (Ex 20:16; cf. Dt 5:20).

A. "Truth or truthfulness is the virtue which consists in showing oneself true in deeds and truthful in words" (CCC 2505). Jesus came to bring us the truth (cf. Jn 18:37). In turn, He referred to Satan as the "father of lies" (Jn 8:44).

B. "The Christian is not to 'be ashamed of testifying to our Lord' (2 Tm 1:8) in deed and word. Martyrdom is the supreme witness given to the truth of the faith" (CCC 2506).

C. "Respect for the reputation and honor of persons forbids all detraction and calumny in word or attitude." To gossip about one's neighbor is also wrong (CCC 2507).

D. "Lying consists in saying what is false with the intention of deceiving one's neighbor" (CCC 2508). "An offense committed against the truth requires reparation" (CCC 2509).

E. "The golden rule helps one discern, in concrete situations, whether or not it would be appropriate to reveal the truth to someone who asks for it" (CCC 2510).

F. "'The sacramental seal [of Confession] is inviolable' (CIC 983 § 1). Professional secrets must be kept" (CCC 2511).

G. "Society has a right to information based on truth, freedom, and justice. One should practice moderation and discipline in the use of the social communications media" (CCC 2512).

H. Art is a distinctively human form of expression based on beauty as a transcendental reflection of the good. The fine arts, and above all sacred art, old and new, add to the expression of the beauty of creative human activity (CCC 2513).

VI. The Tenth Commandment: You shall not covet your neighbor's goods (cf. Ex 20:17; Dt 5:21).

A. "'Where your treasure is, there will your heart be also' (Mt 6:21)" (CCC 2551).

NOTES...

B. The tenth commandment forbids avarice and envy. Both are capital sins (CCC 2552-53).

C. "Detachment from riches is necessary for entering the Kingdom of heaven" (CCC 2556), as seen through the teaching of Jesus to the rich young man (cf. Mk 10:17-27). The Christian must learn to trust in God, not in possessions (cf. Lk 12:13-34).

D. "'I want to see God' expresses the true desire of man. Thirst for God is quenched by the water of eternal life (cf. Jn 4:14)" (CCC 2557).

FOCUS QUESTIONS

1. Discuss the many ways people can affirm the Fifth Commandment in their lives.
2. What are the major implications of breaking the Seventh Commandment?
3. Why is detachment such a blessed virtue?

Concluding prayers
Intercessions
Closing prayer
Hymn (optional)

RESOURCES

Catechism of the Catholic Church, 2196-2557
Essentials of the Faith, McBride, chaps. 47-53

Session Twenty-three

The Mystery of Grace and Justification

LEARNING OBJECTIVE

To present the Catholic teaching on grace with particular attention to its intrinsic nature and capacity to transform the person to the likeness of God.

Hymn: "Amazing Grace"

Invitation to prayer — silent prayer

Oration:

Father, all-powerful and ever-living God,
we do well always and everywhere to give you thanks.

You have no need of our praise,
yet our desire to thank you is itself your gift.
Our prayer of thanksgiving adds nothing to your greatness,
but makes us grow in your grace,
through Jesus Christ our Lord.

Weekday IV
Eucharistic Prayer Preface

Scripture reading: John 15:9-17

"As the Father loves me, so I also love you. Remain in my love. If you keep my commandments, you will remain in my love, just as I have kept my Father's commandments and remain in his love.

"I have told you this so that my joy may be in you and your joy may be complete. This is my commandment: love one another as I love you. No one has greater love than this, to lay down one's life for one's friends. You are my friends if you do what I command you. I no longer call you slaves, because a slave does not know what his master is doing. I have called you friends, because I have told you everything I have heard from my Father. It was not you who chose me, but I who chose you and appointed you to go and bear fruit that will remain, so that whatever you ask the Father in my name he may give you. This I command you: love one another."

NOTES...

TEACHING TO BE PRESENTED

I. Grace and justification.

A. The grace of the Holy Spirit justifies God's sons and daughters.

1. Justification is the cleansing from sin and the communication of "'the righteousness of God through faith in Jesus Christ' and through Baptism (Rom 3:22; cf. 6:3-4)" (CCC 1987).
2. Through Baptism we become members of the Body of Christ, the Church. "Through the power of the Holy Spirit we take part in Christ's Passion by dying to sin, and in his Resurrection by being born to a new life" (CCC 1988).

B. "The first work of the grace of the Holy Spirit is *conversion*" (CCC 1989).

1. Graced by the Holy Spirit, justification takes place according to Jesus' proclamation of Matthew's Gospel: "'Repent, for the kingdom of heaven is at hand' (Mt 4:17)" (CCC 1989).
2. It is only through grace that a person is able to turn towards God and away from sin. In so doing, forgiveness and righteousness from on high are accepted (CCC 1989).
3. As the Council of Trent stated in 1547: "'Justification is not only the remission of sins, but also the sanctification and renewal of the interior man' (Council of Trent [1547]: DS 1528)" (CCC 1989).

C. Justification detaches a person from sin.

1. Sin contradicts the love of God.
2. Justification purifies the heart of sin (CCC 1990).
3. Justification is the gesture of God's merciful love offering forgiveness (CCC 1990).
4. Justification reconciles a person with God (CCC 1990).
5. Justification "frees from the enslavement to sin, and it heals" (CCC 1990).

D. Justification accepts "*God's righteousness* through faith in Jesus Christ" (CCC 1991).

1. Justification in this context means the "rectitude of divine love" (CCC 1991).
2. "With justification, faith, hope, and charity are poured into our hearts, and obedience to the divine will is granted us" (CCC 1991).

E. Justification has been merited by Christ's passion and death (CCC 1992).

1. Christ "offered himself on the cross as a living victim, holy and pleasing to God, and whose blood has become the instrument of atonement for the sins of all men" (CCC 1992).
2. Justification is received in Baptism, the sacrament of faith (CCC 1992).
3. Justification "conforms us to the righteousness of God, who makes us inwardly just by the power of his mercy" (CCC 1992).
4. The purpose of justification is the glory of God and of Christ, and the gift of eternal life (CCC 1992).

F. "Justification establishes *cooperation between God's grace and man's freedom*" (CCC 1993).

1. The covenant response on the part of the person is living the life of faith. This saying "yes" to God through His Word is the assent of faith (CCC 1993).
2. A person is invited to conversion through the promptings of the Holy Spirit who through love "precedes and preserves" the assent of faith (CCC 1993).

3. The Council of Trent explains that when the heart is touched by the Holy Spirit, the person could reject this prompting of grace. However, without God's grace, the person cannot move toward justice. Again, grace precedes and sustains the activity of God (CCC 1993).

G. "Justification is the *most excellent work of God's love*" (CCC 1994).

1. St. Augustine says that justification, made manifest in Christ and granted by the Holy Spirit, is greater than the creation of heaven and earth (CCC 1994). Justification manifests God's mercy.
2. The Holy Spirit nurtures the interior life of the believer. "Justification entails the *sanctification* of his whole being" (CCC 1995).

NOTES...

II. Grace is the "*free and undeserved help*" that God gives to a person so that they may participate in His own divine life and receive eternal life (CCC 1996).

A. Grace introduces us into the intimacy of the Trinitarian life (CCC 1997).

1. The call to eternal life is supernatural. "It depends entirely on God's gratuitous initiative." For only God can reveal and give Himself (CCC 1998).
2. Sanctifying grace is the free gift of God's love which comes to us through Christ, infused by the Holy Spirit. By this grace the soul is healed of sin and sanctified (CCC 2023).

B. In addition to sanctifying/habitual grace, there is also actual grace.

1. Sanctifying grace is a habitual gift which enables the soul to live continuously in God's love as well as to act by His love (CCC 2000).
2. Actual graces are God's interventions which occur at the beginning of conversion or at other times in the work of sanctification (CCC 2000).

C. The preparation of a person "for the reception of grace is already a work of grace" (CCC 2001).

1. Grace "is needed to arouse and sustain our collaboration in justification through faith" (CCC 2001).
2. It is grace that brings us to sanctification through charity (CCC 2001).

D. God's free initiative of love demands a free response from the one who is being invited and gifted by God (CCC 2002).

1. A person is created in God's own image.
2. Being created in God's own image confers on the person freedom to choose, the power to know God, and to love Him (CCC 2002).
3. "The soul only enters freely into the communion of love" (CCC 2002). The human response is a free choice.

E. Grace is the gift of the Holy Spirit who justifies and sanctifies (CCC 2003).

1. Various graces are distinguishable.
    a. The gifts of the Holy Spirit which assist us in our collaboration with God to build up His kingdom (CCC 2003).
    b. Sacramental graces are received through the sacraments (CCC 2003).
    c. Charisms are graces received for the purpose of giving service in the life of the Church. Teaching, preaching, and hospitality are a few examples of charisms (CCC 2003).
    d. The grace of state is given to those with varying responsibilities for Church ministry (CCC 2004).
2. We cannot see or feel grace. It can only be known through faith (CCC 2005).

NOTES...

III. Merit.

A. By its definition, merit refers to recompense owed (CCC 2006).

1. With regard to God, there is no possible way of even conceiving God's greatness and our insignificance before Him (CCC 2007).
2. On His initiative, God invites the person to choose in freedom through His collaboration (CCC 2008).
3. Any "merit of good works" can only be attributed to God's grace (CCC 2008).

B. True merit which may be granted by grace makes us "co-heirs" with Christ (CCC 2009).

1. We become partners by grace in God's divine nature (CCC 2009).
2. The merits of our good works are gifts of the divine goodness (CCC 2009).
3. "*No one can merit the initial grace* of forgiveness and justification, at the beginning of conversion" (CCC 2010).
4. Moved by grace and charity, *"we can then merit* for ourselves and for others the graces needed for our sanctification, for the increase of grace and charity, and for the attainment of eternal life" (CCC 2010).

C. "*The charity of Christ is the source in us of all our merits* before God" (CCC 2011).

IV. The call of all believers is to union with God through the attainment of holiness (CCC 2013).

A. "'All Christians in any state or walk of life are called to the fullness of Christian life and to the perfection of charity' (LG 40 § 2)" (CCC 2013).

1. The romance of faith, being in love with God, realizes that there are no limits as one is progressively drawn into the intimate life of Trinitarian love (CCC 2028).
2. This union with Christ is called "mystical" because it is lived in the realm of mystery (CCC 2014).
3. In the mystery of His love God chooses to work differently with different people. The most important reality of our own personal growth in union, is to do God's will as it is manifested in our own lives (CCC 2014).
4. The ultimate manifestation of the activity of God in our lives is our inner transformation which bears fruit in greater virtue and charity (CCC 2013). "This I command you: love one another" (Jn 15:17).

B. The journey to God in this life can never avoid the Cross in union with Christ (CCC 2015).

1. Because of our wounded nature, there must be denial and spiritual battle (CCC 2015).
2. Various forms of mortification and asceticism assist the self to die in the spiritual sense so that the peace and joy of beatitude living becomes predominant (CCC 2015).
3. A person who strives to do God's will and accepts whatever suffering comes into their lives can live in the hope of final perseverance, that is, receiving eternal life with God after death (CCC 2016).

NOTES...

FOCUS QUESTIONS

1. In some Protestant denominations, grace is not viewed as an inner (intrinsic) transforming reality. How does Catholicism differ?
2. Early in the history of the Church a heresy called Pelagianism manifested itself in subtle ways it exists in contemporary culture. Pelagians knew they needed God's grace, but they felt they could become holy by using their own God-given powers, given creation and revelation. How would Catholicism refute this?
3. Quietism, another heresy, fails to note that we must cooperate willingly for grace to be fully effective. How does the Catholic teaching on grace challenge Quietism?

Concluding prayers
Intercessions
Closing prayer
Hymn (optional)

RESOURCES

Catechism of the Catholic Church, 1987-2029
Lumen Gentium, (Dogmatic Constitution on the Church), Vatican II
Ut unum sint (On Commitment to Ecumenism), John Paul II
Essentials of the Faith, chap. 43

Session Twenty-four

Sin and the Constant Call of Conversion

LEARNING OBJECTIVE

To present the Catholic teaching on sin, God's loving mercy, and the constant call to conversion and repentance.

Hymn: "What Wondrous Love Is This"

Invitation to prayer — silent prayer

Oration:

Father, our source of life,
you know our weakness
May we reach out with joy to grasp your hand
and walk more readily in your ways

We ask this through our Lord Jesus Christ, your Son,
who lives and reigns with you and the Holy Spirit,
one God, for ever and ever.

Opening Prayer
Friday of the Fourth Week of Lent

Scripture reading: 1 John 1:8-10

If we say, "We are without sin," we deceive ourselves, and the truth is not in us. If we acknowledge our sins, he is faithful and just and will forgive our sins and cleanse us from every wrongdoing. If we say, "We have not sinned," we make him a liar, and his word is not in us.

Alternate Scripture: Luke 15:11-24 (The Prodigal Son)

TEACHING TO BE PRESENTED

NOTES...

I. God's love is merciful.

A. Sin is a rejection of God's love.

1. "The Gospel is the revelation in Jesus Christ of God's mercy to sinners" (cf. Lk 15) (CCC 1846).
2. As St. Augustine says: "'God created us without us: but he did not will to save us without us' (St. Augustine, *Sermo* 169, 11, 13: PL 38, 923). To receive his mercy, we must admit our faults" (CCC 1847).
3. The work of grace is to "uncover sin so as to convert our hearts and bestow on us 'righteousness to eternal life through Jesus Christ our Lord' (Rom 5:21)" (CCC 1848).
4. "Sin is an offense against reason, truth, and right conscience; it is failure in genuine love for God and neighbor caused by a perverse attachment to certain goods" (CCC 1849).
5. Sin wounds the dignity of the person and injures human solidarity (CCC 1849).
6. Sin has been defined as "'an utterance, a deed, or a desire contrary to the eternal law' (St. Augustine, *Contra Faustum* 22: PL 42, 418; St. Thomas Aquinas, *STh* I-II, 71, 6)" (CCC 1849).
7. Sin can be described as "an offense against God." It "sets itself against God's love for us and turns our hearts away from it" (CCC 1850).
8. "Like the first sin, it is disobedience, a revolt against God through the will to become 'like gods' (Gn 3:5)" (CCC 1850).
9. "Sin is thus 'love of oneself even to contempt of God' (St. Augustine, *De civ. Dei* 14, 28: PL 41, 436)" (CCC 1850).
10. "Sin is diametrically opposed to the obedience of Jesus, which achieves our salvation" (cf. Phil 2:6-9) (CCC 1850).

B. There are a great many kinds of sins.

1. Scripture provides several lists of them (CCC 1852):
   a. Galatians 5:19-21
   b. Romans 1:28-32
   c. 1 Corinthians 6:9-10
   d. Ephesians 5:3-5
   e. Colossians 3:5-9
   f. 1 Timothy 1:9-10
   g. 2 Timothy 3:2-5
2. "Sins are rightly evaluated according to their gravity. The distinction between mortal and venial sin, already evident in Scripture (cf. 1 Jn 5:16-17), became part of the tradition of the Church" (CCC 1854).
3. Mortal sin causes a complete break in our relationship with God. It destroys charity in the heart of the person by a grave violation of God's law; it turns a person away from God, who is their ultimate end and beatitude. They prefer an inferior good to God (CCC 1855).
4. Then venial sin stains our relationship with God. It allows charity to remain alive even though it offends and wounds it (CCC 1855).
5. Mortal sin attacks the vital principle within us, most especially charity. The only way of initiating God's mercy and the necessary conversion of heart "is normally accomplished within the setting of the sacrament of reconciliation" (CCC 1856).
6. "For a *sin* to be *mortal*, three conditions must together be met:"
   a. Grave matter

NOTES...

   b. Full knowledge
   c. Deliberate consent (CCC 1857).
7. "*Unintentional ignorance* can diminish or even remove the imputability of a grave offense" (CCC 1860).
8. However, "no one is deemed to be ignorant of the principles of the moral law, which are written in the conscience" of every person (CCC 1860).
9. "The promptings of feelings and passions can also diminish the voluntary and free character of the offense, as can external pressures or pathological disorders" (CCC 1860).
10. "Sin committed through malice, by deliberate choice of evil, is the gravest" (CCC 1860).
11. "Mortal sin is a radical possibility of human freedom, as is love itself" (CCC 1861).
12. Because mortal sin results in the loss of charity and the privation of sanctifying grace, "if it is not redeemed by repentance and God's forgiveness, it causes exclusion from Christ's kingdom and the eternal death of hell" (CCC 1861).
13. "Our freedom has the power to make choices for ever, with no turning back" (CCC 1861).
14. "Although we can judge that an act is in itself a grave offense, we must entrust judgment of persons to the justice and mercy of God" (CCC 1861).
15. "One commits *venial sin* when, in a less serious matter," a person does not observe the standard prescribed by the moral law, or when the moral law is disobeyed in a grave matter out of ignorance or without full consent (CCC 1862).
16. "Venial sin weakens charity; it manifests a disordered affection for created goods; it impedes the soul's progress in the exercise of the virtues and the practice of the moral good" (CCC 1863).
17. Venial sin "merits temporal punishment" (CCC 1863).
18. "Deliberate and unrepented venial sin disposes us little by little to commit mortal sin" (CCC 1863).
19. "However venial sin does not break the covenant with God"(CCC 1863).
20. "With God's grace it is humanly reparable. 'Venial sin does not deprive the sinner of sanctifying grace, friendship with God, charity, and consequently eternal happiness' (John Paul II, *RP* 17 § 9)" (CCC 1863).
21. "There are no limits to the mercy of God, but anyone who deliberately refuses to accept his mercy by repenting, rejects the forgiveness of his sins and the salvation offered by the Holy Spirit (cf. John Paul II, DeV 46). Such hardness of heart can lead to final impenitence and eternal loss" (CCC 1864).
22. "Sin tends to reproduce itself and reinforce itself, but it cannot destroy the moral sense at its root" (CCC 1865).
23. "Vices can be classified according to the virtues they oppose, or also be linked to the *capital sins* which Christian experience has distinguished." The capital sins are "pride, avarice, envy, wrath, lust, gluttony, and sloth or acedia" (CCC 1866).

C. The social implications of sins
   1. "Sin is a personal act. Moreover, we have a responsibility for the sins committed by others when *we cooperate in them*" (CCC 1868).
   2. Cooperating would entail:
      a. "— by participating directly and voluntarily in them;
      b. "— by ordering, advising, praising, or approving them;

NOTES...

c. "— by not disclosing or not hindering them when we have an obligation to do so;
d. "— by protecting evildoers" (CCC 1868).

3. "Sins give rise to social situations and institutions that are contrary to divine goodness" (CCC 1869).
4. "'Structures of sin' are the expression and effect of personal sins. They lead their victims to do evil in their turn. In an analogous sense, they constitute a 'social sin' (John Paul II, RP 16)" (CCC 1869).

II. The life of constant conversion.

A. Conversion is God's grace and our response.

1. Jesus calls us to conversion. "This call is an essential part of the proclamation of the kingdom" (CCC 1427).
2. "Baptism is the principal place for the first and fundamental conversion. It is by faith in the Gospel and by Baptism (cf. Acts 2:38) that one renounces evil and gains salvation, that is, the forgiveness of all sins and the gift of new life" (CCC 1427).
3. "Christ's call to conversion continues to resound in the lives of Christians. This *second conversion* is an uninterrupted task for the whole Church who, 'clasping sinners to her bosom, [is] at once holy and always in need of purification, [and] follows constantly the path of penance and renewal' (LG 8 § 3)" (CCC 1428).
4. "This endeavor of conversion is not just a human work. It is the movement of a 'contrite heart,' drawn and moved by grace to respond to the merciful love of God who loved us first" (Ps 51:17; cf. Jn 6:44; 12:32; 1 Jn 4:10) (CCC 1428).
5. "St. Ambrose says of the two conversions that, in the Church, 'there are water and tears: the water of Baptism and the tears of repentance' (St. Ambrose, *ep.* 41, 12: PL 16, 1116)" (CCC 1429).
6. Jesus calls each person to "*conversion of the heart, interior conversion.*" This "interior conversion urges expression in visible signs, gestures and works of penance" (cf. Jl 2:12-13; Is 1:16-17; Mt 6:1-6; 16-18) (CCC 1430).
7. "Interior repentance is a radical reorientation of our whole life, a return, a conversion to God with all our heart, an end of sin, a turning away from evil, with repugnance toward the evil actions we have committed" (CCC 1431).
8. "This conversion of heart is accompanied by a salutary pain and sadness which the Fathers called *animi cruciatus* (affliction of spirit) and *compunctio cordis* (repentance of heart)" (cf. Council of Trent (1551): DS 1676-1678; 1705; cf. *Roman Catechism*, II, V, 4) (CCC 1431).
9. Conversion is "a work of the grace of God who makes our hearts return to him.... God gives us the strength to begin anew" (CCC 1432).
10. It is in discovering the greatness of God's love that our heart is shaken by the darkness of sin and the fear of being separated from God (CCC 1432).

B. The ways of conversion.

1. Conversion calls each person to interior penance. Three major forms are fasting, prayer, and almsgiving. These express conversion in relation to oneself, to God, and to others (CCC 1434).
2. Conversion is accomplished in daily life by gestures of reconciliation, concern for the poor, the exercise and defense of justice and right, by the admission of faults, acceptance of suffering. Taking up one's cross each day and following Jesus is the surest way of penance (CCC 1435).

NOTES...

3. "Daily conversion and penance find their source and nourishment in the Eucharist, for in it is made present the sacrifice of Christ" (CCC 1436).
4. "Reading Sacred Scripture, praying the Liturgy of the Hours and the Our Father — every sincere act of worship or devotion revives the spirit of conversion and repentance within us and contributes to the forgiveness of our sins" (CCC 1437).
5. The seasons and days of penance in the course of the liturgical year are intense moments of the Church's penitential practice (CCC 1438).
6. Christ instituted the sacrament of Penance for all sinful members of His Church. It is through this sacrament that a person undergoes conversion through the action of the Holy Spirit; namely, contrition, confession, and satisfaction; God's action, through the intervention of the Church (bishop and his priests), forgives sins in the name of Jesus Christ (CCC 1448).

FOCUS QUESTIONS

1. Why do we say that conversion must be constant?
2. Why is sinning a lack of freedom?
3. Describe vices and the virtues they oppose.

Concluding prayers
Intercessions
Closing prayer
Hymn (optional)

RESOURCES

Catechism of the Catholic Church, 1426-1454, 1846-1876
Dives in misericordia (The Mercy of God), John Paul II
Lumen gentium, (Dogmatic Constitution on the Church), Vatican II
Essentials of the Faith, McBride, chap. 26

Session Twenty-five

The Liturgical and Sacramental Life

LEARNING OBJECTIVE

To develop an understanding of the deep and profound significance of the liturgical and sacramental life within Catholicism.

Hymn: "Praise, My Soul, the King of Heaven"

Invitation to prayer — silent prayer

Oration:

Almighty and eternal God,
in Christ your Son
you have shown your glory to the world.
Guide the work of your Church:
help it to proclaim your name,
to persevere in faith
and to bring your salvation to people everywhere.

We ask this through our Lord Jesus Christ, your Son,
who lives and reigns with you and the Holy Spirit,
one God, for ever and ever.

Opening Prayer
Mass for the Universal Church (D)

Scripture reading: Ephesians 1:3-6

Blessed be the God and Father of our Lord Jesus Christ, who has blessed us in Christ with every spiritual blessing in the heavens, as he chose us in him, before the foundation of the world, to be holy and without blemish before him. In love he destined us for adoption to himself through Jesus Christ, in accord with the favor of his will, for the praise of the glory of his grace that he granted us in the beloved.

NOTES...

TEACHING TO BE PRESENTED

I. The purpose of the liturgy.

A. The Church confesses the mystery of the Trinity and God's plan of salvation for all creation in the liturgy (CCC 1066).

B. "'The wonderful works of God among the people of the Old Testament were but a prelude to the work of Christ' (SC 5 § 2; cf. St. Augustine, *En. in Ps.* 138, 2: PL 37, 1784-1785)" (CCC 1067).

C. Christ's Paschal Mystery, His Passion, Death, Resurrection, and Ascension accomplished the work of our salvation (CCC 1067).

D. The Church proclaims and celebrates Christ's work in her liturgy so that people may "express in their lives and manifest to others the mystery of Christ and the real nature of the true Church" (SC 2) (CCC 1068).

II. The word "liturgy" explained.

A. Liturgy originally meant "public work" or a "service in the name of/on behalf of the people" (CCC 1069).

B. In the Christian tradition, liturgy means the "participation of the People of God" (CCC 1069).

C. "In the New Testament the word 'liturgy' refers not only to the celebration of divine worship but also to the proclamation of the Gospel and to active charity" (cf. Lk 1:23; Acts 13:2; Rom 15:16, 27; 2 Cor 9:12; Phil 2:14-17, 25, 30) (CCC 1070).

D. In liturgical celebrations, the Church is servant, in the image of her Lord, the one minister of the sanctuary. She shares in Christ's priestly worship, prophetic proclamation, and kingly service of love (CCC 1070).

E. The Church proclaims and celebrates the mystery of Christ in its liturgy so that the faithful might live it and bear witness to it in the world (CCC 1095).

F. "In the liturgy, all Christian prayer finds its source and goal" (CCC 1073).

G. The liturgy provides the opportunity of responding in faith and love to the Father (CCC 1083).

H. "The liturgy is also a participation in Christ's own prayer addressed to the Father in the Holy Spirit" (CCC 1073).

I. A summary "textbook-type" definition: Liturgy is the Church's public worship of God, including the seven sacraments (especially the Eucharist), and many non-sacramental liturgies such as Liturgies of the Word, the Liturgy of the Hours (formerly called the Divine Office), and numerous blessings and sacramentals.

III. Christ's presence in this age of the Church.

A. "The Church was made manifest to the world on the day of Pentecost by the outpouring of the Holy Spirit" (cf. SC 6; LG 2) (CCC 1076). Through the work of the Holy Spirit in the Church, Christ is made present by revealing and communicating His work of salvation through the liturgy of His Church until He comes again.

B. In this age of the Church, Christ lives and acts in and with His Church, in a way appropriate to this new time. Christ acts through the sacraments (CCC 1076).

C. The liturgy — work of the Trinity.
   1. God the Father reveals and communicates His love. His divine and life-giving action comes as Word and Gift. Our blessing is our worship of and surrender to our Creator in thanksgiving (CCC 1078).
   2. "In the Church's liturgy the divine blessing is fully revealed and communicated. The Father is acknowledged and adored as the source and the end of all the blessings of creation and salvation. In his Word who became incarnate, died, and rose for us, he fills us with his blessings. Through his Word, he pours into our hearts the Gift that contains all gifts, the Holy Spirit" (CCC 1082).
   3. "On the one hand, the Church, united with her Lord and 'in the Holy Spirit' (Lk 10:21), blesses the Father 'for his inexpressible gift' (2 Cor 9:15) in her adoration, praise, and thanksgiving" (CCC 1083).
   4. On the other hand, until God's plan in time has been accomplished, "the Church never ceases to present to the Father the offering of his own gifts," beseeching Him to send the Holy Spirit on her offering, on the Church herself, on all the faithful and indeed on the whole world (CCC 1083).
   5. That through our communion with the death and resurrection of Christ, the high priest, and by the power of the Spirit, the divine blessings will bring forth the fruit of life "'to the praise of the his glorious grace' (Eph 1:6)" (CCC 1083).
   6. "During his earthly life Jesus announced his Paschal mystery by his teaching and anticipated it by his actions. When his Hour comes, he lives out the unique event of history which does not pass away: Jesus dies, is buried, rises from the dead, and is seated at the right hand of the Father 'once for all' (Rom 6:10; Heb 7:27; 9:12; cf. Jn 13:1; 17:1). His Paschal mystery is a real event that occurred in our history, but it is unique: all other historical events happen once, and then they pass away." The Paschal mystery never passes away (CCC 1085).
   7. By dying Jesus destroyed death. All that Christ is, and all that He did and suffered for all, takes part in God's eternity and transcends all time, so is present at every moment. "The event of the Cross and Resurrection *abides* and draws everything toward life" (CCC 1085).
   8. "'Christ is always present in his Church, especially in her liturgical celebrations. He is present in the Sacrifice of the Mass ... but especially in the Eucharistic species. By his power he is present in the sacraments so that when anybody baptizes, it is really Christ himself who baptizes. He is present in his word since it is he himself who speaks when the holy Scriptures are read in the Church. Lastly, he is present when the Church prays and sings' (SC 7)" (CCC 1088).
   9. Christ always associated the Church with Himself in that great work in which God is perfectly glorified and we are sanctified. The Church is the Lord's beloved bride, who calls to Him and offers worship to the eternal Father through Him (cf. SC 7) (CCC 1089).
   10. Christ's work in the liturgy is sacramental. His mystery of salvation is made present by the power of the Holy Spirit. Christ's body, the Church, is a kind of sacrament insofar as it is a sign and instrument through which the Holy Spirit dispenses the mystery of salvation (CCC 1111).
   11. "The mission of the Holy Spirit in the liturgy of the Church is to prepare the assembly to encounter Christ; to recall and manifest Christ to the faith of the

NOTES...

NOTES...

assembly; to make the saving work of Christ present and active by his transforming power; and to make the gift of communion bear fruit in the Church" (CCC 1112).

12. In the earthly liturgy, we enjoy a foretaste of heaven. Joined with the Communion of Saints, we praise God's glory (CCC 1090).

D. The Pascal Mystery in the Church's sacraments.

<u>Note</u>: ***See Sessions 26-31 for further development of individual sacraments.***

1. Jesus Christ is the Sacrament, or place of encounter with the Father. "I am the way and the truth and the life. No one comes to the Father except through me. If you know me, then you will also know my Father" (Jn 14:6-7).
2. The Church, or body of Christ, is another kind of sacrament (cf. 1 Cor 12:12-13).
3. The Church has discerned over the centuries that, among liturgical celebrations, there are seven sacraments instituted by the Lord. These are sacraments of the Church in two ways: "by her" and "for her" (CCC 1118).
4. They are dispensed by the Church for she herself is the sacrament of Christ's action, at work, through the mission of the Holy Spirit. They are for the Church in the sense that sacraments build up the Church, since they reveal and communicate to people, especially in the Eucharist, the mystery of communion with the God of love, who is one in three persons (CCC 1210).
5. "The sacraments are efficacious signs of grace, instituted by Christ and entrusted to the Church, by which divine life is dispensed to us. The visible rites by which the sacraments are celebrated signify and make present the graces proper to each sacrament. They bear fruit in those who receive them with the required dispositions" (CCC 1131).
6. The seven sacraments of the New Law are Baptism, Confirmation, the Eucharist, Penance, the Anointing of the Sick, Holy Orders, and Matrimony. "The seven sacraments touch all the stages and all the important moments of Christian life" (cf. St. Thomas Aquinas, *STh* III, 65, 1) (CCC 1210).
7. Baptism, Confirmation, and Eucharist are the sacraments of Christian initiation. Penance and the Sacrament of the Sick are the sacraments of healing. Holy Orders and Matrimony are the sacraments at the service of communion and the mission of the faithful. The Eucharist, the sacrament of sacraments, is the sacrament to which all the others are ordered as their end (CCC 1119).
8. Forming "'one mystical person' with Christ the head, the Church acts in the sacraments as 'an organically structured priestly community' (LG 11; cf. Pius XII, *Mystici Corporis* [1943]). Through Baptism and Confirmation the priestly people is enabled to celebrate the liturgy" (CCC 1119).
9. Those of the faithful consecrated by Holy Orders are appointed to feed the Church in Christ's name with God's Word and with his grace. They are the ministerial priesthood (CCC 1120).
10. The ordained are at the service of the priesthood of the baptized. The ordained priesthood "guarantees that it really is Christ who acts in the sacraments through the Holy Spirit for the Church" (CCC 1120).
11. "The fruit of sacramental life is both personal and ecclesial. For every one of the faithful on the one hand, this fruit is life for God in Christ Jesus; for the Church, on the other, it is an increase in charity and in her mission of witness" (CCC 1134).

IV. How liturgy is celebrated.

NOTES...

A. Signs and symbols.

1. The Liturgy is celebrated through signs and symbols. "Their meaning is rooted in the work of creation and in human culture, specified by the events of the Old Covenant and fully revealed in the person and work of Christ" (CCC 1145).
2. "As a social being, man needs signs and symbols to communicate with others through language, gestures, and actions. The same holds true for his relationship with God" (CCC 1146).
3. God speaks to us through visible creation. "Light and darkness, wind and fire, water and earth, the tree and its fruit speak of God and symbolize both his greatness and his nearness" (CCC 1147).
4. In the liturgy, signs and symbols are a visible, tangible expression of an invisible grace and reality. Symbols are real in the sense that they accomplish what they signify. For example, consecrated bread and wine do not merely represent Jesus: they become his body and blood.

B. Words and actions.

1. "A sacramental celebration is a meeting of God's children with their Father, in Christ and the Holy Spirit; this meeting takes the form of a dialogue" (CCC 1153).
2. "The Liturgy of the Word is an integral part of the celebration. The meaning of the celebration is expressed by the Word of God which is proclaimed and by the response of faith to it" (CCC 1190).
3. "The liturgical word and action are inseparable both insofar as they are signs and instruction and insofar as they accomplish what they signify" (CCC 1155).

C. Singing and music.

1. The musical tradition of the universal Church is a treasure of inestimable value and is of preeminent importance (CCC 1156).
2. "The composition and singing of inspired psalms, often accompanied by musical instruments, were already closely linked to the liturgical celebrations of the Old Covenant. The Church continues and develops this tradition" (CCC 1156).
3. Song and music form "'a necessary or integral part of the solemn liturgy' (SC 112)" (CCC 1156). They fulfill this function when they are:
   a. "the beauty expressive of prayer"
   b. "the unanimous participation of the assembly"
   c. "the sacred character of the celebration" (CCC 1191).

D. Holy images.

1. "Christian iconography expresses in images the same Gospel message that Scripture communicates by words" (CCC 1160).
2. "All the signs in the liturgical celebrations are related to Christ: as are sacred images of the holy Mother of God and of the saints as well. They truly signify Christ, who is glorified in them" (CCC 1161).

E. The liturgical year.

1. "Sunday, the 'Lord's Day,' is the principal day for the celebration of the Eucharist because it is the day of the Resurrection. It is the pre-eminent day of the liturgical assembly, the day of the Christian family, and the day of joy and

NOTES...

rest from work. Sunday is 'the foundation and kernel of the whole liturgical year' (SC 106)" (CCC 1193).

2. "The Church, 'in the course of the year . . . unfolds the whole mystery of Christ from his Incarnation and Nativity through his Ascension, to Pentecost and the expectation of the blessed hope of the coming of the Lord' (SC 102 § 2)" (CCC 1194).
3. The liturgical year should be fully explained. Color and symbol aid in the Church's expressions of the life of Christ in the cycle of the Church year.
4. "By keeping the memorials of the saints — first of all the holy Mother of God, then the apostles, the martyrs, and other saints — on fixed days of the liturgical year, the Church on earth shows that she is united with the liturgy of heaven. She gives glory to Christ for having accomplished his salvation in his glorified members; their example encourages her on her way to the Father" (CCC 1195).
5. The faithful who celebrate the Liturgy of the Hours are united to Christ our high priest, by the prayer of the Psalms, meditation on the Word of God, and canticles and blessings, in order to be joined with his unceasing and universal prayer that gives glory to the Father and implores the gift of the Holy Spirit on the whole world (CCC 1174).

V. Where is the liturgy celebrated?

A. "Christ is the true temple of God, 'the place where his glory dwells'; by the grace of God, Christians also become temples of the Holy Spirit, living stones out of which the Church is built" (CCC 1197).

B. "In its earthly state the Church needs places where the community can gather together. Our visible churches, holy places, are images of the holy city, the heavenly Jerusalem, toward which we are making our way on pilgrimage" (CCC 1198).

C. "It is in these churches that the Church celebrates public worship to the glory of the Holy Trinity, hears the word of God and sings his praise, lifts up her prayer, and offers the sacrifice of Christ sacramentally present in the midst of the assembly. These churches are also places of recollection and personal prayer" (CCC 1199).

D. A tour of the parish church is an excellent way to explain what one sees in a sacred place. A look at the sacred vessels and vestments will aid in an understanding of the richness of Catholicism.

VI. Liturgical diversity

A. "It is fitting that liturgical celebration tends to express itself in the culture of the people where the Church finds herself, though without being submissive to it. Moreover, the liturgy itself generates cultures and shapes them" (CCC 1207).

B. "The criterion that assures unity amid the diversity of liturgical traditions is fidelity to apostolic Tradition, i.e., the communion in the faith and the sacraments received from the apostles, a communion that is both signified and guaranteed by apostolic succession" (CCC 1209).

FOCUS QUESTIONS

1. What is meant by the words "the Paschal mystery of Christ"?
2. What are some of the ways we can become attuned to the rhythms and movements of the liturgical year?
3. Many Catholic churches contain holy images such as statues, icons, and other artwork. What role do these images play in our spiritual life?

Concluding prayers
Intercessions
Closing prayer
Hymn (optional)

RESOURCES

Catechism of the Catholic Church, 1066-1210
Music in Catholic Worship, National Conference of Catholic Bishops
Sacrosanctum concilium (Constitution on the Sacred Liturgy), Vatican II
Essentials of the Faith, McBride, chaps. 30-32

NOTES...

Session Twenty-six

The Sacraments of Baptism and Confirmation

LEARNING OBJECTIVE

To give an understanding that Baptism is the basis of the whole Christian life and that Confirmation is the completion of baptismal grace.

Hymn: "At the Lamb's High Feast We Sing"

Invitation to prayer — silent prayer

Oration:

Father of love and power,
it is your will to establish everything in Christ
and to draw us into his all-embracing love.
Guide the elect of your Church:
strengthen them in their vocation,
build them into the kingdom of your Son,
and seal them with the Spirit of your promise.

We ask this through Christ our Lord.

Prayer Over the Elect (B)
Rite of Election or Enrollment of Names

Scripture reading: Acts 19:1-6

While Apollos was in Corinth, Paul traveled through the interior of the country and came [down] to Ephesus where he found some disciples. He said to them, "Did you receive the holy Spirit when you became believers?" They answered him, "We have never even heard that there is a holy Spirit." He said, "How were you baptized?" They replied, "With the baptism of John." Paul then said, "John baptized with a baptism of repentance, telling the people to believe in the one who was to come after him, that is, in Jesus." When they heard this, they were baptized in the name of the Lord Jesus. And when Paul laid [his] hands on them, the holy Spirit came upon them, and they spoke in tongues and prophesied.

TEACHING TO BE PRESENTED

NOTES...

I. Baptism is the beginning of the Christian life and the door to the other sacraments (CCC 1213).

A. Baptism is the first of three sacraments of initiation.

1. The sacraments of Baptism, Confirmation, and the Eucharist together constitute the "sacraments of Christian initiation," whose unity must be preserved (CCC 1285).
2. "The sacraments of Christian initiation . . . lay the *foundations* of every Christian life" (CCC 1212).
3. The progression of Christian initiation parallels natural human development. "'The faithful are born anew by Baptism, strengthened by the sacrament of Confirmation, and receive in the Eucharist the food of eternal life. By means of these sacraments of Christian initiation, they thus receive in increasing measure the treasures of the divine life and advance toward the perfection of charity' (Paul VI, apostolic constitution, *Divinae consortium naturae*: AAS 63 [1971] 657; cf. RCIA Introduction 1-2)" (CCC 1212).

B. Baptism is the basis of the whole Christian life (CCC 1213).

1. The Trinity gives the baptized sanctifying grace for justification, enabling us by the gift of the theological virtues to believe in God, to hope in Him, and to love Him; giving us the power to live and act under the inspiration of the Holy Spirit by the gifts of the Spirit; and allowing us to increase in goodness by strengthening the moral virtues (CCC 1266).
2. "Thus the whole organism of the Christian's supernatural life has its roots in Baptism" (CCC 1266).
3. Baptism is also a prophetic foretelling of the life to come: Jesus Christ reveals to humanity the fullness of life to which they are called.
4. "The Lord himself affirms that Baptism is necessary for salvation" (cf. Jn 3:5) (CCC 1257).

C. The principal effects of Baptism are purification and new birth (CCC 1262).

1. Through Baptism, we are freed from all sin and are reborn as God's children (CCC 1263, 1265).
2. The different effects of Baptism are expressed by the sensible elements of the sacramental rite: "Immersion in water symbolizes not only death and purification, but also regeneration and renewal" (CCC 1262).
3. The faith required for Baptism need not be perfect and mature. An initial faith is called to increase and the baptized experience continual conversion (CCC 1253).

D. Through Baptism "we become members of Christ, are incorporated into the Church and made sharers in her mission" (CCC 1213).

1. Incorporated into Christ, the baptized are configured to Him and sealed with the indelible spiritual mark of belonging to Christ (CCC 1272).
2. Baptism establishes the foundation for communion among all Christians, even those not yet in full communion with the Catholic Church (CCC 1271).
3. The baptized share in Christ's priestly, prophetic, and royal mission. "*Baptism gives a share in the common priesthood of all believers*" (CCC 1268).

NOTES...

II. Confirmation deepens our baptismal identity and strengthens us for service.

A. Confirmation is a gift of God's grace which increases and deepens baptismal grace (CCC 1303).

1. It "roots us more deeply" in the divine Sonship of Christ — a Sonship which makes us cry, "'Abba! Father' (Rom 8:15)" (CCC 1303). It also brings us into closer union with Christ, "increases the gifts of the Holy Spirit in us" and "renders our bond with the Church more perfect (cf. LG 11)" (CCC 1303).
2. "It is evident from its celebration that the effect of the sacrament of Confirmation is the special outpouring of the Holy Spirit as once granted to the apostles on the day of Pentecost" (CCC 1302).
3. "'The reception of the sacrament of Confirmation is necessary for the completion of baptismal grace' (cf. *Roman Ritual*, Rite of Confirmation [OC], Introduction 1)" (CCC 1285).

B. As true witnesses of Christ, the confirmed are "'more strictly obliged to spread and defend the faith by word and deed' (LG 11; cf. OC, Introduction 2)" (CCC 1285).

1. The sacrament gives us a "special strength of the Holy Spirit . . . to confess the name of Christ boldly, and never to be ashamed of the Cross" (cf. Council of Florence [1439]: DS 1319; LG 11; 12) (CCC 1303).
2. Through Confirmation, Jesus Christ marks a Christian with the seal of his Spirit and clothes that person with divine power to be his witness. This is the "character" of Confirmation — the perfection of the common priesthood of the faithful received in Baptism and the power to profess faith in Christ publicly (CCC 1304-1305).
3. The seal of Confirmation "marks our total belonging to Christ, our enrollment in his service forever, as well as the promise of divine protection" at the end of the world (cf. Rv 7:2-3; 9:4; Ez 9:4-6) (CCC 1296).
4. Like Baptism, Confirmation imparts a character — a permanent change in the soul — and so can only be received once (CCC 1304).

C. The sacrament of Confirmation is conferred through the anointing with chrism (a special blessed oil) on the forehead, the laying on of hands, and the words, "'*Accipe signaculum doni Spiritus Sancti*' (Be sealed with the Gift of the Holy Spirit.)" (CCC 1320).

1. "To receive Confirmation one must be in a state of grace." Candidates should pray intensely in preparation for the sacrament that they might be responsive and docile instruments of the Holy Spirit (CCC 1310).
2. "Candidates for Confirmation, as for Baptism, fittingly seek the spiritual help of a *sponsor.* To emphasize the unity of the two sacraments, it is appropriate that this be one of the baptismal godparents" (cf. OC Introduction 5; 6; CIC, can. 893 §§ 1-2) (CCC 1311).
3. Normally a bishop confers Confirmation — a practice that is appropriate to the very meaning of the sacrament. As one who has received the fullness of the sacrament of Holy Orders, the bishop can best welcome Christians to the task of bearing witness to Christ (CCC 1312-1313).
4. "The sign of peace that concludes the rite of the sacrament signifies and demonstrates ecclesial communion with the bishop and with all the faithful" (cf. St. Hippolytus, *Trad. Ap.* 21: SCh 11, 80-95) (CCC 1301).

FOCUS QUESTIONS

1. Can you think of any biblical stories or images involving water that reflect the meaning of Baptism?
2. How will you live out your Confirmation through witness and service?
3. What does it mean to share in the ministry of Christ as priest, prophet, and king?

Concluding prayers
Intercessions
Closing prayer
Hymn (optional)

RESOURCES

Catechism of the Catholic Church, 1213-1284, 1285-1321
Lumen gentium (Dogmatic Constitution on the Church), Vatican II
Divinae consortium naturae (Apostolic Constitution), Paul VI

NOTES...

Session Twenty-seven

Eucharist

Theology of the Mass

LEARNING OBJECTIVE

To teach that the Eucharist within Catholicism is the heart and the summit of the Church's life, for in it Christ associates his Church and all her members with his sacrifice of praise and thanksgiving.

Hymn: "At That First Eucharist"

Invitation to prayer — silent prayer

Oration:

Lord Jesus Christ,
you gave us the eucharist
as the memorial of your suffering and death.
May our worship of this sacrament of your body and blood
help us to experience the salvation you won for us
and the peace of the kingdom
where you live with the Father and the Holy Spirit,
one God, for ever and ever.

Opening Prayer
Solemnity of the Body and Blood of Christ

Scripture reading: Luke 22:14-20

When the hour came, he took his place at table with the apostles. He said to them, "I have eagerly desired to eat this Passover with you before I suffer, for, I tell you, I shall not eat it [again] until there is fulfillment in the kingdom of God." Then he took a cup, gave thanks, and said, "Take this and share it among yourselves; for I tell you [that] from this time on I shall not drink of the fruit of the vine until the kingdom of God comes." Then he took the bread, said the blessing, broke it, and gave it to them, saying, "This is my body, which will be given for you; do this in memory of me." And likewise the cup after they had eaten, saying, "This cup is the new covenant in my blood, which will be shed for you."

TEACHING TO BE PRESENTED

NOTES...

I. "The Eucharist is 'the source and summit of the Christian life' (LG 11)" (CCC 1324).

A. The Eucharist contains the Church's entire spiritual treasure, that is, Christ Himself. He is our Passover and Living Bread (CCC 1324).

1. The Eucharist is the effective sign and the sublime cause of the sharing in divine life and the unity of the people of God by which the Church exists (CCC 1324).
2. By the Eucharistic Celebration we are already united to the heavenly liturgy and anticipate eternal life when God will be all in all (CCC 1326).
3. The Church calls the Eucharist the Holy Sacrifice because it makes present the one sacrifice of Christ the Savior and includes the Church's own offering.

B. "Jesus chose the time of Passover" to fulfill His mission of salvation (CCC 1339).

1. "By celebrating the Last Supper with his apostles in the course of the Passover meal, Jesus gave the Jewish Passover its definitive meaning" (CCC 1340).
2. The Eucharist "completes and surpasses all the sacrifices of the Old Covenant" (CCC 1330).

C. During the Eucharist, Christ is present to His people in several ways:

1. He is present in the person of the minister.
2. He is present in the proclamation of the Word.
3. He is present in the assembly gathered in His Name.
4. He is present substantially, sacramentally, and permanently under the Eucharistic Elements (CCC 1373).

II. The Eucharistic liturgy is a celebration of both word and sacrament.

A. The liturgical celebration of the Eucharist possesses an essential structure which has remained constant throughout the Church's history.

1. The Eucharistic celebration moves from the Liturgy of the Word, centered on the Scriptures and their interpretation, to the Liturgy of the Eucharist which makes present the living Word: Christ the Lord.
2. "The liturgy of the Word and liturgy of the Eucharist together form 'one single act of worship' (SC 56); the Eucharistic table set for us is the table both of the Word of God and of the Body of the Lord (cf. DV 21)" (CCC 1346).
3. The Eucharistic liturgy "remains the center of the Church's life" (CCC 1343).

B. The gathering and the Liturgy of the Word includes readings, the homily, and general intercessions. When the Scriptures are read in church, God Himself speaks to His people and Christ, present in His own Word, proclaims the Gospel.

C. The Liturgy of the Eucharist includes the presentation of bread and wine, the consecratory prayer of thanksgiving, and the communion rite (CCC 1346).

1. The Sacramental Sacrifice of the Eucharist is:
   a. "— thanksgiving and praise to the *Father*;
   b. "— the sacrificial memorial of *Christ* and his Body;
   c. "— the presence of Christ by the power of his word and of his *Spirit*" (CCC 1358).
2. "In the Eucharistic sacrifice the whole of creation loved by God is presented to the Father through the death and the Resurrection of Christ. Through Christ the Church can offer the sacrifice of praise in thanksgiving for all that God has made good, beautiful, and just in creation and in humanity" (CCC 1359).

NOTES...

3. The Eucharist is a sacrifice because it makes present the sacrifice of the cross. Christ's sacrifice and the Eucharist are one. "'The same Christ who offered himself once in a bloody manner on the altar of the cross is contained and offered in an unbloody manner' (Council of Trent [1562]: *Doctrina de ss. Missae sacrificio*, c. 2: DS 1743; cf. Heb 9:14, 27)" (CCC 1367).

D. The Church, as the body of Christ, offers itself completely in the Eucharistic sacrifice, uniting itself to His intercession before the Father for all people.

1. "The lives of the faithful, their praise, sufferings, prayer, and work, are united with those of Christ and with his total offering, and so acquire a new value" (CCC 1368).
2. To Christ's offering are also united the members of His body in heaven the Blessed Virgin Mary and all the saints. Finally, the faithful departed in Christ, destined for heaven yet undergoing purification, are part of the offering as well (CCC 1370-71).

III. The real presence of Christ in the Eucharist is a profound mystery.

A. Christ's presence in the Eucharist is what we call real presence.

1. "This presence is called 'real' not to exclude the idea that the others are 'real' too, but rather to indicate presence par excellence, because it is substantial and through it Christ becomes present whole and entire, God and man" (MF 39).
2. Through the power of Christ and the action of the Holy Spirit, Christ becomes wholly present in each of the elements of bread and wine, in such a way that the breaking of the bread does not divide Christ (CCC 1374).
3. Since the Eucharistic Celebration is a meal in addition to being a sacrifice, it is fitting that the faithful heed the Lord's command and receive His Body and Blood as spiritual food. Proper dispositions for receiving Holy Communion are:
   a. freedom from serious sin (CCC 1385), and
   b. observance of the Church's law of fasting — one hour from the intake of food and drink, with the exception of water and medicine (CCC 1387).

B. In His Eucharistic presence, Christ remains mysteriously in our midst as the one who loves us and gave Himself up for us, and He remains under signs that express and communicate His love (CCC 1380).

1. In the greatness of His love, Christ wanted to remain present to His Church in this unique way. His visible presence while on earth is exchanged for His sacramental presence in the Eucharist (CCC 1380).
2. The Lord's Eucharistic presence in our midst is real but veiled. Therefore we celebrate the Eucharist with joyful hope as we await Christ's coming at the end of history and as we pray for a share in the eternal vision of God (CCC 1404).

C. When Christ is honored as present in the Blessed Sacrament, it should be remembered that this presence is derived from the sacrifice and is directed toward sacramental and spiritual communion.

1. The celebration of the Eucharist in the Sacrifice of the Mass is the true origin and purpose of the worship celebrated outside the Mass (cf. Paul VI, MF 56) (CCC 1378).
2. The primary and original reason for reservation of the Eucharist outside Mass is the administration of Holy Communion to the sick and the dying (CCC 1379).

3. The secondary reasons are the giving of Communion and the adoration of our Lord Jesus Christ present in the sacrament (CCC 1379).

D. Eucharistic adoration is an invitation to a deeper participation in the Paschal mystery.

1. It makes the faithful respond gratefully to the gifts of Christ who by His humanity continues to pour divine life upon the members of His Body.
2. They achieve a close familiarity with Him and in His presence pour out their hearts for themselves and for those dear to them; they pray for peace and for the salvation of the world. They draw from this wondrous exchange an increase of faith, hope, and love.
3. Thus they nourish the proper disposition to celebrate the Memorial of the Lord as devoutly as possible and to receive frequently the Bread given to us by the Father (*Holy Communion and Worship of the Eucharist Outside Mass*, 80).
4. On Holy Thursday of the year 2003, in the Twenty-fifth year of his pontificate, Pope John Paul II wrote a new encyclical *Ecclesia de Eucharistia* (On the Eucharist in Its Relationship to the Church).

IV. The Pope wishes to rekindle Eucharistic "amazement."

A. This is in continuity with the program that he has sent forth for "the Church at the dawn of the third millennium. summoning her to put out into the deep on the sea of history with the enthusiasm of the new evangelization" (EE 6).

1. To contemplate the face of Christ and to contemplate it with Mary, is the "program" he has sent forth.
2. The Church has received from Christ the Eucharist as *the gift par excellence.*

B. The Pope wishes to reemphasize the reality of the Eucharist as the Sacrifice of Christ's Body and Blood.

1. Highlighting the "oneness" of the sacrifice of Christ and the Eucharist, he quotes St. John Chrysostom: "We always offer the same Lamb, not one today and another tomorrow, but always the same one. For this reason the sacrifice is always only one…" (EE 12).
2. "In giving his sacrifice to the Church, Christ has also made his own the spiritual sacrifice of the Church, which is called to offer herself in union with the sacrifice of Christ" (EE 13).
3. "Those who feed on Christ in the Eucharist need not wait until the hereafter to receive eternal life; *they already posses it on earth* as the first-fruits of a future fullness which will embrace man in his totality" (EE 18).

C. In his great desire to rekindle in all people this Eucharistic "amazement," Pope John Paul II says, "Let us take our place, dear brothers and sisters, *at the school of the saints*, who are the great interpreters of Eucharistic piety. In them the theology of the Eucharist takes on all the splendour of a lived reality; it becomes 'contagious' and, a manner of speaking, it 'warms our hearts.' Above all, let us listen to *Mary Most Holy* in whom the mystery of the Eucharist appears, more than anyone else, as a *mystery of light*. Gazing on Mary, we come to know the *transforming power present in the Eucharist*" (EE 62).

V. The Eucharist is a project for solidarity of all humanity.

A. In his Apostolic Letter, "Stay With Us, Lord," Pope John Paul II highlights that the Eucharist of the Church not only strengthens one's unity with Christ, but also with the entire human race.

NOTES…

NOTES...

B. "The Eucharist not only provides the interior strength needed for this mission, but is also — in some sense — *its plan*. For the Eucharist is a mode of being, which passes from Jesus into each Christian, through whose testimony it is meant to spread throughout society and culture. For this to happen, each member of the faithful must assimilate, through personal and communal meditation, the values which the Eucharist expresses, the attitudes it inspires, the resolutions to which it gives rise" (MND 25).

FOCUS QUESTIONS

1. In what way is the transformation that takes place in the Eucharist like the Incarnation? In what way is it different?
2. What does it mean to you that Christ feeds us with His very self?
3. How can we respond to the Real Presence of the Lord in our churches? How do you think He would have us respond?

Concluding prayers
Intercessions
Closing prayer
Hymn (optional)

RESOURCES

Catechism of the Catholic Church, 1322-1419
Dei verbum (Dogmatic Constitution on Divine Revelation), Vatican II
Ecclesia de Eucharistia (On the Eucharist in its Relationship to the Church), John Paul II
Holy Communion and Worship of the Eucharist Outside Mass, Sacred Congregation for Divine Worship
Mane Nobiscum Domine (Stay With Us, Lord), John Paul II
Mysterium fidei (Mystery of Faith), Vatican II
Sacrosanctum concilium (Constitution on the Sacred Liturgy), Vatican II
Essentials of the Faith, McBride, chaps. 35-36

Session Twenty-eight

Eucharist

Structure of the Mass

LEARNING OBJECTIVE

To give an understanding of both the Liturgy of the Word and the Liturgy of the Eucharist and the meaning behind each of their separate sections.

Hymn: "Gift of Finest Wheat"

Invitation to prayer — silent prayer

Oration:

Lord Jesus Christ,
we worship you living among us
in the sacrament of your body and blood.

May we offer to our Father in heaven
a solemn pledge of undivided love.
May we offer to our brothers and sisters
a life poured out in loving service of that kingdom
where you live with the Father and the Holy Spirit,
one God, for ever and ever.

Alternate Opening Prayer
Solemnity of the Body and Blood of Christ

Scripture reading: Luke 24:28-35

As they approached the village to which they were going, he gave the impression that he was going on farther. But they urged him, "Stay with us, for it is nearly evening and the day is almost over." So he went in to stay with them. And it happened that, while he was with them at table, he took bread, said the blessing, broke it, and gave it to them. With that their eyes were opened and they recognized him, but he vanished from their sight. Then they said to each other, "Were not our hearts burning [within us] while he spoke to us on the way and opened the scriptures to us?" So they set out at once and returned to Jerusalem where they found gathered together the eleven and those with them who were saying, "The Lord has truly been raised and has appeared to Simon!" Then the two recounted what had taken place on the way and how he was made known to them in the breaking of the bread.

NOTES...

TEACHING TO BE PRESENTED

I. Gathering Rites — "Christians come together in one place for the Eucharistic assembly" (CCC 1348).

A. Order
1. Song and opening procession
2. Sign of the Cross
3. Greeting
4. Rite of blessing and sprinkling of holy water (Sundays) *or* the penitential rite with the *Kyrie, eleison* ("Lord, have mercy")
5. Gloria (solemnities, feasts, and Sundays outside Advent and Lent)
6. Opening prayer (the Collect)

B. All of Christ's members have a part to play in the Eucharistic Celebration.
1. Christ is "the principal agent of the Eucharist." Unseen but active, He is at the head of every liturgical assembly (CCC 1348).
2. "It is in representing him that the bishop or priest acting *in the person of Christ the head* (*in persona Christi capitis*) presides over the assembly, speaks after the readings, receives the offerings, and says the Eucharistic Prayer" (CCC 1348).
3. "*All* have their own active parts to play in the celebration, each in his own way: readers, those who bring up the offerings, those who give communion, and the whole people whose 'Amen' manifests their participation" (CCC 1348).

II. The Liturgy of the Word.

A. Order — The Scripture readings for Mass are organized according to a three-year Sunday cycle and a two-year weekday cycle.
1. First reading: Sundays — Old Testament (Acts of the Apostles during Easter); Weekdays — Old Testament or New Testament
2. Responsorial Psalm (usually sung)
3. Second reading: Sundays, solemnities, and major feasts — New Testament
4. Gospel verse: This is omitted if not sung. During Lent, the Alleluia is replaced by another acclamation.
5. Gospel reading
6. Homily (may be omitted except on Sundays and Holy Days of Obligation)
7. Profession of Faith: Nicene Creed (The Apostles' Creed may be used in Masses with Children)
8. General intercessions

B. The Liturgy of the Word is an encounter with the Word of God proclaimed.
1. "The *Liturgy of the Word* includes 'the writings of the prophets,' that is, the Old Testament, and 'the memoirs of the apostles' (their letters and the Gospels)" (CCC 1349).
2. The homily is an exploration of the Scripture readings for the purpose of integrating God's Word into the minds, hearts, and wills of the assembly (CCC 1349).
3. Intercessions for all people follow the homily. This conforms to St. Paul's exhortation to St. Timothy: "'I urge that supplications, prayers, intercessions, and thanksgivings be made for all men, for kings, and all who are in high positions' (1 Tm 2:1-2)" (CCC 1349).

III. The Liturgy of the Eucharist.

A. Order

1. Preparation of the altar and gifts — presentation of offerings at altar (bread, wine, collection); preparation of altar; prayer during preparation of gifts; prayer over gifts.
2. Eucharistic Prayer — four versions for general use; two forms for Masses of Reconciliation; three forms for Masses with children.
    a. Preface
    b. First acclamation — *Sanctus* or "Holy, Holy, Holy" (usually sung)
    c. Invocation of the Holy Spirit *(Epiclesis)*
    d. Institution narrative and Consecration
    e. Second acclamation — The Memorial (four versions, usually sung)
    f. Memorial Prayer *(Anamnesis)* and Offering
    g. Intercessions of priest
    h. Third acclamation — the Doxology and Great Amen (usually sung)
3. Rite of Communion
    a. The Lord's Prayer
    b. The Sign of Peace
    c. The Fraction Rite (breaking of the bread) with Lamb of God *(Agnus Dei)*
    d. Reception of Holy Communion (procession, song, meditation)
    e. Prayer after Communion

B. The Liturgy of the Eucharist is an encounter with the Word of God celebrated.

1. In the offertory, bread and wine are brought forward and presented to the priest. He will in turn offer those gifts in the Eucharistic sacrifice and they will become the body and blood of Christ (CCC 1350).
    a. "'The Church alone offers this pure oblation to the Creator, when she offers what comes forth from his creation with thanksgiving' (St. Irenaeus, *Adv. haeres.* 4, 18, 4: PG 7/1, 1027; cf. Mal 1:11)" (CCC 1350).
    b. "The presentation of the offerings at the altar . . . commits the Creator's gifts into the hands of Christ who, in his sacrifice, brings to perfection all human attempts to offer sacrifices" (CCC 1350).
    c. "From the very beginning Christians have brought, along with the bread and wine for the Eucharist, gifts to share with those in need. This custom of the *collection,* ever appropriate, is inspired by the example of Christ who became poor to make us rich" (cf. 1 Cor 16:1; 2 Cor 8:9) (CCC 1351).
2. "The *anaphora:* with the Eucharistic Prayer — the prayer of thanksgiving and consecration — we come to the heart and summit of the celebration" (CCC 1352).
    a. "In the *preface,* the Church gives thanks to the Father, through Christ, in the Holy Spirit, for all his works: creation, redemption, and sanctification. The whole community thus joins in the unending praise that the Church in heaven, the angels and all the saints, sing to the thrice-holy God" (CCC 1352).
    b. "In the *epiclesis,* the Church asks the Father to send his Holy Spirit (or power of his blessing) (cf. *Roman Missal,* EP I [Roman Canon] 90) on the bread and wine, so that by his power they may become the body and blood of Jesus Christ and so that those who take part in the Eucharist may be one body and one spirit" (CCC 1353).
    c. "In the *institution narrative,* the power of the words and the action of Christ, and the power of the Holy Spirit, make sacramentally present

NOTES...

NOTES...

under the species of bread and wine Christ's body and blood, his sacrifice offered on the cross once for all" (CCC 1353).

d. "In the *anamnesis* that follows, the Church calls to mind the Passion, resurrection, and glorious return of Christ Jesus; she presents to the Father the offering of his Son which reconciles us with him" (CCC 1354).

3. "In the *intercessions,* the Church indicates that the Eucharist is celebrated in communion with the whole Church in heaven and on earth, the living and the dead, and in communion with the pastors of the Church, the Pope, the diocesan bishop, his presbyterium and his deacons, and all the bishops of the whole world together with their Churches" (CCC 1354).
4. "In the communion, preceded by the Lord's prayer and the breaking of the bread, the faithful receive 'the bread of heaven' and 'the cup of salvation,' the body and blood of Christ who offered himself 'for the life of the world' (Jn 6:51)" (CCC 1355).

IV. Dismissal Rite.

A. Order
   1. Brief announcements
   2. Blessing
   3. Dismissal (recession and song)

B. The Mass concludes with a blessing over the people and a dismissal, "so that each may go out to do good works, praising and blessing God" (GIRM 90c).

FOCUS QUESTIONS

1. "The Church has always venerated the divine Scriptures just as she venerates the body of the Lord" (DV 21). How is our liturgical experience of the proclaimed Word of Scripture similar to our experience of the celebrated, sacramental Word? How are they different?
2. The Church is the people of God, and everyone present at Mass has a role to play — there are no spectators. How can we, the congregation, best enter into the Mysteries being celebrated?
3. The celebrant often dismisses the assembly with the words, "Go in peace to love and serve the Lord." How does our reception of Holy Communion affect our ability to go forth and live lives of true charity and service?

Concluding prayers
Intercessions
Closing prayer
Hymn (optional)

RESOURCES

Catechism of the Catholic Church, 1348-1355
Dei verbum (Dogmatic Consitution on Divine Revelation), Vatican II
General Instruction of the Roman Missal, United States Conference of Catholic Bishops

Session Twenty-nine

The Sacraments of Healing

Penance and Anointing of the Sick

LEARNING OBJECTIVE

To present the Catholic teaching on the two sacraments of healing: Penance and Reconciliation, and The Anointing of the Sick.

Hymn: "O Christ, the Healer"

Invitation to prayer — silent prayer

Oration:

All powerful Father,
God of mercy,
look kindly on us in our suffering.
Ease our burden and make our faith strong
that we may always have confidence and trust
in your fatherly care.

Grant this through our Lord Jesus Christ, your Son,
who lives and reigns with you and the Holy Spirit,
one God, for ever and ever.

Opening Prayer (B)
Mass for Any Need

Scripture reading: Luke 5:12-16

Now there was a man full of leprosy in one of the towns where he was; and when he saw Jesus, he fell prostrate, pleaded with him, and said, "Lord, if you wish, you can make me clean." Jesus stretched out his hand, touched him, and said, "I do will it. Be made clean." And the leprosy left him immediately. Then he ordered him not to tell anyone, but "Go, show yourself to the priest and offer for your cleansing what Moses prescribed; that will be proof for them." The report about him spread all the more, and great crowds assembled to listen to him and to be cured of their ailments, but he would withdraw to deserted places to pray.

NOTES...

TEACHING TO BE PRESENTED

I. The sacrament of Penance is an opportunity to encounter a God of mercy through the person of Jesus Christ.

A. The human heart can never be satisfied with a life oriented away from God.
   1. The greatest gift for each person is to know and accept God's love.
   2. In Baptism we receive God's new life in Christ, but this life does not take away human frailty and the inclination to sin (CCC 1426).

B. Sin is an offense against God, a rupture of an already existing relationship with Him and his Church (CCC 1440).
   1. Sin can weaken and destroy our life as God's sons and daughters.
      a. Mortal sin attacks the vital principle within us — charity. It destroys love in the human heart by a serious infraction of God's law. By choosing a lesser good, we turn away from God, the supreme good (CCC 1855).
      b. Venial sin allows love to remain, even though it offends and wounds it (CCC 1855).
   2. The mystery of sin has both a personal and a social dimension.
   3. To return to communion with God after having lost it through sin is a movement granted by the God who is rich in mercy and concerned for the salvation of all men and women.

C. Penance is a sacrament of conversion because it is the first step of our return to God, from whom we alienate ourselves by sin (CCC 1423).
   1. Conversion of heart is a radical reorientation of our lives to God resulting in an avoidance of evil and a desire, with God's grace, to always do good (CCC 1423).
   2. Conversion is a work of God's grace that makes our hearts return to Him (CCC 1432). It touches the past and the future and is nourished by hope in God's mercy.
   3. Conversion is also accomplished in daily life by prayer, gestures of reconciliation, care of the poor, regular examination of conscience, acceptance of suffering, and endurance of persecution for the sake of righteousness (CCC 1435).

D. The sacrament is called by a variety of names.
   1. It is called "Penance" because "it consecrates the Christian sinner's personal and ecclesial steps of conversion, penance, and satisfaction" (CCC 1423).
   2. It is called "confession" because the admission of sins to a priest "is an essential element of this sacrament" (CCC 1424).
   3. It is called the "*sacrament of forgiveness*, since by the priest's sacramental absolution God grants the penitent 'pardon and peace' (OP 46: formula of absolution)" (CCC 1424).
   4. It is called "reconciliation" because it imparts the love of the reconciling God to all sinners and bids us to live in charity with one another (CCC 1424).

E. The sacrament of Penance comprises three acts of the penitent: contrition, confession to a priest, and the intention to make satisfaction (CCC 1448).
   1. The movement of returning to God — conversion and repentance — implies sorrow for and an aversion to sins committed and the firm intention of avoiding all sin in the future (CCC 1431).
   2. The oral confession of sins to a priest is rooted in the Lord's institution of the sacrament the evening of the Resurrection (cf. Jn 20). Confession and self-accusation represents a recognition and praise of God's holiness and mercy.

3. The sacrament is fully effected when the penitent receives absolution from the priest-confessor.

F. According to Church law, one is obligated to receive this sacrament only when conscious of having committed mortal sin (CCC 1457).

1. Regular confession, even when there is no mortal or grave sin, is strongly recommended by the Church.
2. "The regular confession of our venial sins helps us form our conscience, fight against evil tendencies, let ourselves be healed by Christ and progress in the life of the Spirit" (CCC 1458).

NOTES...

II. Indulgences.

"The doctrine and practice of indulgences in the Church are closely linked to the effects of the sacrament of Penance" (CCC 1471).

A. What is an indulgence?

1. "'An indulgence is a remission before God of the temporal punishment due to sins whose guilt has already been forgiven, which the faithful Christian who is duly disposed gains under certain prescribed conditions through the action of the Church which, as the minister of redemption, dispenses and applies with authority the treasury of the satisfactions of Christ and the saints' (Paul VI, apostolic constituion, *Indulgentiarum doctrina*, Norm 1).

   "'An indulgence is partial or plenary according as it removes either part or all of the temporal punishment due to sin' (*Indulgentiarum doctrina*, Norm 2; cf. Norm 3)" (CCC 1471).
2. "The faithful can gain indulgences for themselves or apply them to the dead" (CIC, can. 994) (CCC 1471).

III. The sacrament of Anointing of the Sick is an opportunity to encounter a God of compassion through the person of Jesus Christ.

A. Illness and suffering have always been among the gravest problems confronted in human life.

1. In illness, a person experiences powerlessness, limitations, and finitude. "Every illness can make us glimpse death" (CCC 1500).
2. Illness can be either an occasion for turning away from God or turning toward Him (CCC 1501). Without minimizing the pain and suffering of serious illness, it can nevertheless be an opportunity for making great strides in the life of the soul.

B. "By his passion and death on the cross Christ has given a new meaning to suffering: it can henceforth configure us to him and unite us with his redemptive Passion" (CCC 1505).

1. "On the cross Christ took upon himself the whole weight of evil and took away the 'sin of the world' (Jn 1:29; cf. Is 53:4-6), of which illness is only a consequence" (CCC 1505).
2. "Christ's compassion toward the sick and his many healings of every kind of infirmity are a resplendent sign that 'God has visited his people' (Lk 7:16; cf. Mt 4:24)" (CCC 1503).
3. In the New Testament, Jesus often "makes use of signs to heal: spittle and the laying on of hands (cf. Mk 7:32-36; 8:22-25), mud and washing (cf. Jn 9:6-7). The sick try to touch him.... And so in the sacraments Christ continues to 'touch' us in order to heal us" (CCC 1504).

NOTES...

C. "The Church believes and confesses that among the seven sacraments there is one especially intended to strengthen those who are being tried by illness, the Anointing of the Sick" (CCC 1511).

   1. "The sacrament of Anointing of the Sick has as its purpose the conferral of a special grace on the Christian experiencing the difficulties inherent in the condition of grave illness or old age" (CCC 1527).
   2. "The proper time for receiving this holy anointing has certainly arrived when the believer begins to be in danger of death because of illness or old age" (CCC 1528).
   3. "Each time a Christian falls seriously ill, he may receive the Anointing of the Sick, and also when, after has received it, the illness worsens" (CCC 1529).
   4. Only bishops and priests can confer the Anointing of the Sick. In the Roman rite, the celebrant applies a specially blessed oil to the forehead and hands of the sick person and prays to God to impart the sacrament's special graces (CCC 1530-31).

D. The effects of this sacrament include:

   "— the uniting of the sick person to the passion of Christ, for his own good and that of the whole Church;
   "— the strengthening, peace, and courage to endure in a Christian manner the sufferings of illness or old age;
   "— the forgiveness of sins, if the sick person was not able to obtain it through the sacrament of Penance;
   "— the restoration of health, if it is conducive to the salvation of his soul;
   "— the preparation for passing over to eternal life" (CCC 1532).

E. The Church has received this charge to continue to heal the sick as well as accompany them with prayers of intercession (CCC 1509).

   1. The Church believes in the life-giving presence of Christ, the physician of souls and bodies. "This presence is particularly active through the sacraments, and in an altogether special way through the Eucharist, the bread that gives eternal life and that St. Paul suggests is connected with bodily health" (cf. Jn 6:54, 58; 1 Cor 11:30) (CCC 1509).
   2. "The Holy Spirit gives to some a special charism of healing (cf. 1 Cor 12:9, 28, 30) so as to make manifest the power of the grace of the risen Lord" (CCC 1508).

FOCUS QUESTIONS

1. Why is it important that the sacrament of Penance reconcile the sinner with both God and the Church?
2. Why do many people blame God for suffering in the world or deny God's existence because of suffering? Can He really understand human pain?
3. The healing experienced through the sacrament of Anointing may or may not entail physical healing. What other kinds of healing are there?

Concluding prayers
Intercessions
Closing prayer
Hymn (optional)

RESOURCES

Catechism of the Catholic Church, 1420-1532, 1855
Indulgentiarum doctrina (On Indulgences), Paul VI
Essentials of the Faith, McBride, chaps. 37-38

NOTES...

Session Thirty

The Sacrament of Matrimony

LEARNING OBJECTIVE

To present the vocation of marital love as expressed in the teaching of the Catholic Church on the Sacrament of Matrimony and the sixth and ninth commandments.

Hymn: "When Love Is Found"

Invitation to prayer — silent prayer

Oration:

Father, keep them always true to your commandments.
Keep them faithful in marriage
and let them be living examples of Christian life.
Give them the strength which comes from the gospel
so that they may be witnesses of Christ to others.
(Bless them with children
and help them to be good parents.
May they live to see their children's children.)
And, after a happy old age,
grant them fullness of life with the saints
in the kingdom of heaven.

We ask this through Christ our Lord.

From the Nuptial Blessing
Wedding Mass

Scripture reading: Ephesians 5:2a, 21-33

Live in love, as Christ loved us....

Be subordinate to one another out of reverence for Christ. Wives should be subordinate to their husbands as to the Lord. For the husband is head of his wife just as Christ is head of the church, he himself the savior of the body. As the church is subordinate to Christ, so wives should be subordinate to their husbands in everything. Husbands, love your wives, even as Christ loved the church and handed himself over for her to sanctify her, cleansing her by the bath of water with the word, that he might present to himself the church in splendor, without spot or wrinkle or any such thing, that she might be holy and without blemish. So [also] husbands should love their wives as their own bodies. He who loves his wife loves himself. For no one hates his own flesh but rather nourishes and cherishes it, even as Christ does the church, because we are members of his body.

> "For this reason a man shall leave [his]
> father and [his] mother
> and be joined to his wife,
> and the two shall become one flesh."
>
> This is a great mystery, but I speak in reference to Christ and the church. In any case, each one of you should love his wife as himself, and the wife should respect her husband.

NOTES...

TEACHING TO BE PRESENTED

I. "'God himself is the author of marriage' (GS 48 § 1)" (CCC 1603).

A. "The vocation to marriage is written in the very nature of man and woman as they came from the hand of the Creator" (CCC 1603).

1. God created man and woman through love and also calls them to love, the fundamental and innate vocation of every human person, for we are created in the image and likeness of God, Who is love (CCC 1604).
2. Since God created man and woman in His own image, their mutual love expresses their likeness to Him (CCC 1604).
3. Marital love is an image of the absolute and unfailing love with which God loves us all. True marital love is taken up into divine love (CCC 1604).

B. "'The intimate community of life and love which constitutes the married state has been established by the Creator and endowed by him with its own proper laws' (GS 48 § 1)" (CCC 1603).

1. "Holy Scripture affirms that man and woman were created for one another." The woman is man's equal partner. The Lord Jesus showed that this means a permanent union of their two lives so that they become one flesh (CCC 1605).
2. "Everyone, man and woman, should acknowledge and accept his sexual *identity*. Physical, moral, and spiritual *difference* and *complementarity* are oriented toward the goods of marriage and the flourishing of family life. The harmony of the couple and of society depends in part on the way in which the complementarity, needs, and mutual support between the sexes are lived out" (CCC 2333).
3. "'In creating men "male and female," God gives man and woman an equal personal dignity (FC 22; cf. GS 49 § 2). Man is a person, man and woman equally so, since both were created in the image and likeness of the personal God' (MD 6)" (CCC 2334).
4. "'The well-being of the individual person and of both human and Christian society is closely bound up with the healthy state of conjugal and family life' (GS 47 § 1)" (CCC 1603).
5. A covenant is a sacred bond between two sides (people). In the Old Testament God established a covenant between Himself and his Chosen people. God's promise in the Covenant was "steadfast love" and "absolute fidelity." In the New Testament Christ continued with the "new covenant" with his sacrifice on the cross. Thus, the matrimonial covenant is profoundly rooted in Scripture. This covenant, "'by which a man and a woman establish between themselves a partnership of the whole of life, is by its nature ordered toward the good of the spouses and the procreation and education of offspring' (CIC, can. 1055 § 1; cf. GS 48 § 1)" (CCC 1601). Through the matrimonial covenant a man and woman establish between themselves a lifelong covenant.

NOTES...

C. "After the fall, marriage helps to overcome self-absorption, egoism, pursuit of one's own pleasure, and to open oneself to the other, to mutual aid and to self-giving" (CCC 1609).
   1. Because of the reality of sin, there is always a challenge in the relations between a man and woman. "Their union has always been threatened by discord, a spirit of domination, infidelity, jealousy, and conflicts that can escalate into hatred and separation" (CCC 1606). The love expressed between a couple in marriage helps to overcome the disordered inclination of man and woman to self-absorption.
   2. "To heal the wounds of sin, man and woman need the help of the grace that God in his infinite mercy never refuses them (cf. Gn 3:21). Without his help man and woman cannot achieve the union of their lives for which God created them 'in the beginning'" (CCC 1608).
   3. Spouses are called to grow continually in their communion through day-to-day fidelity to their marriage promise of total mutual self-giving.

II. The marital covenant "'between baptized persons has been raised by Christ the Lord to the dignity of a sacrament' (CIC, can. 1055 § 1; cf. GS 48 § 1)" (CCC 1601).

A. "Since it signifies and communicates grace, marriage between baptized persons is a true sacrament of the New Covenant" (cf. DS 1800; CIC, can. 1055 § 2) (CCC 1617).
   1. "The Church attaches great importance to Jesus' presence at the wedding at Cana. She sees in it the confirmation of the goodness of marriage and the proclamation that thenceforth marriage will be an efficacious sign of Christ's presence" (CCC 1613).
   2. "Baptism, the entry into the People of God, is a nuptial mystery: it is so to speak the nuptial bath (cf. Eph 5:26-27) which precedes the wedding feast, the Eucharist. Christian marriage in its turn becomes an efficacious sign, the sacrament of the covenant of Christ and the Church" (CCC 1617).

B. In the Roman rite, the spouses, as ministers of Christ's grace, are usually understood to confer the sacrament of Matrimony on each other by expressing their consent before the Church (CCC 1623).
   1. "In the epiclesis of this sacrament, the spouses receive the Holy Spirit as the communion of love of Christ and the Church (cf. Eph 5:32). The Holy Spirit is the seal of their covenant, the ever-available source of their love and the strength to renew their fidelity" (CCC 1624).
   2. Bride and groom should prepare themselves for the worthy celebration of their marriage by receiving the sacrament of Penance, especially if the ceremony is to take place during Holy Mass (CCC 1622).
   3. Through the Eucharist, the memorial of the New Covenant, Christ is united forever with the Church, his beloved bride, for whom He gave his life (cf. LG 6). "It is therefore fitting that the spouses should seal their consent to give themselves to each other through the offering of their own lives by uniting it to the offering of Christ for his Church made present in the Eucharistic sacrifice" (CCC 1621).

C. A baptized man and a baptized woman may enter into the marriage covenant if they are free to contract marriage and if they freely express their consent.
   1. "To be free" to marry means that neither partner can be acting "under constraint" or be "impeded by any natural or ecclesiastical law" (CCC 1625).
   2. The Church teaches that the exchange of consent between the spouses is the indispensable element that brings marriage into being. "This consent that

binds the spouses to each other finds its fulfillment in the two 'becoming one flesh' (Gn 2:24; cf. Mk 10:8; Eph 5:31)" (CCC 1627).

3. Consent must be a free act of the will of both contracting partners, without coercion or serious fear arising from external circumstances. "No human power can substitute for this consent (cf. CIC, can. 1057 § 1). If this freedom is lacking the marriage is invalid" (CCC 1628).
4. Preparation for a marriage is of great importance so that the consent of the spouses may be a free and responsible act.

NOTES...

III. Married people are called to live in conjugal chastity.

A. The virtue of chastity consists in the successful integration of sexuality within the person and fosters the inner unity of body and soul.
   1. Chastity fosters self-control and authentic freedom. The alternatives are clear: either people govern their passions and attain inner peace and freedom, or they allow themselves to be enslaved by them and become unhappy (CCC 2339).
   2. All the baptized in Christ are called to love chastely in keeping with their particular state in life (CCC 2337).
   3. Lust, masturbation, fornication, pornography, prostitution, rape, and homosexual acts are offenses against the virtue of chastity (CCC 2351-56).
   4. The virtue of purity and modesty are an integral aspect of temperance. Modesty protects the mystery of persons and calls for behavior appropriate to the dignity of persons and their relationships.

B. Sexuality is directed to the conjugal love of man and woman (CCC 1643).
   1. In marriage the couple's bodily intimacy becomes a pledge of spiritual communion.
   2. The union of the spouses achieves the twofold end of marriage: the good of the spouses, and the transmission of life (CCC 1652).
   3. Adultery is marital infidelity. It is an offense against the virtue of justice for it violates commitment, the sign of the covenant, and the marriage bond (CCC 2380).

C. Engaged couples are also called to live chastely in continence.
   1. "They should see in this time of testing a discovery of mutual respect, an apprenticeship in fidelity, and the hope of receiving one another from God" (CCC 2350).
   2. Couples should reserve for marriage the expressions of affection specific to married love.
   3. In this way, engaged couples will help each other grow in virtue and will be better equipped to fulfill the demands of marital fidelity and chastity.

IV. The Church stands for life and teaches that all marriage acts must remain open to the transmission of life.

A. A child arises from the very heart of the mutual self-giving of each spouse.
   1. Every child has the right to be the fruit of a natural act of conjugal love between a husband and a wife and has the right to be respected as an individual human person from the moment of conception (CCC 2366).
   2. The Second Vatican Council calls the family a "domestic church" (cf. LG 11; FC 21). Within the family, parents should be the first to preach the faith to their children by their word and example (CCC 1656).

B. Couples may seek to space the births of their children for just reasons.
   1. Periodic continence and methods of natural family planning conform to the practice of conjugal chastity and safeguard the unitive and procreative aspects of

NOTES...

conjugal love. Such methods respect the spouses' bodies, encourage tenderness between them, and foster self-control and authentic freedom.

2. The desire to space children must be in keeping with the generosity of responsible parenthood and not merely an outgrowth of selfish motives.
3. Birth control pills and devices that have a contraceptive or abortifacient effect do not foster respect, tenderness, self-control, or authentic freedom. These methods are intrinsically evil.

C. The child is fruit and fulfillment and a gift from God.

1. A child is not something owed to parents.
2. Techniques which seek to assist infertile couples must respect the virtue of chastity and the rights of a child.
3. Married couples experiencing physical sterility, after exhausting the legitimate potential of medicine, should unite themselves to the Lord's cross, the source of all spiritual fruitfulness.
4. Childless couples may adopt or undertake necessary or special service for others as a manifestation of spiritual fruitfulness (CCC 2373-2379).

V. Scripture attests to Jesus' unequivocal insistence on the indissolubility of the marriage bond (CCC 1614).

A. "The Lord Jesus insisted on the original intention of the Creator who willed that marriage be indissoluble (cf. Mt 5:31-32; 19:3-9; Mk 10:9; Lk 16:18; 1 Cor 7:10-11). He abrogates the accommodations that had slipped into the old Law (cf. Mt 19:7-9)" (CCC 2382).

1. "Between the baptized, 'a ratified and consummated marriage cannot be dissolved by any human power or for any reason other than death' (CIC, can. 1141)" (CCC 2382).
2. "The *separation* of spouses while maintaining the marriage bond can be legitimate in certain cases provided for by canon law" (cf. CIC, cann. 1151-1155) (CCC 2383).
3. Divorce attempts to break a lifelong covenant to which spouses freely consented and is thus a serious offense against the natural law (CCC 2384).
4. Divorce is gravely detrimental to abandoned spouses, to children traumatized by their parents' separation, and to the stability of society (CCC 2385).
5. By following Christ, denying themselves and taking up their crosses, spouses will be able with Christ's help to embrace and live out the original meaning of marriage (CCC 1615).
6. A spouse who is the innocent victim of civil divorce has not violated the moral law (CCC 2386).

B. While the Church upholds the sanctity and permanency of marriage, she wishes to console and offer healing to those who entered into the covenant without the intention of permanent commitment (CCC 2382-2386).

1. Divorced Catholics are not broken off from the Church and the sacraments can be worthily received. However, one who enters into a subsequent marriage without first obtaining a declaration of nullity may not receive any sacraments, including the sacrament of Penance.
2. Under certain circumstances and after carefully scrutinizing all available evidence, the Church can issue a declaration of nullity to separated or divorced couples. Commonly known as an annulment, a declaration of nullity is a canonical judgment that a sacramental bond never existed, thus freeing the couple to remarry in the Church (CCC 1629).

3. Because of the life investment already at work in any marriage, the Church prefers to seek reconciliation between estranged partners and will "use pastoral means to induce the spouses, if at all possible, to convalidate the marriage and to restore conjugal living" (CIC 1676).

NOTES...

VI. The issue of "same-sex unions."

A. Certain segments of contemporary society encourage the recognition of two people of the same sex to enter into a marital union. God created male and female with a human sexuality that is complementary both physically and emotionally. This union, and it alone, is ordered to the perfecting goal of the gift of sexuality: being united as mother and father in one's children, and one's children being conceived and raised in the loving union of their mother and father.

B. So-called "same-sex unions" are by their nature untruthful: the body of a man is not designed to receive and be united to that of another man. The same is true of women. There is no possibility of two men or two women conceiving a child through the gift of one to the other in sexual union.

C. Any law that practically mistakes and equates same-sex unions with that of husband and wife is erroneous. The institution of marriage has been safeguarded from the beginning of human history by the law of God written into human nature and revealed by Christ to the Church. Thus, same-sex unions defy God's natural law.

FOCUS QUESTIONS

1. Married couples are called to imitate the relationship between Christ and His Church. What does this mean to you?
2. Christ raised the natural good of marriage to the supernatural level of a sacrament. Why do you think God chose to provide married people with this special outpouring of grace?
3. How has our modern culture contributed to a breakdown of the family and marital chastity?

Concluding prayers
Intercessions
Closing prayer
Hymn (optional)

RESOURCES

Catechism of the Catholic Church, 1601-1658, 2331-2391, 2514-2527
Codex Iuris Canonici (Code of Canon Law)
Familiaris consortio (The Role of the Christian Family in the Modern World), John Paul II
Gaudium et spes (Pastoral Constitution on the Church in the Modern World), Vatican II
Humanae vitae (On the regulation of Birth), Paul VI
Mulieris Dignitatem (On the Dignity and Vocation of Women), John Paul II
Essentials of the Faith, McBride, chaps. 40-41

Session Thirty-one

The Sacrament of Holy Orders

LEARNING OBJECTIVE

To present Holy Orders as a sacrament in the mission entrusted by Christ to his apostles and directed towards the salvation of the People of God.

Hymn: "Alleluia! Sing to Jesus"

Invitation to prayer — silent prayer

Oration:

Father,
you have appointed your Son Jesus Christ eternal High Priest.
Guide those he has chosen to be ministers of word and sacrament
and help them to be faithful
in fulfilling the ministry they have received.

Grant this through our Lord Jesus Christ, your Son,
who lives and reigns with you and the Holy Spirit,
one God, for ever and ever.

Opening Prayer
Mass for Priests

Scripture reading: 2 Timothy 1:6-14

For this reason, I remind you to stir into flame the gift of God that you have through the imposition of my hands. For God did not give us a spirit of cowardice but rather of power and love and self-control. So do not be ashamed of your testimony to our Lord, nor of me, a prisoner for his sake; but bear your share of hardship for the gospel with the strength that comes from God.

He saved us and called us to a holy life, not according to our works but according to his own design and the grace bestowed on us in Christ Jesus before time began, but now made manifest through the appearance of our savior Christ Jesus, who destroyed death and brought life and immortality to light through the gospel, for which I was appointed preacher and apostle and teacher. On this account I am suffering these things; but I am not ashamed, for I know him in whom I have believed and am confident that he is able to guard what has been entrusted to me until that day. Take as your norm the sound words that you heard from me, in the faith and love that are in Christ Jesus. Guard this rich trust with the help of the holy Spirit that dwells within us.

TEACHING TO BE PRESENTED

NOTES...

I. The sacrament of Holy Orders initiates the recipient into a special group singled out for service to Christ and his Church.

A. The word "order" refers to an established civil body, especially a governing body.

1. Sacred Scripture and Tradition have spoken of such sacred bodies — or "*ordines*" (CCC 1537).
2. The ancient Liturgy speaks of various orders in the Church including the order of bishop, the order of priest, and the order of deacon. Groups of catechumens, virgins, spouses, and widows were similarly referred to as orders (CCC 1537).
3. Integration into one of these sacred "bodies" was accomplished by a rite called "ordination." Ordination is a liturgical act which was either a consecration, a blessing, or a sacrament.

B. Today the word "ordination" is reserved for the sacramental act which integrates a man into the order of bishop, presbyter (priest), or deacon.

1. Such a sacramental action goes far beyond a simple election, designation, delegation, or institution by the community.
2. The sacrament of Holy Orders confers a gift of the Holy Spirit that permits the exercise of a "sacred power" coming from Christ and his Church.
3. "Ordination is also called *consecratio*, for it is a setting apart and an investiture by Christ himself for his Church" (CCC 1538).

II. "Ordained ministers exercise their service for the People of God by teaching (*munus docendi*), divine worship (*munus liturgicum*) and pastoral governance (*munus regendi*)" (CCC 1592).

A. An ordained, ministerial priesthood is rooted in the Old Testament and the Levitical priesthood of ancient Israel.

1. The Old Testament records that God chose the Levites from among the twelve tribes of Israel and set them apart for liturgical service (cf. Nm 1:48-52; Jos 13:33).
2. Historically, it is quite clear that the chief function of the priest was "'to act on behalf of men in relation to God, to offer gifts and sacrifices for sins' (Heb 5:1; cf. Ex 29:1-30; Lv 8)" (CCC 1539).

B. The sacrament of Holy Orders confers a sacred power for the service of the faithful (CCC 1592).

1. "The whole Church is a priestly people. Through Baptism all the faithful share in the priesthood of Christ. This participation is called the 'common priesthood of the faithful'" (CCC 1591).
2. "Based on this common priesthood and ordered to its service, there exists another participation in the mission of Christ: the ministry conferred by the sacrament of Holy Orders, where the task is to serve in the name and in the person of Christ the Head in the midst of the community" (CCC 1591).
3. The term *"in persona Christi"* ("in the person of Christ") points to the difference in essence between the common priesthood of the faithful and the ministerial, ordained priesthood: "Through the ordained ministry, especially that of bishops and priests, the presence of Christ as head of the Church is made visible in the midst of the community of believers" (cf. LG 21) (CCC 1549).

NOTES...

C. The sacrament of Orders "configures the recipient to Christ by a special grace of the Holy Spirit" in order to make Him an effective instrument in service to the People of God (CCC 1581).
   1. Like Baptism and Confirmation, Holy Orders "confers an *indelible spiritual character* and cannot be repeated or conferred temporarily" (cf. Council of Trent: DS 1767; LG 21; 28; 29; PO 2) (CCC 1582).
   2. Since it is Christ Himself who saves and sanctifies through his ministers, no sin or failing can prevent a validly ordained priest from being a vehicle of God's grace (CCC 1584).

III. Since the beginning of the Church, the ordained ministry has been conferred and exercised in three degrees — bishops, presbyters, and deacons — and each is irreplaceable for the structure of the Church (CCC 1593).

A. Bishops receive the fullness of the sacrament of Holy Orders (CCC 1594).
   1. Bishops have the duty of authentically teaching the faith, celebrating the sacraments (particularly the Eucharist), and guiding their churches as true pastors (shepherds).
   2. The bishop and his priests have been entrusted with a unique responsibility and high privilege: to care for the Eucharist and to be stewards of the grace of Christ's supreme priesthood (cf. LG 26).
      a. It is through the celebration of the Eucharist that the bishop and his co-workers, his brother priests, assure the sanctifying office of the Church.
      b. The Eucharist is the center of each particular church's life (CCC 1561).
   3. "As successors of the apostles and a members of the college, the bishops share in the apostolic responsibility and mission of the whole Church under the authority of the Pope, successor of St. Peter" (CCC 1594).
      a. A bishop who has jurisdiction over a particular ecclesial region (diocese) is called the Ordinary of that diocese.
      b. He may be assisted in the episcopal ministry by one or more "auxiliary" bishops.
   4. Only bishops may confer the sacrament of Holy Orders in the three degrees.

B. Priests are called to be the bishop's prudent co-workers (CCC 1595).
   1. Priests (presbyters) are united with their bishop in priestly dignity and receive their pastoral responsibilities from him (CCC 1595).
   2. Priests receive from their Ordinary "the charge of a parish community or a determinate ecclesial office" (CCC 1595).
   3. The priest strives to sanctify the People of God through the celebration of all the sacraments, except the conferral of Holy Orders.
      a. Priests may administer the sacrament of Confirmation under certain circumstances, but in the Roman rite, bishops remain the ordinary ministers of Confirmation (CCC 1313).
      b. In addition to his high dignity as celebrant of the Eucharistic mysteries, the priest humbly shows himself to be a living sign of Christ's compassion in the sacrament of Penance. St. John Vianney, the patron saint of parish priests, remains an example and model of the office of "confessor."

C. Deacons are ministers ordained to serve the Church.
   1. Although they do not receive the ministerial priesthood, deacons receive an important call in the ministry of the Church. Representing Christ as Servant, they are called firstly to the service of charity and to the Word and divine wor-

ship. Such tasks must always be carried out under the pastoral authority of the diocesan bishop (CCC 1596).

2. In certain circumstances, deacons may baptize, officiate at marriage ceremonies, celebrate the Rite of Christian Burial, distribute Holy Communion, proclaim the Gospel and preach at liturgical functions.
3. Ordination to the diaconate may be transitional (as in the case of men preparing for the priesthood) or permanent. Permanent deacons promise to remain in their present state in life and assist in the order of service in the Church (CCC 1570-1571).

NOTES...

IV. All three ordinations — that of bishops, priests, and deacons — follow the same movement and basic structure (CCC 1572).

A. The sacrament of Holy Orders is conferred by the bishop through the imposition (laying on) of hands and a solemn prayer of consecration (CCC 1573-1576).

1. The New Testament pastoral letters of St. Paul demonstrate that the practice of laying on of hands has apostolic precedent (cf. 1 Tm 4:14; 2 Tm 1:6).
2. The conferring of Holy Orders is a sign of the love of Christ who imparts sacramental grace and carries on his earthly ministry through ordinary, humble men.

B. A Mass of Ordination is a moment of special grace for the local church, an event which sparks great promise and excitement for the local church.

1. The faithful should be encouraged to promote a positive attitude towards the role of the priest in the community and to foster vocations to the priesthood through prayer and example.
2. The seeds of priestly vocations are planted primarily through strong Catholic family life as well as through the good example of holy pastors.

C. "The Church confers the sacrament of Holy Orders only on baptized men (*viri*), whose suitability for the exercise of the ministry has been duly recognized" (CCC 1598).

1. "The Lord Jesus chose men (*viri*) to form the college of the twelve apostles, and the apostles did the same when they chose collaborators to succeed them in their ministry (cf. Mk 3:14-19; Lk 6:12-16; 1 Tm 3:1-13; 2 Tm 1:6; Ti 1:5-9; St. Clement of Rome, *Ad Cor.* 42, 4; 44, 3: PG 1, 292-293; 300).... The Church recognizes herself to be bound by this choice made by the Lord himself (cf. John Paul II, MD 26-27; CDF, declaration, *Inter insigniores*: AAS 69 [1977] 98-116)" (CCC 1577).
2. "If Christ — by his free and sovereign choice, clearly attested to by the Gospel and by the Church's constant Tradition — entrusted only to men the task of being an *'icon' of his countenance as 'shepherd' and 'bridegroom' of the Church through the exercise of the ministerial priesthood*, this in no way detracts from the role of women, or for that matter from the role of the other members of the Church who are not ordained to the sacred ministry, since *all* share equally in the dignity proper to the *'common priesthood'* based on Baptism" ("Letter to Women," Pope John Paul II, June 29, 1995, #11).
3. Candidates for the priesthood prepare for ordination through intense prayer and study. Generally this preparation takes place at seminaries where the "seed" (*"semini"*) of their vocations mature and bear fruit.

D. The rites of Ordination require that candidates make certain promises before God and his Church.

NOTES...

1. Ordination to the diaconate includes promises to obey one's Ordinary (or religious superior); to pray for the Church, especially using the Liturgy of the Hours; and, for transitional deacons and unmarried permanent deacons, to freely embrace celibacy for the love of God's kingdom.
   a. "Celibacy is a sign of this new life to the service of which the Church's minister is consecrated; accepted with a joyous heart celibacy radiantly proclaims the Reign of God" (cf. PO 16) (CCC 1579).
   b. "In accordance with the traditional discipline of the Church, a married deacon who has lost his wife cannot enter a new marriage" (Pope Paul VI, Apostolic letter laying down certain norms regarding the Holy Order of Deacons, 6).
2. Priestly ordination includes promises to maintain obedience to one's Ordinary and his successors; to celebrate the sacraments with love and devotion; to worthily preach the Gospel and explain the Catholic faith; and to make one's life an offering in imitation of Christ and for the salvation of souls.
3. Before ordination to the episcopate (the order of bishops), a priest will promise to guard and proclaim the full deposit of faith; to remain united to the Catholic Church; to obey the Pope, the successor of the apostle Peter; and, in cooperation with his brother priests and deacons, to be a worthy shepherd of the church entrusted to his care.

FOCUS QUESTIONS

1. Why are there three ordained ministries rather than one?
2. How do the orders of bishop, priest, and deacon work together for the good of the Church and the building up of Christ's kingdom?
3. A priest is shepherd, servant, teacher, and father to his people. What are some attributes that would be important in the priestly ministry?

Concluding prayers
Intercessions
Closing prayer
Hymn (optional)

RESOURCES

Catechism of the Catholic Church, 874-896, 1536-1600
Letter of Pope John Paul II to Women, June 29, 1995
Lumen gentium (Dogmatic Constitution on the Church), Vatican II
Ordinatio Sacerdotalis (On Reserving Priestly Ordination to Men Alone), John Paul II
Sacerdotalis caelibatus (On the celibacy of the priest), Paul VI
Essentials of the Faith, McBride, chap. 39

Session Thirty-two

Prayer in the Christian Life

LEARNING OBJECTIVE

To present the Church's teachings on the ways we can grow in our relationship with God through prayer.

Hymn: "All People That On Earth Do Dwell"

Invitation to prayer — silent prayer

Oration:

God our Father,
you have promised your kingdom
to those who are willing to become like little children.
Help us to follow the way of St. Theresa with confidence
so that by her prayers
we may come to know your eternal glory.

Grant this through our Lord Jesus Christ, your Son,
who lives and reigns with you and the Holy Spirit,
one God, for ever and ever.

Opening Prayer
Memorial of St. Theresa of the Child Jesus

Scripture reading: Matthew 6:5-6

"When you pray, do not be like the hypocrites, who love to stand and pray in the synagogues and on street corners so that others may see them. Amen, I say to you, they have received their reward. But when you pray, go to your inner room, close the door, and pray to your Father in secret. And your Father who sees in secret will repay you."

TEACHING TO BE PRESENTED

I. **Prayer is the great gift and activity of communication with our loving God.**

   A. In Baptism we enter into a covenant relationship with God through Jesus Christ.

      1. God, through the covenant relationship with His people is constantly revealing Himself.

NOTES...

2. One of our great responses is, through faith in God, to pray both personally and liturgically.
3. The life of faith through the exercise of prayer is a way of communication with God.
4. Prayer is described as a covenant relationship between God and a person living in Christ through Baptism (CCC 2565).

B. Prayer is communion with the One who loves us.

1. Prayer brings us into relationship with the Trinity: Father, Son and Holy Spirit.
2. Prayer is essential to our relationship with God.
3. Using a human analogy, a relationship dies when it does not experience the gift of communication.
4. Because prayer is "communion with Christ," it "extends throughout the Church, which is his Body" (cf. Eph 3:18-21) (CCC 2565).

II. God is the initiator of the covenant relationship, always proclaiming steadfast love and absolute fidelity.

A. The Old Testament portrays God's invitation to Abraham and his descendants to be His chosen people.

1. Abraham and Sarah, our ancestors in faith, portray hearts open to God's will through discerning obedience (CCC 2570).
2. Moses is the great Old Testament example of intercessory prayer (CCC 2574).
3. David prays for his people and in their name (CCC 2579).
4. In the Psalms, David gives praise to God, exhibits repentance and submission to God's will. He is a model of prayer for all people (CCC 2579).
5. The Psalms are both personal and communal prayer (CCC 2586).

B. The covenant relationship of prayer is fully revealed to us through Jesus Christ who is the fulfillment of God's plan of salvation.

1. Throughout the accounts of Jesus in the New Testament writings we recognize the role of prayer.
   a. Jesus learns to pray from His mother (CCC 2599).
   b. The "*filial prayer*" of Jesus is "lived out by the only Son in his humanity," with and for all people (CCC 2599).
   c. "Jesus prays *before* the decisive moments of his mission" (CCC 2600).
   d. Jesus prays alone. He prays for all people in His time alone before and with God (CCC 2602).
   e. Jesus teaches us to pray in the Our Father (CCC 2607).
   f. Jesus challenges us to "*conversion of heart*" through the Sermon on the Mount (CCC 2608).
   g. St. Luke in his Gospel gives us the principal *parables* of prayer (CCC 2613).
   h. Jesus hears our prayer (CCC 2616).
2. Jesus entrusts to His disciples the call to prayer. This call, in imitation of Christ, is extended to all God's people (CCC 2614).
3. The fruit of prayer is conversion and charity.

III. There are five forms of prayer.

A. Blessing and adoration.

NOTES...

1. In "*Blessing*," God's gift and the human acceptance of it are united in dialogue with each other (CCC 2626).
2. "*Adoration*" is the attitude of those who acknowledge themselves to be creatures before their Creator (CCC 2628).

B. Petition is that form of prayer in which we ask, beseech, call insistently, invoke, entreat, cry out, and even "struggle in prayer" (cf. Rom 15:30; Col 4:12) (CCC 2629; CCC 2630-2633).

C. "Intercession is a prayer of petition which leads us to pray as Jesus did" on behalf of all people (CCC 2634; CCC 2635-2636).

D. "Thanksgiving characterizes the prayer of the Church which, in celebrating the Eucharist, reveals and becomes more fully what she is" (CCC 2637). "Every event and need can become an offering of thanksgiving" (CCC 2638).

E. "Praise is the form of prayer which recognizes most immediately that God is God.... It shares in the blessed happiness of the pure of heart who love God in faith before seeing him in glory" (CCC 2639).

IV. Liturgical and personal prayer are two dimensions of prayer entered into by God's people.

A. In personal prayer the person is alone before God.

B. In liturgical prayer one accompanies the body of believers. One enters in a special way the Paschal Mystery, uniting with Christ own response to His Father.

V. The life of prayer is expressed in three main ways.

A. Vocal prayer, involving the senses, calls a person to pray with his or her entire being. Vocal prayer is internalized to the extent that we recognize God's presence (CCC 2700-2704).

B. In meditation the person seeks an understanding of the way of Christ and His teachings (CCC 2705-2708).

C. Contemplative prayer is the ultimate gift and highest form of prayer. Contemplative prayer has the incredible simplicity of being merely "a *gaze* of faith" (CCC 2715) fixed upon the person of Jesus Christ (CCC 2709-2724).

VI. The struggle of prayer arises from our condition of being people wounded by sin.

A. A spiritual struggle often surfaces as we attempt to give ourselves to God through prayer.

1. Because of our inclination to sin (concupiscence) we are drawn to self-satisfaction.
2. The intent of prayer is to communicate with God by letting go of preoccupation with self.

B. A person must recognize the various aspects of the spiritual struggle.

1. Distractions (CCC 2729).
2. Vigilance (CCC 2730).
3. Dryness (CCC 2731).

NOTES...

FOCUS QUESTIONS

1. When a person prays, he or she is never the same. Explain.
2. Why is environment important for prayer?
3. Name three of the greatest obstacles to prayer in our time.

Concluding prayers
Intercessions
Closing prayer
Hymn (optional)

RESOURCES

Catechism of the Catholic Church, 2558-2731
The Way of Perfection, St. Teresa of Ávila, chaps. 19-31
Essentials of the Faith, McBride, chap. 54

Session Thirty-three

Developing a Life of Prayer

LEARNING OBJECTIVE

To provide traditional methods of how to develop and strengthen the life of prayer.

Hymn: "Go Make of All Disciples"

Invitation to prayer – silent prayer

Oration:

Lord Jesus,
in the unity of the Trinity,
you are a communion of love
with the Father and the Holy Spirit.
Teach us to pray
that we may be drawn into union with the Trinity.

We ask this through our Lord Jesus Christ,
your Son, who lives and reigns
with you and the Holy Spirit,
one God, for ever and ever.

Scripture reading: Mark 1:35-39

Rising very early before dawn, he left and went off to a deserted place, where he prayed. Simon and those who were with him pursued him and on finding him said, "Everyone is looking for you." He told them, "Let us go on to the nearby villages that I may preach there also. For this purpose have I come." So he went into their synagogues, preaching and driving out demons throughout the whole of Galilee.

TEACHING TO BE PRESENTED

I. **The act of praying, which involves thought and love for God, draws a person into a transforming relationship of love. God responds uniquely to each individual person. The lives of the three women doctors of the Church, St. Teresa of Ávila, St. Catherine of Siena, and St. Thérèse of Lisieux, provide insight into the uniqueness of an individual's journey to God through prayer.**

   A. Every human heart has an unfathomable space which can only be filled by God. This yearning, when properly recognized, leads to the choice of making prayer part of one's daily life.

   B. Choosing to lead a life of prayer requires planning and a firm resolution.

NOTES...

C. Each person needs to develop certain practices which strengthen daily fidelity
   1. Set aside a regular time each day for prayer.
   2. Find a space that will provide quiet. Learn to feel comfortable with the quiet.
   3. Decide on a particular amount of time. Fifteen minutes is a good way to begin. Stay with that time even if you have distractions.
   4. Ask God to teach you to pray. Trust that God will do this if you persevere.
   5. Allow the desire for God to stir prayerful words such as simply, "Come to me," or "I desire to love and please you." Find short lines from the Psalms such as, "O God, you are my God – / for you I long" (Ps 63:2).
   6. Believe that through the life of faith, a person entrusts oneself to God. Never fear to live the romance of faith with God. He will embrace each person uniquely.
   7. Feelings of consolation may be experienced or darkness may be present. Do not give up prayer if feelings of dryness continue. A person must believe that feeling God's absence does not mean He is not present. As the psalmist says, "Hear my voice, LORD, when I call; / have mercy on me and answer me" (Ps 27:7).
   8. The purpose of prayer is to encounter God for God Himself. This will require a self-forgetfulness, a dying to the self, and self transcendence in order to be present to God in the gaze of faith – "while keeping our eyes fixed on Jesus, the leader and perfecter of faith" (Heb 12:2).
   9. God's love is steadfast. At the end of the allotted time give him thanks and praise, because He will never abandon you.

II. Praying with Scripture.

A. The practice of prayer with the use of Scripture has a long tradition in the life of the Church. This method is also called *Lectio Divina.*

B. There are four steps in the practice of *Lectio Divina.*
   1. Choose a passage of Scripture and *read* it carefully. It may be read several times.
   2. Using the mind, *meditate* on the various aspects of the Scripture passage. The Holy Spirit will guide one to be moved by certain thoughts or images.
   3. Allow the heart to become engaged in this experience of reflection. This leads to *oratio,* or prayer. What does the heart desire in this prayerful experience of Scripture? Trust that one will be led into prayer by the Holy Spirit. If you feel nothing, stay with the attitude of trust.
   4. Move into a silent stillness before God. This time may lead to moments of contemplation. These moments can lead to greater depths of the contemplative life.

C. All are called from Baptism to a life of truth and love. This is also called holiness. The faithful practice of prayer is a sure road of growth in holiness. Every person is called to contemplation. Lives of the great mystics model heroic virtue. Many faithful Catholics become contemplative. The use of the *Lectio Divina* method provides a path that is clear and profound. The Holy Spirit is always present when Scripture is used in the context of prayer.

III. Eucharistic devotions.

A. The Roman Catholic Tradition has a rich treasury of pious practices and devotions. The Decree of the Sacred Liturgy of Vatican II states, "Popular devotions of the Christian people, provided that they conform to the laws and norms of the

Church, are to be highly recommended, especially where they are ordered by the Apostolic See" (SC #13).

B. The Celebration of the Eucharistic Liturgy by which the Sacrifice of Christ on Calvary is made present and is the source and summit of the Church's life of prayer. Flowing from the Holy Sacrifice of the Mass are Eucharist devotions. Most forms of Eucharistic devotion pertain to the reserving of the Sacrament. These devotions are exposition, benediction, processions, congresses, and spiritual communion.

1. Exposition of the Blessed Sacrament occurs when a priest or deacon removes the Sacred Host from the tabernacle, puts it in a monstrance and places it on the altar for adoration by the faithful. Christ is present to be adored.
2. Benediction of the Blessed Sacrament honors the Real Presence of Christ in the Eucharist. A consecrated host is placed in a monstrance and enthroned on an altar between lighted candles. Incense is used. A period of silent adoration is offered. The gathered assembly participate in the singing of special hymns and receive the blessing of the Eucharist. A priest or deacon officiates at this celebration.
3. Corpus Christi is the yearly Feast honoring the Real Presence of Christ in the Eucharist. It usually occurs on the Sunday after Trinity Sunday. In many parishes a Eucharistic devotion occurs as the priest, holding the Blessed Sacrament, leads the faithful through a procession.
4. Eucharistic Congresses are held to foster devotion to Christ in the Blessed Sacrament. Lectures and discussions foster greater awareness and devotion to the Blessed Eucharist. Congresses are held as national and diocesan events.
5. In his encyclical letter, *Ecclesia de Eucharistia*, Pope John Paul II reminds us of the ancient practice of spiritual Communion. He quotes St. Teresa of Ávila: "When you do not attend Mass, you can make a spiritual Communion, which is a most beneficial practice; by it the love of God will be greatly impressed on you" (*The Way of Perfection*, Ch. 35).

   Here is a suggested prayer to use:

   > O Lord Jesus , since I am unable at this time to receive You in the holy sacrament of the Eucharist, I beg you to come spiritually into my heart in the spirit of Your holiness, in the truth of Your goodness, in the fullness of Your power, in the communion of Your mysteries and in the perfection of Your ways. O Lord, I believe, I trust, I glorify You, I am sorry for all my sins. O Sacrament most Holy, O Sacrament divine, all praise and all thanksgiving be every moment thine.
   >
   > From "Spiritual Communion,"
   > *Encyclopedia of Catholic Devotions and Practices*, by Ann Ball

IV. Devotion to Mary.

The Church's devotion to the Blessed Virgin is intrinsic to Christian worship (MC 56).

A. The *Catechism of the Catholic Church* clearly states:

> The Church rightly honors "the Blessed Virgin with special devotion. From the most ancient times the Blessed Virgin has been honored with the title of 'Mother of God,' to whose protection the faithful fly in all their dangers and needs.... This very special devotion ... differs essen-

NOTES...

NOTES...

tially from the adoration which is given to the incarnate Word and equally to the Father and the Holy Spirit, and greatly fosters this adoration" (LG 66). The liturgical feasts dedicated to the Mother of God and Marian prayer, such as the Rosary, an "epitome of the whole Gospel," expresses this devotion to the Virgin Mary (cf. Paul VI, MC 42; SC 103) (CCC 971).

B. The Rosary.

1. The Rosary is a form of mental and vocal prayer centered on the events in the lives of Jesus and Mary. There are four sets of sacred Mysteries:
   a. The Joyful Mysteries
      1. The Annunciation
      2. The Visitation
      3. The Nativity
      4. The Presentation
      5. The Finding in the Temple
   b. The Luminous Mysteries
      1. The Baptism of Jesus
      2. The Miracle at the Wedding in Cana
      3. The Proclamation of the Kingdom
      4. The Transfiguration of Jesus
      5. The Institution of the Holy Eucharist
   c. The Sorrowful Mysteries
      1. The Agony in the Garden
      2. The Scourging at the Pillar
      3. The Crowning of Thorns
      4. The Carrying of the Cross
      5. The Crucifixion
   d. The Glorious Mysteries
      1. The Resurrection
      2. The Ascension
      3. The Descent of the Holy Spirit
      4. The Assumption
      5. The Crowning of the Blessed Virgin
2. Rosary beads are composed of five decades. At the beginning of each decade there is a bead singularly set apart on which the Our Father is prayed. This is then followed by the ten beads on which the Hail Mary is prayed. Depending upon which set of Mysteries of the Rosary is being recited, each Mystery is announced prior to the Our Father. At the end of each decade, the Glory Be to the Father is said. Each Rosary begins with the Apostles' Creed. Then follows an Our Father, three Hail Marys and the Glory Be to the Father prior to actually beginning the five Mysteries.
3. Traditionally the Joyful Mysteries are recited on Mondays and Saturdays, the Sorrowful on Tuesdays and Fridays, the Luminous on Thursdays, and the Glorious on Wednesdays and Sundays.

C. A beautiful Marian prayer which many Catholics memorize and pray is the *Memorare*. It is attributed to St. Bernard of Clairvaux (circa 1090-1153). The prayer is as follows:

Remember, O most gracious Virgin Mary, that never was it know that anyone who fled to your protection, implored your help, or sought your intercession was left unaided.

Inspired by this confidence, I fly unto you, O Virgin of Virgins, my Mother. To you I come, before you I stand, sinful and sorrowful. O Mother of the Word Incarnate, despise not my petitions, but in your mercy hear and answer me.

Amen.

D. The Liturgy of the Hours.

1. The *Divine Office*, also known as the Liturgy of the Hours, is the official daily prayer of the Church. This is primarily a public prayer but many recite it privately. Within Monastic Communities it is prayed seven times a day.
2. Those called to the sacrament of Holy Orders are obliged to pray the Divine Office. The majority of consecrated men and women are expected to pray this prayer. Many laity are choosing to make this prayer a part of their lives.
3. The Liturgy of the Hours consist of hymns, antiphons, psalms, selections from Sacred Scripture, readings from the Church Fathers, writings from the Saints and other Catholic Prayers. It is arranged according to a four-week cycle (CCC 1174-1178).

NOTES...

VI. Stations of the Cross.

The Way of the Cross is a devotional practice that re-enacts major events of the Passion of Christ from his trial to his entombment. There are fourteen stations. Some modern stations add a Resurrection. They may either be prayed in private or be prayed publicly, which is common during Lent. Most churches have the stations well-displayed on both sides of the Church building (CCC 1674, 2669).

VII. Morning and Evening Prayer.

A. This devotion goes back to the early Church when people observed the beautiful significance of the rising of the Sun and the setting of the moon. At these times, morning and evening, they turned to God in prayer.

B. The morning practice of offering one's day to God is a profound way of uniting ones joys and suffering in union with Christ. This self-offering brings about many graces for the Mystical Body of Christ.

1. The most common form of this prayer is as follows:
   O Jesus, through the Immaculate Heart of Mary, I offer you all my prayers, works, joys and suffering of this day, for all the intentions of your Sacred Heart, in union with the Holy Sacrifice of the Mass throughout the world, in reparation for my sins, for the intentions of all our associates, and for the general intention recommended this month.
2. A worldwide association known as the Apostleship of Prayer promotes the glory of God through this Morning Offering. The intention each month reflects various intentions of the Pope.

C. Evening Prayer usually consists of thanking God for the blessings of the day, a prayer of forgiveness for any failings of the day and a request for protection during the night.

NOTES...

VIII. Novenas and litanies.

A. A novena is a public or private devotional practice that is prayed over nine consecutive days. The word novena means "nine." A novena is usually prayed for favors or special graces. The majority of novenas are prayed in honor of Mary, signifying the nine months that Christ was in her womb. Other novenas are to the Holy Spirit, the Sacred Heart, St. Joseph, St. Ann, St. Jude, or other saints of particular devotion.

B. A litany is a prayer in the form of responsive petitions. Having its origins in the Old Testament, the early Church retained this practice. Approved litanies for public use are those in honor of the Holy Name of Jesus, the Sacred Heart, the Blessed Virgin and St. Joseph.

IX. Guardian angels and patron saints.

A. Guardian angels are spiritual beings created by God who are personal and immortal. "Angels are *servants* and messengers of God" (CCC 329). "The whole life of the Church benefits from the mysterious and powerful help of angels" (cf. Acts 5:18-20; 8:26-29; 10:3-8; 12:6-11; 27:23-25) (CCC 334). "'Beside each believer stands an angel as protector and shepherd leading him to life'" (St. Basil, *Adv. Eunomium* III, 1: PG 29, 656B) (CCC 336). Thus, prayer to the angels is a longstanding devotion in the Church.

B. Patron saints.

1. The Church teaches that within the communion of saints – souls in heaven, purgatory and the faithful on earth – there is a constant communion of charity. The holiness of one is of benefit to another.
2. The veneration of saints by celebrating their feasts, naming children and churches after them, and invoking their support enriches Catholic life.
   a. The Church not only calls on the faithful to have devotion to Mary, but also encourages the practice of imploring the aid of the saints in heaven who are closely joined with Christ.
1. Just as we can ask our Christian brothers and sisters on earth to pray for us, so too we can ask those in heaven to pray for us.
3. The lives of the saints are both inspirational and encouraging to all Christians. Their heroic virtue, integrity, and faith encourage all to hope and perseverance.

X. Holy images.

Sacred images are beneficial to prayer. They are visual reminders and inspirations of God's infinite beauty. For this reason "the church has always been a friend of the fine arts....They are dedicated to God, they praise him and extend his glory to the extent that their only purpose is to turn people's spirits devotedly toward God" (SC # 122).

XI. Spiritual reading.

A. A long tradition in the Church is the practice of spiritual reading. It is a constant reminder of the sacred and encourages a commitment to strengthening the spiritual life.

B. There are two main categories of spiritual reading. One is the classical treasures of the Church which are primarily always kept in print. The other are contemporary books. Often it is a challenge to know whether a recently written book is sound spiritually. Certain publishers only print very acceptable materials and this helps in decision making.

C. Another consideration is the complexity of the reading materials. Some of the classics are not for beginners. One needs to read foundational materials to gain experience in understanding spiritual concepts.

D. The lives of the saints provide great reading. An all-time favorite is the autobiography of St. Thérèse of Lisieux entitled *Story of a Soul.*

E. Other classic books are:
- *The Practice of the Presence* of God by Brother Lawrence
- *Introduction to the Devote Life* by St. Francis de Sales
- *Revelations of Divine Love* by Julian of Norwich
- *Seven Storey Mountain* by Thomas Merton

F. Some books for more advanced spiritual reading are:
- *The Complete Works of St. John of the Cross* (three volumes)
- *The Complete Works of St. Teresa of Ávila* (three volumes)
- *The Cloud of Unknowing* (Anonymous)
- *The City of God* by St. Augustine

G. The *Catechism of the Catholic Church*, Part IV, is also a profound reading on the life of prayer. It needs to be read slowly and in a meditative manner.

H. Whoever decides to embark on the journey of spiritual reading will recognize that their life of prayer will be strengthened. It is a discipline but a golden opportunity to fill one's life with holy thoughts and hopeful yearnings.

NOTES...

FOCUS QUESTIONS

1. What are the challenges of committing to a life of prayer?
2. Why do Catholics pray to Mary?
3. Why are devotions helpful to a life of prayer?

Concluding prayers
Intercessions
Closing prayer
Hymn (optional)

RESOURCES

The Bible
Catechism of the Catholic Church, 2558-2758
Ecclesia de Eucharistia (On the Eucharist in Its Relationship to the Church), John Paul II
Ann Ball, *Encyclopedia of Catholic Devotions and Practices*
The Way of Perfection, Teresa of Ávila, chap. 35

Session Thirty-four

Our Father

The Spirituality of Gospel Living

LEARNING OBJECTIVE

To present the spiritual significance of praying the Our Father as a summary of the whole Gospel. Life which reflects this quality of living brings about the kingdom of God.

Hymn: "Gather Us In"

Invitation to prayer — silent prayer

Oration:

God our Father,
in your care and wisdom
you extend the kingdom of Christ to embrace the world
to give all men redemption.
May the Catholic Church be the sign of our salvation,
may it reveal for us the mystery of your love,
and may that love become effective in our lives.

Grant this through our Lord Jesus Christ, your Son,
who lives and reigns with you and the Holy Spirit,
one God, for ever and ever.

Opening Prayer
Mass for the Universal Church (A)

Scripture reading: Matthew 6:7-15

In praying, do not babble like the pagans, who think that they will be heard because of their many words. Do not be like them. Your Father knows what you need before you ask him.

This is how you are to pray:

Our Father in heaven,
hallowed be your name,
your kingdom come,
your will be done,
on earth as in heaven.
Give us today our daily bread;

and forgive us our debts,
as we forgive our debtors;
and do not subject us to the final test,
but deliver us from the evil one.

If you forgive others their transgressions, your heavenly Father will forgive you. But if you do not forgive others, neither will your Father forgive your transgressions.

NOTES...

TEACHING TO BE PRESENTED

I. The Our Father: The prayer Jesus taught.

A. "The Lord's Prayer 'is truly the summary of the whole gospel' (Tertullian, *De orat.* 1: PL 1, 1155)" (CCC 2761).

1. The Our Father is a prayer, in the Lord's Spirit and gives new form to our desires, those inner movements that inspire our life. "Jesus teaches us this new life by his words; he teaches us to ask for it by our prayer" (CCC 2764).
2. The authenticity of our life will depend on the authenticity of our prayer (CCC 2764).
3. The Lord's Prayer, which comes to us "from Jesus is truly unique: it is 'of the Lord'" (CCC 2765).
4. Through this prayer Jesus gives us the words the Father gave Him and as well, realizing the needs of each human heart, Jesus reveals them to us: He is the model of our prayers (CCC 2765).
5. Since our prayer interprets our desires before Him, God, who searches the heart, "'knows what is the mind of the Spirit, because the Spirit intercedes for [us] according to the will of God' (Rom 8:27)" (CCC 2766).

B. The Our Father is trinitarian in nature.

1. "The prayer to Our Father is inserted into the mysterious mission of the Son and of the Spirit" (CCC 2766).
2. The Lord's Prayer is the prayer of the Church *par excellence*. It is an integral part of the Liturgy of the Hours and Christian initiation. "Integrated into the Eucharist it reveals the eschatological character [i.e. of the last things — death, judgment, and eternal life] of its petitions, hoping for the Lord, 'until he comes' (1 Cor 11:26)" (CCC 2776).

II. The first three petitions of the Our Father.

A. *Our Father who art in heaven*

1. The first three petitions of the Our Father help us to focus on the glory of God without mentioning ourselves.
2. Before one prays the Our Father one must purify one's heart from false paternal and maternal images stemming from personal experience (CCC 2779).
3. The Our Father transcends the categories of the created world. If we ascribe to God ideas derived from experiences of this world, we may create an idol(s) to worship. Knowledge of the true God demands that we destroy all our "false images" (CCC 2779).
4. "To pray to the Father is to enter into his mystery as he is and as the Son has revealed him to us" (CCC 2779).

NOTES...

5. "The free gift of adoption requires on our part continual conversion and *new life*. Praying to our Father should develop in us two fundamental dispositions" (CCC 2784).
   a. "*The desire to become like him*" (CCC 2784).
   b. "*A humble and trusting heart* that enables us 'to turn and become like children' (Mt 18:3)" (CCC 2785).

B. When praying "'our' Father," each of the baptized prays in the communion of the whole Church (CCC 2787).
   1. The Holy Trinity is one being and indivisible. "When we pray to the Father, we adore and glorify him together with the Son and the Holy Spirit" (CCC 2789).
   2. "If we pray the Our Father sincerely," the love we welcome sets us free from narrow individualism. "The 'our' at the beginning of the Lord's Prayer, like the 'us' of the last four petitions, excludes no one." So that we may say it with full effect, our divisions and oppositions must be overcome (cf. Mt 5:23-24; 6:14-15) (CCC 2792).
   3. "When we say 'Our' Father," we invoke the new covenant in Jesus Christ. Our communion with the Holy Trinity, in God's love, spreads through the Church to encompass the world (CCC 2801).
   4. The biblical expression "in heaven" does not mean a place (i.e. space) but a way of being. Our Father is not "elsewhere;" His holiness surpasses anything we can imagine. God is altogether close to humble and contrite hearts (CCC 2794).
   5. The symbol of heaven brings us back to the mystery of the covenant we live when we pray to the Father. Sin exiles us while conversion of heart enables us to return to the Father (CCC 2795).
   6. "After we have placed ourselves in the presence of God our Father to adore and to love and to bless him, the Spirit of adoption stirs up in our hearts seven petitions, seven blessings" (CCC 2803).

C. *Hallowed be thy name*
   1. Jesus taught us this petition as a request, an expression of desire and expectation in which God and humanity are involved. "Beginning with this first petition to our Father, we are immersed in the innermost mystery of his Godhead and the drama of the salvation of our humanity" (CCC 2807).
   2. Asking that His name be made holy draws us into God's plan for the fullness of time, according to His good pleasure set forth in Christ, that we may be holy and blameless before Him in love (CCC 2807).
   3. "This petition embodies all the others. Like the six petitions that follow, it is fulfilled by *the prayer of Christ*. Prayer to our Father is our prayer, if it is prayed *in the name* of Jesus" (cf. Jn 14:13, 15:16; 16:24, 26) (CCC 2815).

D. *Thy kingdom come*
   1. In the Lord's Prayer this petition refers primarily to the final coming of God's kingdom through Christ's return (CCC 2816).
   2. It also prays for the growth of the kingdom in the here and now (CCC 2859).
   3. Each Christian needs to discern between the growth of God's kingdom and the progress of culture and society in which they are involved. This distinction is not a separation. Our vocation to eternal life does not lessen but reinforces our duty to serve justice and peace in this world with all the powers and skills the Creator has given us (CCC 2859).

NOTES...

III. The last four petitions of the Our Father.

A. *Thy will be done on earth as it is in heaven*

1. The last four petitions are involved with our life in the world.
2. God's "commandment is 'that you love one another; even as I have loved you, that you also love one another' (Jn 13:34; cf. 1 Jn 3; 4; Lk 10:25-37). This commandment summarizes all the others and expresses his entire will" (CCC 2822).
3. Through this petition we insistently ask that this divine plan should be fully realized on earth as it already is in heaven (CCC 2823).
4. "By prayer we can discern 'what is the will of God' and obtain the endurance to do it (Rom 12:2; cf. Eph 5:17; cf. Heb 10:36). Jesus teaches us that one enters the kingdom of heaven not by speaking words, but by doing 'the will of my Father in heaven' (Mt 7:21)" (CCC 2826).

B. *Give us this day our daily bread*

1. "'*Give us*': The trust of children who look to their Father for everything is beautiful.... Jesus teaches us this petition, because it glorifies our Father by acknowledging how good he is, beyond all goodness" (CCC 2828).
2. "'*Give us*' also expresses the covenant" (CCC 2829). We are God's own and He is with us and for us. But by saying "us" we also recognize God as the Father of all people and so "pray to him for them all, in solidarity with their needs and sufferings" (CCC 2829).
3. "'*Our bread*': The Father who gives us life cannot but give us the nourishment life requires — all appropriate goods and blessings, both material and spiritual" (CCC 2830).
4. "In the Sermon on the Mount, Jesus insists on the filial trust that cooperates with our Father's providence" (cf. Mt 6:25-34) (CCC 2830).
5. "The drama of hunger in the world calls Christians who pray sincerely to exercise responsibility toward their brethren, both in their personal behavior and in their solidarity with the human family" (CCC 2831).
6. "'Our' bread is the 'one' loaf for the 'many.' In the Beatitudes 'poverty' is the virtue of sharing; it calls us to communicate and share both material and spiritual goods, not by coercion but out of love, so that the abundance of some may remedy the needs of others" (cf. 2 Cor 8:1-15) (CCC 2833).
7. "Pray and work" (cf. St. Benedict, *Regula*, 20, 48). Even when we have done our work, the food we receive is still a gift. It is right to ask God for it and to thank Him (CCC 2834).
8. This petition also involves the hunger of the heart for God's word. People are perishing because there is a famine of the spirit. Christians must make every effort to preach the Good News to the poor (CCC 2835).
9. "This 'today' is not only that of our mortal time, but also the 'today' of God" (CCC 2836). In a temporal sense, daily means today. In a qualitative sense it means what is necessary for life. Taken literally from the Greek word *epiousios,* meaning "super-essential," it refers directly to the Bread of Life, Christ's Body (CCC 2837).
10. Thus, "'this day' is the Day of the Lord, the day of the feast of the kingdom, anticipated in the Eucharist that is already the foretaste of the kingdom to come" (CCC 2837).

C. *And forgive us our trespasses as we forgive those who trespass against us*

NOTES...

1. Our petition will not be heard unless we have first met a demand. "Our petition looks to the future, but our response must come first, for the two parts are joined by the single word 'as'" (CCC 2838).
2. God's outpouring of mercy can penetrate our hearts only to the extent that we forgive those who trespass against us. In refusing to forgive others our hearts are hardened and closed. This impenetrability blocks God's merciful love (CCC 2840).
3. "In confessing our sins, our hearts are open to his grace" (CCC 2840).
4. "This petition is so important that it is the only one to which the Lord returns and which he develops explicitly in the Sermon on the Mount" (cf. Mt 6:14-15; 5:23-24; Mk 11:25) (CCC 2841).
5. "Christian prayer extends to the *forgiveness of enemies* (cf. Mt 5:43-44), transfiguring the disciple by configuring him to his Master. Forgiveness is a high-point of Christian prayer" (CCC 2844).
6. "Forgiveness also bears witness that, in our world, love is stronger than sin" (CCC 2844).

D. *And lead us not into temptation*

1. "This petition goes to the root of the preceding one, for our sins result from our consenting to temptation" (CCC 2846).
2. The Greek word translated as "lead" means "both 'do not to allow us to enter into temptation' and 'do not let us yield to temptation'" (cf. Mt 26:41). We therefore ask Him not to allow us to take the way that leads to sin (CCC 2846).
3. "'Lead us not into temptation' implies a *decision of the heart.*" We are free persons. God does not impose on us. By wrestling with temptations we become aware of our evil inclinations (CCC 2848).
4. "Such a battle and such a victory become possible only through prayer" (CCC 2849).
5. "This petition takes on all its dramatic meaning in relation to the last temptation of our earthly battle; it asks for *final perseverance.* 'Lo, I am coming like a thief! Blessed is he who is awake' (Rv 16:15)" (CCC 2849).

E. *But deliver us from evil*

1. This last petition to God is also included in Jesus' prayer found in the Last Supper Discourse: "'I am not asking you to take them out of the world, but I ask you to protect them from the evil one' (Jn 17:15)" (CCC 2850).
2. "In this petition, evil is not an abstraction, but refers to a person, Satan, the Evil One, the angel who opposes God. The devil (*dia-bolos*) is the one who 'throws himself across' God's plan and his work of salvation accomplished in Christ" (CCC 2851).
3. "When we ask to be delivered from the Evil One, we pray as well to be freed from all evils, present, past and future, of which he is the author or instigator" (CCC 2854).
4. "The final doxology, 'For the kingdom, the power and the glory are yours, now and forever,' takes up again, by inclusion, the first three petitions to our Father: the glorification of his name, the coming of his reign, and the power of his saving will" (CCC 2855).

F. *Amen*

1. "Amen" expresses our *fiat* concerning the seven petitions: "So be it" (CCC 2856).

FOCUS QUESTIONS

1. Many people say the Our Father without realizing the depth of prayer it contains. What touched you most in hearing the Our Father? Explain.
2. The Our Father is the very prayer Christ taught as Scripture tells us. What do the first three petitions say about Christ's relationship to His Father?
3. How would you describe the Our Father as being the summary of Gospel living?

Concluding prayers
Intercessions
Closing prayer
Hymn (optional)

RESOURCES

Catechism of the Catholic Church, 2777-2856
The Way of Perfection, Teresa of Ávila, chaps. 30-42
Essentials of the Faith, McBride, chap. 55

NOTES...

Session Thirty-five

The Liturgical Year

LEARNING OBJECTIVE

To present an understanding of how and why the Church follows the Liturgical Year.

Hymn: "To Jesus Christ Our Sovereign King"

Invitation to prayer – silent prayer

Oration:

Lord Jesus Christ,
you give us the sacredness of time.
Teach us how to live,
celebrating each day
the mystery of your love.
Help us find meaning in
the many signs that
constantly remind us of your eternal presence.

We ask this through our Lord Jesus Christ, your Son,
who lives and reigns with you and the Holy Spirit,
one God, for ever and ever.

Scripture reading: John 1:14-18

And the Word became flesh
and made his dwelling among us,
and we saw his glory,
the glory as of the Father's only Son,
full of grace and truth.

John testified to him and cried out, saying, "This was he of whom I said, 'The one who is coming after me ranks ahead of me because he existed before me.'" From his fullness we have all received, grace in place of grace, because while the law was given through Moses, grace and truth came through Jesus Christ. No one has ever seen God. The only Son, God, who is at the Father's side, has revealed him.

TEACHING TO BE PRESENTED

NOTES...

I. The Church, as the Spouse of Christ, lives according to the way of the Liturgical Year.

A. The central focus and mystery of this holy year is the person of Jesus Christ, the fullness of God's revelation.

B. Catholics who follow the various seasons of the Liturgical Year open themselves to ongoing conversion by:
1. Following the way of Christ and all that He teaches.
2. Constantly being open to ongoing conversion of mind and heart.
3. Constantly being drawn to strengthening their personal relationship with Christ.

C. "Every week, on the day which she has called the Lord's day, she keeps the memory of the Lord's resurrection, which she also celebrates once a year, together with His blessed passion, in the most solemn festival of Easter" (SC #102).

Thus, the Paschal Mystery of Christ's death and resurrection is the high point of the Liturgical Year.

II. Advent Season.

A. The format of the Liturgical Year begins with Advent. This four week season is filled with themes of joyful expectation and encouragement towards conversion. The faithful remember Christ's first coming through the Incarnation and recall that He will come again at the end of time.

B. On December 17, the O Antiphons begin. They continue until December 23. Each antiphon is found in the beautiful Advent Hymn "O Come, O Come Emmanuel." The antiphons are derived from the Old Testament prophecies which Christ fulfilled. They are:
1. December 17, O Wisdom
2. December 18, O Lord of Might
3. December 19, O Flower of Jesse's Stem
4. December 20, O Key of David
5. December 21, O Rising Dawn
6. December 22, O King of Nations
7. December 23, O Emmanuel

C. There are two popular symbols of the Advent Season.
1. The color purple.
2. The Advent Wreath.
   a. The wreath is made of fir branches and constructed to hold four candles, three purple and one rose, representing the four Sundays of Advent.
   b. These wreathes are popular in churches and in homes. The candles are lighted on each consecutive Sunday of Advent. All are burning by the fourth Sunday. This practice is meant to cultivate a deeper sense of this beautiful liturgical season which is characterized as a time of waiting.

III. Christmas Season.

A. December 24 is the Vigil of Christmas. A vigil, coming from the Latin word meaning awake, is a "watch" on the eve of a religious feast. On December 24, the Church reflects on the words of the prophet Isaiah:

NOTES...

Awake, awake!
  Arise, O Jerusalem....
Break out together in song,
  O ruins of Jerusalem!
For the LORD comforts his people,
  he redeems Jerusalem.
The LORD has bared his holy arm
  in the sight of all the nations;
All the ends of the earth will behold
  the salvation of our God (Is 51:17; 52:9-10).

B. Christmas Day celebrates the Incarnation of Jesus Christ. "Jesus fulfilled the messianic hope of Israel in his threefold office of priest, prophet, and king" (CCC 436). The angels announced his birth: "'To you is born this day in the city of David a Savior, who is Christ the Lord' (Lk 2:11)" (CCC 437).

C. In the Roman Catholic Church Christmas culminates on the feast of Epiphany, which is from a Greek word meaning manifestation. January 6 (or on the Sunday closest to this date) the Church commemorates the manifestation of Christ to the whole world as represented by the Magi from the East (Mt 2:1-12).

IV. Ordinary Time.

A. This period of the Liturgical Year begins after Epiphany. It is temporarily suspended during Lent.

1. The Sunday after Epiphany begins Ordinary Time by celebrating the Baptism of the Lord and introducing us to the public life of Christ. Ordinary Time then unfolds during two periods of time.
2. The first period ends at the beginning of the Season of Lent.
3. The second, longer period of Ordinary Time starts after the Feast of Pentecost and continues until the last Sunday of the Liturgical Year, the Feast of Christ the King.

V. The Lenten Season.

A. Lent begins with Ash Wednesday. On this day ashes are blessed and imposed upon the heads of the faithful as a sign of penitence and mortality.

B. Lent, reflecting Christ's forty days in the desert prior to his public ministry, is a time of fasting, prayer, and almsgiving in preparation for the great feast of our believing, the Resurrection of his Body following Christ's passion and death. "'Christ died for our sins in accordance with the scriptures' (1 Cor 15:3). Our salvation flows from God's initiative of love for us, because 'he loved us and sent his Son to be the expiation for our sins' (1 Jn 4:10). 'God was in Christ reconciling the world to himself' (2 Cor 5:19)" (CCC 619-620).

C. Popular symbols of Lent are the color purple and the crown of thorns. The environment of Lent is somber and pensive.

VI. The Easter Season.

A. Christ rose from the dead after his passion and death. This is the greatest mystery of our faith. Christ emptied himself to save all. This "kenosis" of Christ is a model for all Christians.

1. Kenosis is from a Greek word meaning "emptying." Christ's emptying of himself is his free renunciation of his right to divine status, "the form of God," by reason of the Incarnation.
2. As proclaimed in the New Testament Christological hymn Philippians 2:6-11, Christ took the form of a slave, born in the likeness of man, thus fully human and yet totally integrated with his divinity. Christ was totally dependent on God the Father, from whom he had descended to earth (CCC 461-463).

B. The Paschal Candle is the great symbol of the Easter Season. This large wax candle is blessed after the Easter fire during the Service of the Light which begins the Easter Vigil.

1. The Paschal Candle symbolizes the light of Christ rising in glory that scatters the darkness of sin and death.
2. On the Paschal Candle is a cross and the *alpha* and the *omega* symbol, which mean Christ is "the first and the last, the one who lives" (Rv 1:17-18).
    a. It has the numerals of the current year on it.
    b. Grains of incense and wax nails are implanted at the ends of crossbars and in the center of the cross.

C. Another great symbol of Easter is the holy water blessed during the celebration of the Easter Vigil.

1. It is used for Christian Initiation at the Easter Vigil and throughout the Liturgical Year.
2. This water may be taken home for special devotions and family or personal prayer.

D. Easter Season is a joyous time lasting for fifty days.

1. After forty days, Christ's Ascension into Heaven is celebrated.
2. The following nine days to the Vigil of Pentecost prepare in a special way for the coming of the Holy Spirit. After Christ ascended to Heaven, as he had promised, he sent his Holy Spirit.

> "The Church was made manifest to the world on the day of Pentecost by the outpouring of the Holy Spirit (cf. SC 6; LG 2). The gift of the Spirit ushers in a new era in the 'dispensation of the mystery' — the age of the Church, during which Christ manifests, makes present, and communicates his work of salvation through the liturgy of his Church, 'until he comes' (1 Cor 11:26). In this age of the Church Christ now lives and acts in and with his Church, in a new way appropriate to this new age. He acts through the sacraments in what the common Tradition of the East and the West calls 'the sacramental economy'; this is the communication (or 'dispensation') of the fruits of Christ's Paschal mystery in the celebration of the Church's 'sacramental' liturgy" (CCC 1076).

VII. The colors of the Liturgical Year.

A. To help celebrate the liturgical year, the Church uses liturgical colors. Celebration remembers a sacred event. After it is remembered it is then affirmed by the act of believing. This leads to hope because of the fidelity of Christ to his people. The liturgical colors are white, green, red, purple, rose, gold, and, rarely, black.

B. The liturgical colors are:

1. White is the color of radiance and light used at Christmas, Easter, other feasts of Christ, Mary, and the saints. It is also used for Masses of Christian burial.

NOTES...

NOTES...

2. Purple is the color of Advent and Lent. It reminds us of our need to do penance and be contrite because of our tendency to sinfulness.
3. Green is the color of life. It is used during the season of Ordinary Time.
4. Red is the color of blood and fire. It is used on Passion Sunday, Good Friday, Pentecost, and for the feasts of saints who shed their blood for martyrdom.
5. Rose is a color of joy and hope. It is used twice during the Liturgical Year; first in Advent, on Gaudete, the third Sunday, and then on Laetare, the fourth Sunday of Lent. It is a reminder that in the midst of penance, joy is always part of life in Christ.
6. Gold is the color of beauty and precious metal. It may be used to celebrate special occasions.
7. Black is a color of mourning. It is an option for funerals. Because white is the color of light and resurrection, in recent times white has come to be preferred.

VIII. Feasts of Mary, the Mother of God.

A. As the Church focuses on Christ throughout the Liturgical Year, she honors Mary. As the Constitution on the Sacred Liturgy describes, Mary "is inseparably linked with her Son's saving work. In her the church admires and exalts the most excellent fruit of the redemption, and joyfully contemplates, as in a faultless image, the goal it anticipates and desire for all its members" (SC #103).

B. Major Feasts of Mary are:
1. The Feast of Mary, Mother of God – January 1
2. The Feast of the Assumption – August 15
3. The Feast of the Immaculate Conception – December 8

IX. Sunday, the Day of the Lord.

A. Sunday, the day of Jesus' resurrection, from the time of the earliest Christians, was the day that Christians met for "the breaking of the bread" (Acts 2:42). "From that time on down to our own day the celebration of the Eucharist has been continued so that today we encounter it everywhere in the Church with the same fundamental structure. It remains the center of the Church's life" (CCC 1343).

B. Sunday is observed as a holy day of obligation. "'On Sundays and other holy days of obligation the faithful are bound to participate in the Mass'" (CIC, can. 1247) (CCC 2192).

C. Sunday as the Lord's Day should be given to "'the proper relaxation of mind and body' (CIC, can. 1247)" (CCC 2193).

D. "Every Christian should avoid making unnecessary demands on others that would hinder them from observing the Lord's Day" (CCC 2195).

E. On Sunday Sacred Scripture is proclaimed in a three-year cycle: A, B, and C.

X. Days of the week.

A. On weekdays during the Liturgical Year there is a two-year cycle.

B. The Church during the week days includes "memorial days of the martyrs and other saints.... Raised up to perfection by the manifold grace of God and already in possession of eternal salvation, they sing God's perfect praise in heaven and pray for us. By celebrating the days on which they died, the Church proclaims the paschal mystery in the saints who have suffered and have been glorified with Christ" (SC #104).

C. An enriching practice is to learn the feasts of the many saints whose lives are remembered. Of great benefit is to read and be inspired by their lives, commitment, and conversion to discipleship with Christ.

NOTES...

FOCUS QUESTIONS

1. How does following the Liturgical Year strengthen one's spiritual life?
2. Why is Sunday a holy day of obligation?
3. What is the significance of Liturgical seasons and colors?

Concluding prayers
Intercessions
Closing prayer
Hymn (optional)

RESOURCES

Catechism of the Catholic Church, 1163-1178
Sacrosanctum Concilium (Constitution on the Sacred Liturgy), Vatican II

Session Thirty-six

Catholic Social Teaching

LEARNING OBJECTIVE

To acquaint each person with major themes of Catholic Social Teaching.

Hymn: "Anthem"

Invitation to prayer – silent prayer

Oration:

Lord Jesus,
give us the grace
to help change the world.
Change the hearts of people
so that they may
assist the poor,
feed the hungry,
clothe and shelter the abandoned.
Give workers their rights.
Let the forgotten receive justice.
We ask this through Christ our Lord.

Adapted from a reflection by Dorothy Day

Scripture reading: Matthew 25:31-40

"When the Son of Man comes in his glory, and all the angels with him, he will sit upon his glorious throne, and all the nations will be assembled before him. And he will separate them one from another, as a shepherd separates the sheep from the goats. He will place the sheep on his right and the goats on his left. Then the king will say to those on his right, 'Come, you who are blessed by my Father. Inherit the kingdom prepared for you from the foundation of the world. For I was hungry and you gave me food, I was thirsty and you gave me drink, a stranger and you welcomed me, naked and you clothed me, ill and you cared for me, in prison and you visited me.' Then the righteous will answer him and say, 'Lord, when did we see you hungry and feed you, or thirsty and give you drink? When did we see you a stranger and welcome you, or naked and clothe you? When did we see you ill or in prison, and visit you?' And the king will say to them in reply, 'Amen, I say to you, whatever you did for one of these least brothers of mine, you did for me.'"

TEACHING TO BE PRESENTED

NOTES...

Catholic social teachings emerge from the richness of the Tradition, reflecting both Scripture and essential doctrines. These teachings bid the conscience of each responsible Catholic to act with wisdom and justice. The *Catechism of the Catholic Church* states, "Social justice can be obtained only in respecting the transcendent dignity of man" (CCC 1929). Respect for the common good proceeds from the principle that "'everyone should look upon his neighbor (without any exception) as "another self"' (GS 27 § 1)" (CCC 1931). The format of this session follows the seven major themes based on the 1998 Reflection of the United States Catholic Bishops, *Sharing Catholic Social Teaching: Challenges and Directions.* These major themes are:

- The Life and Dignity of the Human Person
- The Call to Family, Community, and Participation
- Rights and Responsibilities
- Option for the Poor and Vulnerable
- The Dignity of Work and the Rights of Workers
- Solidarity
- Care for God's Creation

I. **The Life and Dignity of the Human Person**

  A. Each person is created in the Image and Likeness of God (Gn 1:27). Each person, in light of his or her creation by God, has rights.

  B. The fundamental right to have human life "must be respected and protected absolutely from the moment of conception" (CCC 2270).

  C. Each human life has the right to proper development.
    1. Life is to be respected not only in the womb, but throughout every stage of life until natural death (CCC 2319).
    2. Food, clothing, shelter, rest, medical care and necessary social services are the right of each person (PT 11).
    3. The common good of all people requires that society uphold the rights and responsibilities of each person.

  D. Life is to be protected whenever it is vulnerable.
    1. In the Old Testament, requirements were made for safeguarding life when it was weak or threatened (Ex 22:20-26).
    2. In the New Testament, Jesus gave of His life so that we "might have life and have it more abundantly" (Jn 10:10b).
    3. Contemporary culture manifests injustices which harm and threaten the lives of the vulnerable.
      a. The diminished, weak, handicapped and sick "deserve special respect" (CCC 2276).
      b. The dying deserve special attention and care (CCC 2299).
      c. The poor must be embraced in their human dignity. People are more important than any material thing.
      d. Criminals, in spite of their human failures and crimes retain their human dignity. The story of Cain and Abel manifests how God does not take Cain's life, but marks him so that no one else will kill him (Gn 4:14-15). The purpose of punishment is not to destroy but "to redress the disorder caused by the offense" (EV 56).

NOTES...

4. The world's population has the right of protection.
   a. Arms development and accumulation are a threat to all global citizens. "*Over-armament* multiplies reasons for conflict and increases the danger of escalation" (CCC 2315).
   b. The organization of society directly affects human dignity and human development.
      1. What does the economy do for people?
      2. What does the economy do *to* people?
      3. How are people permitted to participate in it?

E. A summary statement from the United States Bishops on the Life and Dignity of the Human Person:

> In a world warped by materialism and declining respect for human life, the Catholic Church proclaims that human life is sacred and that the dignity of the human person is the foundation of moral vision for society. Our beliefs in the sanctity of human life and the inherent dignity of the human person is the foundation of all the principles of our social teaching. In our society, human life is under attack from abortion and assisted suicide. The value of human life is being threatened by increasing use of the death penalty. The dignity of life is undermined when the creation of human life is reduced to the manufacture of a product, as in human cloning or proposals for genetic experiments to "create perfect human beings." We believe that every person is precious, that people are more important than things, and that the measure of every institution is whether it threatens or embraces the dignity of the human person.

II. The Call to Family, Community, and Participation

A. The human person is not only sacred but also social.
1. The family is the foundational to society and is called "the domestic church" (CCC 1666) because in the family one first lives in community.
2. The family has the right to be supported by the government and other institutions (SCST).
3. Excessive individualism, competition and greed mitigate against community and the common good (SCST).
4. St. Paul gives the image of the Mystical Body of Christ. Christ is the Head. People are members of the Body. When one suffers, all suffer (Eph 4:25).

III. Rights and Responsibilities

A. Each person has the right to all things necessary for their dignity and decency. This includes food, shelter, health care, education, and employment. People have a right to participate in the decision that affect their lives.

B. With every right there is a corresponding duty and responsibility. These are ordered to the common good. All people have a responsibility to uphold the common good. Excessive greed, individualism, and competition mitigate against community and the common good.
1. "By means of society, each man is established as an 'heir' and receives certain 'talents' that enrich his identity and whose fruits he must develop (cf. Lk 19:13, 15). He rightly owes loyalty to the communities of which he is part and respect to those in authority who have charge of the common good" (CCC 1880).

2. Respect for the human person proceeds by way of respect for the principle that everyone should look upon his or her neighbor (with no exceptions) as "another self."
3. Relationships which are just are interdependent. This means they are reciprocal, benefiting both parties. By the very fact all are created by God, all are interdependent because of being children of God. "God, Who has fatherly concern for everyone, has willed that all men should constitute one family" (GS 2 #24).
4. In view of the large number of countries which exists, international brotherhood is a social reality. "Christians should cooperate willingly and wholeheartedly in establishing an international order that includes a genuine respect for all freedoms and amicable brotherhood between all men" (GS 5 #88).

NOTES...

IV. Option for the Poor and Vulnerable

A. "'The Church's love for the poor … is part of her constant tradition.' This love is inspired by the Gospel of the Beatitudes, of the poverty of Jesus, and of his concern for the poor (CA 57; cf. Lk 6:20-22, Mt 8:20; Mk 12:41-44). Love for the poor is even one of the motives for the duty of working so as to 'be able to give to those in need' (Eph 4:28)" (CCC 2444).

1. Consumerism detracts from the call of each Christian to help the poor.
2. St. John Chrysostom profoundly reminds Christians, "'Not to enable the poor to share in our goods is to steal from them and deprive them of life. The goods we possess are not ours, but theirs' (St. John Chrysostom, *Hom. in Lazaro* 2, 5: PG 48, 992)" (CCC 2446).
3. Rich nations have a duty to help poor nations (MM 157).
4. Catholic teaching proclaims that the moral test of a society is how it treats its most vulnerable members (SCST).

V. The Dignity and the Right of Workers

A. Every person has the right to work. "*Unemployment* almost always wounds its victim's dignity and threatens the equilibrium of his life. Besides the harm done to him personally, it entails many risks for his family" (cf. LE 18) (CCC 2436).

B. People have a right to proper working conditions, productive work, and fair wages (SCST).

1. Just wage is the adequate remuneration for work which "'should guarantee man the opportunity to provide a dignified livelihood for himself and his family' (GS 67 § 2)" (CCC 2434).
2. Defrauding "anyone of the wage due him is a great crime that calls down avenging wrath from Heaven" (RN 32).
3. Economy serves the people as opposed to the people serving the economy. "Work is for man, not man for work" (LE 6).
4. Workers are entitled to just working conditions. "Workers are not to be treated as slaves" (RN 31).
5. Workers have a right to form unions which are the mouthpiece for the struggle for social justice (LE 20).
6. Created in the image of God, "man shares by his work in the activity of the Creator" (LE 25).
7. Work is a vocation. There is spirituality to all labor. No matter what type of work man is called to accomplish, "he shows himself to be a disciple of Christ by carrying his cross daily" (LE 27).

NOTES...

VI. Solidarity

Solidarity recognizes the unity that exists between all people. As the Mystical Body, all people, created by God, are bonded by care and concern for one another. There is an innate responsibility for all which crosses the boundaries of race, nationality, cultural and economic differences.

> All must consider it their sacred duty to count social obligations among their chief duties today and observe them as such. For the more closely the world comes together, the more widely do people's obligations transcend particular groups and extend to the whole world. This will be realized only if individuals and groups practice moral and social virtues and foster them in social living.
>
> GS 57

VII. Care for God's Creation

The beauty of God's creation comes as gift. Humanity is given dominion over the earth and all creation (Gn 1:28). All are called to be stewards of the earth, animals, and various creatures. The environment deserves particular consideration more than ever before. Natural resources are important for the continuation of life on earth but are threatened by carelessness and lack of awareness of destructive potential.

Catholic social teaching is at the core of Christian principles. Every Catholic should be aware of the major aspects of social teachings. They are inherent to the life of love to which all are called.

VIII. Church Documents on Catholic Social Teaching

A. Major Encyclicals

1. *Rerum Novarum* (On the Condition of Labor) – Pope Leo XIII, 1891
2. *Quadragesimo Anno* (After Forty Years) – Pope Pius XI, 1931
3. *Mater et Magistra* (Christianity and Social Progress) – Pope John XXIII, 1961
4. *Pacem in Terris* (Peace on Earth) – Pope John XXIII, 1963
5. *Gaudium et Spes* (Pastoral Constitution on the Church in the Modern World) – Vatican II, 1965
6. *Populorum Progressio* (On the Development of Peoples) – Pope Paul VI, 1967
7. *Octogesima Adveniens* (A Call to Action) – Pope Paul VI, 1971
8. *Justicia in Mundo*(Justice in the World) – Synod of Bishops, 1971
9. *Laborem Exercens* (On Human Work) – Pope John Paul II, 1981
10. *Solicitudo Rei Socialis* (On Social Concern) – Pope John Paul II, 1987
11. *Evangelium Vitae* (The Gospel of Life) – Pope John Paul II, 1995
12. *Fides et Ratio* (Faith and Reason) – Pope John Paul II, 1998

B. United States Bishops' Statements

1. *Capital Punishment* – 1980
2. *Economic Justice for All* – 1986
3. *Called to Global Solidarity* – 1997
4. *Living the Gospel of Life: A Challenge to American Catholics* – 1998
5. *Sharing Catholic Social Teaching: Challenges and Directions* – 1998
6. *Catholic Perspective on Crime and Criminal Justice* – 2001
7. *Everyday Christianity: To Hunger and Thirst for Justice* – 2001
8. *Faithful Citizenship: A Catholic Call to Political Responsibility* – 2003

C. *Compendium of Social Doctrine of the Church* – Pontifical Council for Justice and Peace, 2004

NOTES...

FOCUS QUESTIONS

1. Why is the dignity of the human person a central theme of Catholic Social Teaching?
2. Sometimes it is said that the poor have no one to blame but themselves. What arguments can be made for and against this statement?
3. Of the seven themes presented, which aspect of Social Justice is in greatest jeopardy in contemporary life?

Concluding prayer
Intercessions
Closing prayer
Hymn (optional)

RESOURCES

Catechism of the Catholic Church
The Poor and Vulnerable: 1397, 2443-2449
Dignity of Work and Rights of Workers: 2426-2436, 2402-2406
Human Solidarity: 1939-1942
Care for Creation: 373, 1049

Evangelium vitae (The Gospel of Life), John Paul II

Gaudium et Spes (Pastoral Constitution on the Church in the Modern World), Vatican II

Laborem Exercens (On Human Work), John Paul II

Mater et Magistra (On Christianity and social progress), John XXIII

Pacem in Terris (Peace on Earth), John XXIII

Rerum Novarum (On the condition of the working class), Leo XIII

Sharing Catholic Social Teaching: Challenges and Directions, United States Conference of Catholic Bishops

Session Thirty-seven

Sacred Scripture in Catholic Tradition

LEARNING OBJECTIVE

To deepen the understanding of how Catholics interpret and revere the Sacred Scriptures.

Hymn: "The Church's One Foundation"

Invitation to prayer – silent prayer

Oration:

Father,
you gave St. Jerome delight
in his study of holy scripture.
May your people find in your word
the food of salvation and the foundation of life.

We ask this through our Lord Jesus Christ, your Son,
who lives and reigns with you and the Holy Spirit,
one God, for ever and ever.

Opening Prayer
Memorial of St. Jerome

Scripture reading: 2 Thessalonians 2:13-17

But we ought to give thanks to God for you always, brothers loved by the Lord, because God chose you as the firstfruits for salvation through sanctification by the Spirit and belief in truth. To this end he has [also] called you through our gospel to possess the glory of our Lord Jesus Christ. Therefore, brothers, stand firm and hold fast to the traditions that you were taught, either by an oral statement or by a letter of ours.

May our Lord Jesus Christ himself and God our Father, who has loved us and given us everlasting encouragement and good hope through his grace, encourage your hearts and strengthen them in every good deed and word.

TEACHING TO BE PRESENTED

NOTES...

I. The sacred deposit of faith.

A. God's revelation was received by the Apostles, to whom the original deposit of faith (*depositum fidei*) was given (Mt 28:19-20; 1 Thes 2:13; 1 Tm 6:20; CCC 84). They handed on this deposit to others as an authoritative *tradition* — literally, "that which is handed on" (CCC 75-79, 96).

1. Part of this tradition was *oral* — that is, spoken and enacted (CCC 81, 98):
   a. Homilies (preaching) (1 Tm 4:13).
   b. Oral catechesis (instruction) (Acts 10:42; 2 Tm 2:1-2).
   c. Provision of the sacraments (Acts 2:38; 6:6; 8:17; 19:6; 1 Cor 11:23-26; 2 Tm 1:6; Jas 5:14-16; Jn 20:23; Heb 13:4).
   d. Essential elements of the liturgy (Acts 2:42).
   e. Essential administrative structure: bishops, presbyters (priests), deacons (Mt 16:18-19; 1 Tm 3:1-13; 4:17; Acts 6:2-6, 14:23; CCC 1554).
   f. Personal example, modeling moral standards, charity, witness through martyrdom (1 Tm 4:11-12; Acts 7:59-60; 2 Cor 8:1-7).
2. Part of this tradition was *written* and became recognized as Scripture (CCC 81):
   a. Scriptures inherited from the Jewish community, which we call the *Old Testament* (Lk 24:25-27; Acts 17:1-3; 2 Tm 3:16-17).
   b. Scriptures written with apostolic authority, which we call the *New Testament* (2 Cor 13:10; 2 Pt 3:15-16).

B. God's revelation has been preserved across the generations through the *apostolic succession*, by which the Apostles' teaching and preaching is handed on.

1. *Bishops* are the successors of the Apostles (2 Tm 1:6; Ti 1:5; CCC 1555-1556).
2. The *Magisterium* (authoritative teaching office of the Church) is composed of the bishops in communion with the successor of St. Peter, the bishop of Rome, who is the Pope (Mt 16:18-19; CCC 85).

C. How are Scripture, Tradition, and Magisterium related?

1. Sacred Tradition came before the New Testament and gave birth to it; the first Christians, who received the oral tradition of the Apostles, did not yet have a New Testament. "The New Testament itself demonstrates the process of living Tradition" in its creation (CCC 83).
2. Sacred Tradition and Sacred Scripture are inseparable. They have a common source and a common goal; they "'form one thing.'" They "'are bound closely together and communicate one with the other' (DV 9)" (CCC 80).
3. "'Both Scripture and Tradition must be accepted and honored with equal sentiments of devotion and reverence' (DV 9)" (CCC 82; cf. 2 Thes 2:15).
4. Scripture is central to Tradition (2 Tm 3:14-15; CCC 104, 131-132).
5. Not all traditions handed down by Catholics are part of the authoritative, unchanging Sacred Tradition. These varying traditions, though they may be beneficial in expressing the eternal truths of Sacred Tradition through particular forms, may be changed or even discontinued over time under the guidance of the Magisterium (CCC 83).

II. The history of Scripture.

A. The Old Testament.

1. The oldest textual material in Scripture began as oral traditions thousands of years ago, passed down through the generations.

NOTES...

2. These traditions were eventually written down, collected, selected, and edited, along with later traditions, to create the scriptural texts we now have in the Old Testament.
3. These texts, written in ancient Hebrew, Aramaic, and Greek, were included in the *Septuagint,* an ancient Greek version of the Old Testament with 46 books used by early Christians, which was accepted as a part of Scripture by the ancient Church.

B. The New Testament.

1. The New Testament books were written after Christ's Ascension, which took place about A.D. 29 or 30. Its earliest books, some of St. Paul's letters, were composed around A.D. 50; the latest writings were probably completed in the early years of the second century.
2. The *Gospels* were formed in three stages (CCC 126):
   a. The *life and teaching of Jesus* provide the basis of the Gospels.
   b. After Christ's Ascension, the Apostles handed on an *oral tradition* about the things Jesus had said and done, "'but with that fuller understanding which they, instructed by the glorious events of Christ and enlightened by the Spirit of truth, now enjoyed' (DV 19)" (CCC 126).
   c. The four evangelists composed the *written Gospels,* which they crafted from both oral and written elements of the Sacred Tradition handed on by the Apostles. They "'synthesized or explained [these elements] with an eye to the situation of the churches' (DV 19)" (CCC 126). Their reasons for writing down elements of the apostolic oral tradition:
      1. Jesus did not return right away as they had expected, and the eyewitnesses to His life and teaching were dying off.
      2. New converts could receive instruction in written as well as oral form.
      3. False teachings were being circulated and needed to be corrected.
3. The *Book of Acts* was originally part of a longer work that also included the Gospel of Luke.
4. The *Epistles* were letters written by St. Paul and other early Church leaders to teach and counsel Christians; some were addressed to particular local churches, while others were intended for a more general Christian audience. Even the letters addressed to a particular church, however, came to be circulated to other churches and read publicly.
5. The *Book of Revelation* is one of the later New Testament texts, reflecting the Church's situation under persecution, and offering hope as similar Old Testament texts had done for the ancient Jews.
6. Taken together, the New Testament books contain material reflecting the apostolic oral tradition (both spoken and enacted) in all its various forms: preaching and instruction, sacraments and liturgy, and organizational structures and personal example.

III. The canon of Scripture.

A. The Church discerned, by the apostolic Tradition, which writings were to be included in the list of sacred books, called the scriptural *canon* (literally, "measuring rod," the standard by which teaching is measured).

B. The Church accepted into the canon as the *Old Testament* the sacred books of the Jewish community:

1. The Law (in Hebrew, *Torah;* also called the Pentateuch): Genesis, Exodus, Leviticus, Numbers, and Deuteronomy. These books contain not only laws of

the ancient Jewish people, but also numerous ancient stories about various subjects: the creation of the world, characters and events of the distant past, and the beginnings of the ancient Jewish people and their liberation from slavery in Egypt.

2. The prophets: books such as Isaiah, Jeremiah, Joel, and Malachi that offer divine warnings of chastisement and promises of redemption and hope; divided into the *major* prophets (longer prophetic works) and *minor* prophets (shorter prophetic works).
3. Other writings:
   a. The historical books, such 1 and 2 Chronicles, Ezra, and 1 and 2 Maccabees, which tell about events in the life of ancient Israel.
   b. The wisdom books, such as Proverbs, Ecclesiastes and Sirach, which are collections of reflections on life and how it should be lived.
   c. The Psalms, the "prayer book" of the ancient Jewish people.

C. The Church accepted into the canon as the *New Testament* certain books written with apostolic authority in the early years of the Church:
   1. The four *Gospels* (Matthew, Mark, Luke, and John) "are the heart of all the Scriptures 'because they are our principal source for the life and teaching' (DV 18)" of Jesus (CCC 125).
   2. The *Book of Acts* tells about the birth and early days of the Church at Jerusalem and nearby places after Jesus' Ascension, as well as the missionary travels of St. Paul.
   3. The *Epistles* are letters that were written to early Christians by St. Paul and other early Church leaders, such as Romans, 1 and 2 Timothy, Hebrews, and Jude.
   4. The *Book of Revelation* belongs to a type of literature known as *apocalyptic,* written in highly dramatic and symbolic language, which encourages believers suffering persecution and gives them hope in God's final triumph over evil. (Certain Old Testament books, such as Daniel, also contain apocalyptic passages.)

D. The Old and New Testaments display a deep inner unity: "All sacred Scripture is but one book, and this one book is Christ" (CCC 134; see also CCC 128-130). As St. Augustine explained, "In the Old Testament, the New Testament is concealed. In the New Testament, the Old Testament is revealed."

E. Why was a scriptural canon necessary?
   1. The divine inspiration and authority of some scriptural books received within the apostolic Tradition (such as the Old Testament texts) were being challenged in the early centuries by heretical teachers such as Marcion. The Church had to affirm these challenged books.
   2. In some local churches in the early centuries there were doubts about the inspiration of a few books that were part of the apostolic deposit of faith. The Church had to affirm these books as well (examples: Hebrews, Jude, 3 John).
   3. Heretical teachers (usually Gnostic) were claiming that certain texts, which contradicted the teaching of the apostolic Tradition, were divinely inspired as Scripture, handed down by a "secret" apostolic tradition. The Church had to reject these books (examples: Gospel of Thomas, Gospel of Truth, Gospel of Mary).
   4. In the liturgy of some of the local churches, alongside the books that belonged to the apostolic deposit of faith, there were other books being read, which contained sound teaching but were nevertheless not part of that deposit (examples: Shepherd of Hermas, Epistle of Barnabas). The canon distinguished

NOTES...

NOTES...

between these two types of books to clarify that the others did not have the same authority as Scripture.

F. What were the Church's criteria for accepting a book into the scriptural canon?

1. Was it of apostolic origin? That is, was it connected with an Apostle or an associate of an Apostle?
2. Did it accord with the rule of faith? That is, was it in keeping with what the Church knew to be true by means of the (oral) Sacred Tradition?
3. Was it widely accepted and in use throughout the Church in many places, or was its acceptance and use limited?

G. When did the Church formally recognize the scriptural canon?

1. The oldest surviving list of New Testament books that is exactly the same as the canon we have today comes from St. Athanasius, bishop of Alexandria, in A.D. 367.
2. Pope St. Damasus presided over a regional council, probably held in Rome, in A.D. 382, which issued a complete list of both Old and New Testament books as we know them in the canon today.
3. Martin Luther and some other leaders of the Protestant movement challenged the Church's inclusion of several Old and New Testament books in the canon. The Catholic Church responded in 1546 when the Council of Trent (a general council) formally defined the canon as we know it today. Most Protestants eventually came to accept the New Testament canon as the Catholic Church had defined it, but they refused to recognize the full Old Testament canon.

IV. The study of Scripture.

A. Why should we study Scripture?

1. Our loving Creator and Father speaks to us in Scripture, so we should listen to what He says there. "'*Sacred Scripture* is the speech of God as it is put down in writing under the breath of the Holy Spirit' (DV 9)'" (CCC 81; cf. CCC 104, 135; Dt 5:27; Ps 85:8; Jn 14:10; 1 Thes 1:13; 2 Tm 3:16).
2. Inspired by God, Scripture is trustworthy; we can rely on it to teach us "'firmly, faithfully and without error … that truth which God, for the sake of our salvation, wished to see confided to the Sacred Scriptures' (DV 11)" (CCC 107).
3. In Scripture, God tells us about *Himself.*
   a. It shows us how He has revealed Himself in His dealings with humankind throughout the ages — what we call *salvation history* (Pss 78, 105, 106, 136; Acts 7:2-53).
   b. It leads us to Jesus Christ, the God-man who reveals to us most fully and perfectly who God truly is (Lk 24:25-27; Jn 5:39; Col 1:19, 2:9; CCC 133, 134). "'Ignorance of the Scriptures is ignorance of Christ' (DV 25; cf. St. Jerome, *Commentariorum in Isaiam libri xviii* prol.: PL 24, 17b)" (CCC 133).
4. In Scripture, God tells us who *we* are.
   a. It shows us that God has created us for Himself in love (Gn 1:27; Ps 139:13-18; Jas 1:18; Rv 4:11).
   b. It shows us that we are fallen creatures in need of the healing and salvation God offers us in Jesus Christ (Ps 51; Rom 3:21-26; 8:31-39; 1 Cor 15:22; Eph 4:22-24; Col 1:11-14).
   c. It shows us the destiny God intends for us in Christ — what we were created to be (Eph 2:10; 1 Jn 3:2-3; 1 Cor 15:22-28; 51-57; 2 Cor 5:17).

NOTES...

5. In Scripture, God tells us *how to live* in accordance with the truth about who He is and who we are.
   a. It guides us in our thoughts, behaviors, and attitudes (Ps 119; Jn 17:17; 2 Tm 3:16-17).
   b. It draws us into communion with Christ (2 Tm 3:14-15; Jn 5:24; 14:21, 23).
   c. It nourishes our faith, hope, and love so that we become more like God and can live with Him in joy forever (Rom 10:17; 15:4; Jn 15:10; CCC 104, 131).
6. For all these reasons, "the Church 'forcefully and specifically exhorts all the Christian faithful … to learn "the surpassing knowledge of Jesus Christ," by frequent reading of the divine Scriptures' (DV 25; cf. Phil 3:8)" (CCC 133).

B. How is Scripture to be interpreted?

1. The Magisterium has been given by God the task of authentic and authoritative interpretation of both Scripture and Tradition (Acts 15:12-21; CCC 85).
   a. In this task the Magisterium is not superior to the Word of God received in the deposit of faith, but is its servant (Acts 26:16-18; 1 Tm 4:6; CCC 86).
   b. Catholics should receive such guidance with confidence so that they are in harmony with the whole Church in interpreting Scripture (Heb 13:17; CCC 85, 87).
2. "In Sacred Scripture, God speaks to man in a human way. To interpret Scripture correctly, the reader must be attentive to what the human authors truly wanted to affirm and to what God wanted to reveal to us by their words" (cf. DV 12 § 1) (CCC 109).
   a. To discover the intention of the human authors, the reader must take the following into account (CCC 110):
      1. The conditions of their particular historical setting (geography, culture, society, language, politics, science, technology, and so on).
      2. The literary genres (types of literature) in use at that time (history, poetry, prophecy, and so on).
      3. The modes of speaking, feeling, and narrating events that were current at that time.
   b. For the reader to discover what God wants to reveal by the words of the human authors, "'Sacred Scripture must be read and interpreted in the light of the same [Holy] Spirit by whom it was written' (DV 12 § 3)" (CCC 111). Three criteria must be employed for interpretation in accordance with the Spirit (CCC 111; cf. DV 12 § 4):
      1. When interpreting any particular passage, the reader must be "*attentive 'to the content and unity of the whole Scripture*'" (CCC 112), keeping in mind the larger context of the passage to assure an interpretation that is in harmony with the rest of Scripture (2 Pt 1:20-21).
      2. Scripture must be interpreted "within '*the living Tradition of the whole Church*'" (CCC 113), not in isolation from this wider Tradition or in opposition to it (Acts 7:27-31; 2 Thes 2:15).
      3. Scripture must be interpreted according to the "*analogy of faith* (cf. Rom 12:6)" — that is, in harmony with "the coherence of the truths of faith among themselves and within the whole plan of Revelation" (CCC 114).

NOTES...

3. The interpretation of a scriptural passage is not necessarily limited to one meaning. Readers should keep in mind the traditional *four senses* of Scripture (CCC 115-119):
   a. The *literal* sense: the literal meaning of the text as intended by the human author. The literal sense is the foundation of all the other senses.
   b. The *spiritual* sense, which includes:
      1. The *allegorical* sense: a symbolic sense, in which the literal sense serves as a sign to point toward a greater significance in Christ.
      2. The *moral* sense, which leads us to do the right thing (to act justly).
      3. The *anagogical* sense, which points toward eternal realities, leading us toward our true home with God in heaven.
      4. As a commonly cited example of the four senses, consider the Old Testament references to Jerusalem (such as Ps 122:2, 3, 6). The literal sense of the word is the ancient city of Jerusalem, capital of the Jewish nation. The allegorical sense refers to the Church, the "Jerusalem [who] ... is our mother" (Gal 4:26). The moral sense of the verse exhorting us to pray "for the peace of Jerusalem" (Ps 122:6) tells us it is right to pray for the peace of the Church. The anagogical sense refers to heaven, or "the heavenly Jerusalem" (Heb 12:22; see also Rv 3:12; 21:2, 10).
      5. The interpretations of individuals must be subject to the final "'judgment of the Church which exercises the divinely conferred commission and ministry of watching over and interpreting the Word of God' (DV 12 § 3)" (CCC 119).

FOCUS QUESTIONS

1. How can the Bible assist in discussions with non-Catholics in light of how to understand oral tradition?
2. What are the major differences between Catholic and Protestant Bibles?
3. Have we let God's revelation challenge us to be active in our proclamation of the Gospel through living our faith?

Concluding prayers
Intercessions
Closing prayer
Hymn (optional)

RESOURCES

The Biblical Basis for the Catholic Faith
Catechism of the Catholic Church, 105-117
Dei Verbum (Dogmatic Constitution on Divine Revelation), Vatican II
Dictionary of the Bible
Dictionary of Biblical Theology, 2nd Edition
How to Read the New Testament
How to Read the Old Testament
The New Catholic Answer Bible
Where We Got the Bible: Our Debt to the Catholic Church

Session Thirty-eight

Ecumenism

LEARNING OBJECTIVE

To present the Catholic teaching on Ecumenism and our desire for Christian unity with the Orthodox and the Christian denominations of the West.

Hymn: "One Bread, One Body"

Oration:

Almighty and Eternal God,
you keep together those you have united.
Look kindly on those who follow Jesus your Son.
We are all consecrated to you by our common baptism;
make us one in the fullness of faith
and keep us one in the fellowship of love.

We ask this through our Lord Jesus Christ, your Son,
who lives and reigns with you and the Holy Spirit,
one God, for ever and ever.

Opening Prayer
Mass for Unity of Christians

Scripture reading: John 17:17-23

"Consecrate them in the truth. Your word is truth. As you sent me into the world, so I sent them into the world. And I consecrate myself for them, so that they also may be consecrated in truth.

"I pray not only for them, but also for those who will believe in me through their word, so that they may all be one, as you, Father, are in me and I in you, that they also may be in us, that the world may believe that you sent me. And I have given them the glory you gave me, so that they may be one, as we are one, I in them and you in me, that they may be brought to perfection as one, that the world may know that you sent me, and that you loved them even as you loved me."

TEACHING TO BE PRESENTED

I. The unity of all divided humanity is the will of God.

II. Ecumenism and the ecumenical movement.

A. The desire to recover the unity of all Christians is a gift of Christ and a call of the Holy Spirit.

NOTES...

1. The Ecumenical movement is made up of those who believe in the Triune God and profess Jesus as Lord and Savior.
2. This movement is fostered by the grace of the Holy Spirit and seeks to heal the division of unity which so openly contradicts the will of Christ, scandalizes the world, and damages that most holy cause, the preaching of the Gospel to everyone (UR 1).

B. The Church's mission is "to gather all people and all things into Christ, so as to be for all an 'inseparable sacrament of unity'" (UUS 5).

1. Christ established the Church on earth and entrusted it to the Apostles and their successors to preach the Gospel faithfully, administer the sacraments, and rule the Church in love (UR 2).
3. Jesus Christ wishes his people to increase, under the action of the Holy Spirit; and he perfects its fellowship in unity: in the confession of one faith; in the common celebration of divine worship, and in the "fraternal harmony of the family of God" (UR 2).
4. From the beginning there arose rifts to this unity which the Apostles condemned (1 Cor. 11:18-19; Gal 1:6-9; 1 Jn 2: 18-19; 1 Cor. 1:11).
5. "But in subsequent centuries much more serious dissensions appeared and large communities became separated from full communion with the Catholic Church, for which, often enough, men of both sides were to blame" (UR 3).

C. Those who are born into these communities of separated brothers and sisters cannot be charged with the sin of separation. "For men who believe in Christ and have been properly baptized have been put in some, though imperfect, communion with the Catholic Church....they have a right to be called Christians...and to be accepted as brothers" (UR 3).

D. Many elements of the Catholic Church exist outside her visible boundaries. These include the Word, grace, faith, hope, charity, and the gifts of the Holy Spirit. "Nevertheless,... they are not blessed with the unity that Christ wished to bestow on all those to whom he has given new birth into one body....For it is through Christ's Catholic Church alone, which is the universal help towards salvation, that the fullness of the means of salvation can be obtained. It was to the apostolic college alone, of which Peter is the head, that we believe that our Lord entrusted all the blessings of the New Covenant, in order to establish on earth, the one Body of Christ into which all those should be fully incorporated who belong in any way to the people of God" (UR 3).

E. Christian unity is promoted by "avoiding expressions, judgments and actions which do not represent the condition of our separated brethren with truth and fairness and so make mutual relations with them more difficult" (UR 4).

F. Common prayer holds a primacy of place in the Ecumenical movement. It is the soul of the Ecumenical movement. "Even when prayer is not specifically offered for Christian unity, but for other intentions such as peace, it actually becomes an expression and confirmation of unity. The common prayer of Christians is an invitation to Christ himself to visit the community of those who call upon him; 'Where two or three are gathered in my name, there am I in the midst of them'(Mt 18:20)" (UUS 21).

G. There must be dialogue between experts of the different Churches, cooperation between the communities in carrying out the duties of Christian life, common prayer, and an examination of conscience (UR 4). Common worship is not to be seen as an ordinary means to unity (UR 8).

H. Catholics, clergy and laity, must pray for their separated brothers and sisters, approach them first, and renew the Catholic Church, "in order that its life may bear witness more clearly and faithfully to the teachings and institutions which have been handed down from Christ through the Apostles" (UR 4). "The faithful should remember that they promote union among Christians better, that indeed they live it better, when they try to live holier lives according to the Gospel" (UR 7).

I. "It is essential that (Catholic) doctrine be presented in its entirety. Nothing is so foreign to the spirit of ecumenism as a false irenicism [the promotion of peace and conciliation among individuals and churches, in matters of theological dispute, with an emphasis on theological agreement and convergence rather than on divisive issues] which harms the purity of Catholic doctrine and obscures its genuine and certain meaning. At the same time, Catholic belief must be explained more profoundly and precisely, in such a way and in such terms that our separated brethren can also really understand it. Furthermore, in ecumenical dialogue, Catholic theologians, standing fast by the teachings of the Church yet searching together with separated brethren into the divine mysteries, should do so with love for the truth, with charity, and with humility." (UR 11)

NOTES...

III. Stumbling blocks to unity.

A. In addition to doctrinal differences, "Christians cannot underestimate the burden of long-standing misgivings inherited from the past, and of mutual misunderstandings and prejudices. Complacency, indifference and insufficient knowledge of one another often make the situation worse" (UUS 2).

IV. The special position of the Eastern Churches (Orthodox).

A. "The Catholic Church desires nothing less than full communion between East and West" (UUS 61).
   1. In the East, there are many Churches which take their origins from the Apostles. The liturgy and spiritual traditions of the East have helped shape those of the West. The dogmas on the Trinity and the Incarnation were defined by Ecumenical Councils held in the East (UR 14).
   2. "However, the heritage handed down by the apostles was received differently and in different forms, so that from the very beginning of the Church its development varied from region to region and also because of differing mentalities and ways of life. These reasons, plus external causes, as well as a lack of charity and mutual understanding, left the way open to divisions" (UR 14).
      a. Although we have become separated, the Churches of the East, "possess true sacraments, above all — by apostolic succession — the priesthood and the Eucharist, whereby they are still joined to us in closest intimacy. Therefore some worship in common, given suitable circumstances and the approval of Church authority, is not merely possible but encouraged" (UR 15).
      b. "From the earliest times the Churches of the East followed their own disciplines, sanctioned by the holy Fathers, by Synods, and even by ecumenical Councils. Far from being an obstacle to the Church's unity, such diversity of customs and observances only adds to her beauty and contributes greatly to carrying out her mission...." (UR 16).
      c. "In order to restore communion and unity or preserve them [with the Churches of the East]. One must 'impose no burden beyond what is indispensable'" (UR 18).

NOTES...

V. The Separated Churches and Ecclesial Communities in the West.

A. Between the Separated Churches themselves and the Catholic Church there exist "very weighty differences not only of a historical, sociological, psychological and cultural character, but especially in the interpretation of revealed truth" (UR 19).

B. "But we rejoice that our separated brethren look to Christ as the source and center of ecclesiastical communion. There longing for communion with Christ impels them evermore to seek unity, and also to bear witness to there faith among the peoples of the earth" (UR 20).

C. They have great love and reverence for Holy Scripture and recognize its divine authority. "They think differently from us – different ones in different ways – about the relationship between the scriptures and the Church. For in the Church, according to the Catholic belief, its authentic teaching office has a special place in expounding and preaching the written Word of God. Nevertheless, in the dialogue itself, the sacred Word is a precious instrument in the mighty hand of God for attaining to that unity which the Savior holds out to all men" (UR 21).

D. Baptism incorporates man into the life of Christ and allows him to become a partaker in the divine life. "Baptism, therefore, constitutes the sacramental bond of unity existing among all who through it are reborn. But baptism, of itself, is only a beginning, a point of departure, for it is wholly directed toward the acquiring of fullness of life in Christ. Baptism is thus ordained toward a complete profession of faith, a complete incorporation into the system of salvation such as Christ himself willed it to be, and finally, toward a complete integration into eucharistic communion" (UR 22).

E. "Although the ecclesial communities separated from us lack the fullness of unity with us which flows from baptism, and although we believe that they have not preserved the proper reality of the eucharistic mystery in its fullness, especially because of the absence of the sacrament of Orders, nevertheless when they commemorate the Lord's death and resurrection in the Holy Supper, they profess that it signifies life in communion with Christ and await his coming in glory. For these reasons, the doctrine about the Lord's Supper, and the other sacraments, worship and ministry in the Church, should form subjects of dialogue" (UR 22).

FOCUS QUESTIONS

1. What do you feel is the most effective tool in the ecumenical movement?
2. Why is it important that the Church apologize for the times in her history that some of her members have not dealt fairly with others?
3. Why is it important that the teachings of the Church are presented in a full and complete manner?

Concluding prayers
Intercessions
Closing prayer
Hymn (optional)

RESOURCES

Unitatis redintegratio (Decree on Ecumenism), Vatican II
Ut Unum Sint (On Commitment to Ecumenism), John Paul II

NOTES...

Session Thirty-nine

The Catholic Church's Relations to Non-Christians and the Missionary Mandate

LEARNING OBJECTIVE

To present the Catholic teaching on the Church's relationship to non-Christians, especially the Muslims and the Jewish people, and an understanding of the missionary mandate.

Hymn: "Where Charity and Love Prevail"

Oration:

God our Loving Father, we pray that every person throughout the world comes to know and love your Son, Jesus Christ, as Savior and Redeemer. May they feel his love and imitate his mercy. Lead those who, through no fault of their own, are ignorant of the Gospel. Grant this through Christ, Our Lord, one God forever and ever.

Scripture reading: Romans 11:16-24

If the firstfruits are holy, so is the whole batch of dough; and if the root is holy, so are the branches.

But if some of the branches were broken off, and you, a wild olive shoot, were grafted in their place and have come to share in the rich root of the olive tree, do not boast against the branches. If you do boast, consider that you do not support the root; the root supports you. Indeed you will say, "Branches were broken off so that I might be grafted in." That is so. They were broken off because of unbelief, but you are there because of faith. So do not become haughty, but stand in awe. For if God did not spare the natural branches, [perhaps] he will not spare you either. See, then, the kindness and severity of God: severity toward those who fell, but God's kindness to you, provided you remain in his kindness; otherwise you too will be cut off. And they also, if they do not remain in unbelief, will be grafted in, for God is able to graft them in again. For if you were cut from what is by nature a wild olive tree, and grafted, contrary to nature, into a cultivated one, how much more will they who belong to it by nature be grafted back into their own olive tree.

TEACHING TO BE PRESENTED

I. **The Church has a duty to promote unity among individuals and nations.**

  A. All men form but one community.
    1. All stem from the one stock God created to people the entire earth (NA 1).
    2. All share a common destiny, namely God (NA 1).

  B. "Men look to their different religions for an answer to the unsolved riddles of human existence" (NA 1).

1. What is the purpose of life?
2. What is man?
3. How does one find happiness?
4. What follows death? (NA 1)

C. "Throughout history there has been an "awareness of a hidden power, which lies behind the course of nature and the events of human life" (NA 2).
1. A supreme being
2. A Father
3. Philosophy
4. Meditation
5. Moral precepts
5. Sacred rites (NA 2)

D. "The Catholic Church rejects nothing of what is true and holy in these religions" (NA 2).
1. "Yet she proclaims and is duty bound to proclaim without fail, Christ who is the way, the truth and the life (Jn 14:6). In him, in whom God reconciled all things to himself (cf. 2 Cor 5:18-19), men find the fullness of their religious life" (NA 2).
2. The Church urges us to enter into dialogue with non-Christians, never forgetting the importance of charity and witness (NA 2).

E. The Church has high regard for the Muslims (NA 3):
1. They worship the one God.
2. They profess to hold the faith of Abraham.
3. They venerate Jesus as a prophet.
4. They have high regard for Mary.
5. They believe in the resurrection of the dead.
6. They honor an upright life.
7. They esteem prayer, fasting and almsgiving.

F. The Church recognizes her own ties to the people of the Old Covenant, the Jews (NA 4). The Jewish faith, unlike other non-Christian religions, is already a response to God's revelation in the Old Covenant (CCC 839).
1. Although the Church is the new people of God, "the gifts and the call of God" to the people of the Old Covenant "are irrevocable" (Rom 11:29).
2. God's plan of salvation began with the patriarchs, Moses, and the prophets.
3. Christ made Jews and Gentiles one in himself (cf. Eph 2: 14-16).
4. The Apostles were of Jewish descent.

G. "Even though the Jewish authorities and those who followed their lead pressed for the death of Christ, neither all Jews indiscriminately at the time, nor Jews today, can be charged with the crimes committed during his passion" (NA 4).
1. Jews are not rejected or accursed.
2. The Church rejects all forms of discrimination and anti-Semitism.
3. Christ underwent His passion and death freely because of the sins of all people.

II. The missionary mandate of the Church.

A. The obligation to proclaim the faith comes from Christ.
1. "Go, therefore, and make disciples of all nations, baptizing them in the name of the Father, and of the Son, and of the holy Spirit, teaching them to observe all that I have commanded you" (Mt 28:19-20).

NOTES...

2. "Go into the whole world and proclaim the gospel to every creature. Whoever believes and is baptized will be saved; whoever does not believe will be condemned" (Mk16:15-16).
3. "He appointed twelve [whom he also named apostles] that they might be with him and he might send them forth to preach" (Mk 3:14).

B. The Church on earth is by its very nature missionary.

1. "...according to the plan of the Father, it has its origin in the mission of the Son and the Holy Spirit ... God graciously calls us to share in his life and glory" (AGD 2).
2. God sent his Son into the world to save men from the power of darkness and sin ... to give his life as ransom for all ... to save what was lost (AGD 3).
3. "But you will receive power when the holy Spirit comes upon you, and you will be my witnesses in Jerusalem, throughout Judea and Samaria, and to the ends of the earth" (Acts 1:8).

C. The mission of the Church is the mission of Christ.

1. The Church, "urged on by the Spirit of Christ, must walk the road Christ himself walked, a way of poverty and obedience, of service and self-sacrifice even to death..."(AGD 5).
2. Christ asserted the necessity of faith and baptism. "Hence those cannot be saved, knowing that the Catholic Church was founded through Jesus Christ, by God, as something necessary, still refuse to enter it, or to remain in it" (AGD 7).
3. "So, although in ways known to himself God can lead those who, through no fault of their own, are ignorant of the Gospel to that faith without which it is impossible to please him, the Church, nevertheless, still has the obligation and also the sacred right to evangelize" (AGD 7).

FOCUS QUESTIONS

1. What does the Church believe in common with the Muslims?
2. "In respect to the gospel, they are enemies on your account; but in respect to election, they are beloved because of the patriarchs. For the gifts and the call of God are irrevocable"(Rom 11: 28-29). How does this passage from Scripture reflect the Church's understanding of God's plan for the Jewish people?
3. Explain this sentence: "The most loving thing I can do for others is bring them to the Catholic Church."

Concluding prayers
Intercessions
Closing prayer
Hymn (optional)

RESOURCES

Catechism of the Catholic Church, 759-762, 839-856

Nostra aetate (Declaration on the Relationship of the Church to Non-Christian Religions), Vatican II

Ad gentes divinitus (Decree on the Church's Missionary Activity), Vatican II

Session Forty

Stewardship

LEARNING OBJECTIVE

To examine the Christian meaning of stewardship as a way of life. God, Creator of all, entrusts to each person the responsibility to share the goods received.

Hymn: "Will You Let Me Be Your Servant"

Invitation to prayer – silent prayer

Oration:

Lord God,
you have enriched all people
with the many gifts of your creation.
In imitation of your Son,
Jesus Christ,
teach us how to be generous,
inspire us to be disciples
and stewards
living with joy and gratitude
for your greater honor and glory.

Scripture reading: Matthew 25:14-30

"It will be as when a man who was going on a journey called in his servants and entrusted his possessions to them. To one he gave five talents; to another, two; to a third, one – to each according to his ability. Then he went away. Immediately the one who received five talents went and traded with them, and made another five. Likewise, the one who received two made another two. But the man who received one went off and dug a hole in the ground and buried his master's money. After a long time the master of those servants came back and settled accounts with them. The one who had received five talents came forward bringing the additional five. He said, 'Master, you gave me five talents. See, I have made five more.' His master said to him, 'Well done, my good and faithful servant. Since you were faithful in small matters, I will give you great responsibilities. Come, share your master's joy.' [Then] the one who had received two talents also came forward and said, 'Master, you gave me two talents. See, I have made two more.' His master said to him, 'Well done, my good and faithful servant. Since you were faithful in small matters, I will give you great responsibilities. Come, share your master's joy.' Then the one who had received the one talent came forward and said, 'Master, I knew you were a demanding person, harvesting where you did not plant and gathering where you did not scatter; so out of fear I went off and buried your talent in the ground. Here it is back.' His master said to him in reply, 'You wicked, lazy servant! So you knew that I harvest where I did not plant and gather where I did not

NOTES...

scatter? Should you not then have put my money in the bank so that I could have got it back with interest on my return? Now then! Take the talent from him and give it to the one with ten. For to everyone who has, more will be given and he will grow rich; but from the one who has not, even what he has will be taken away. And throw this useless servant into the darkness outside, where there will be wailing and grinding of teeth."

TEACHING TO BE PRESENTED

I. A trusting relationship – stewardship.

A. Stewardship is a fairly new term in the vocabulary of the modern American Catholic. The term, and concept, of stewardship is older than Christianity itself — dating back to the creation of the world in the Book of Genesis. God is the source of all things and God gives His creation to human beings, who are made in His image and likeness. God's people are not made to be passive recipients, merely accepting and consuming God's gifts. To take these gifts for granted is an extreme misinterpretation of a relationship with a loving Father. To be like God is to share the gifts of His creation, just as God shares.

1. Stewardship defines our relationship with our Creator. Stewardship is an invitation to each person to draw closer to God with a prayerful response, asking: "What does God want to do through me?" The focus of stewardship is on the Giver — our loving Father — not on the gifts.
2. The English word "steward" comes from the Anglo-Saxon words "stig" or "stye," meaning an enclosure or a hall, and "wéord," which means keeper. A steward is a stye-keeper. A steward is a person in charge of property or affairs of another person, who is the true owner. A steward also often acts as a supervisor, an administrator of finances and property on behalf of the owner of the property.
3. The Greek and Hebrew equivalence express similar ideas. The term Jesus used for "steward" is "*oikonomos,*" naming the person in charge of the household. In the Greco-Roman world, this included more than 100 slaves who engaged in family services and the family's business ventures. The *oikonomos* was most often a slave to whom the master of the household had entrusted the management of his possessions. The Hebrew term "*ben bieth*" literally translates as "son of the house." The term could mean son or steward, which would be a trusted slave, set by the master over the household.
4. The English, Greek, and Hebrew definition for steward clarifies that the word indicates more about relationship than it does about who manages the property. The relationship is one of trust. A steward must be a person of trust.
5. In Matthew 25:14-30, Jesus tells a story of a man entrusting an amount of money to three servants. In each case, the amount transferred corresponds to the individual's ability. Two of the servants realize that the master is showing them trust by asking them to take care of the sum of money. They accept the responsibility of stewardship and the risk that goes with it. They use initiative, their talents and abilities and manage to double what was entrusted to them. When they gave an account of their stewardship, they were praised and rewarded. The third man misjudged the master; he did not know the intent of

the master, nor did he seek to know his will. For him, the handing over of the money was not a sign of trust, but a trap to get him into trouble. He refused to use his gifts and abilities; he simply ensured that he could return the money in the end. Instead of praise, he stands condemned at the time of reckoning. Jesus' parable adds a valuable insight that stewardship involves hard work and effort and taking appropriate risks courageously. Fear is the great enemy of being a good steward. Fear is the opposite of faith. Throughout the Scriptures, we are commanded to "be not afraid" and to "fear not." Fear draws attention away from acting upon the intentions of the True Owner; faith steadies the focus on the Master.

B. The fundamental character traits of a steward are integrity and trustworthiness. A steward manages the owner's property. The steward needs to be faithful to the owner, and he or she must act according to the owner's intention. God is the owner of the entire world and all people are his faithful stewards. They must act according to his intention.

1. A steward can be faithful only if he or she knows the mind of the owner since the steward's authority is delegated; he or she is accountable to the owner for its exercise.
2. Stewardship is a matter of the heart, not about money or possessions or even skills and talents. It is about the trusting relationship between the owner and the steward.
3. No person truly owns anything. At the time of death, this reality will be obvious. Some people have more responsibility than others. If people are to be great, they must take on Jesus' mind and attitude and follow his actions of service. Jesus said he did not come to be served, but to serve.
4. Stewards should not be afraid to seek the intentions of the true owner and to give all their effort in living His will. In the end they will be overjoyed to hear, "Well done, my good and faithful servant."

II. Disciple — a follower of Jesus.

A. A Christian steward and the title "disciple" are one in the same.

1. Both titles describe an individual who applies the Gospel to his or her life and who recognizes that every moment of life is a call to draw closer to God.
2. Jesus is the ultimate example of a Christian steward. Jesus lived a life one with the Father, living and acting upon the Father's Will moment to moment. Christian stewards are called to collaborate with God in His work of creation and re-creation throughout all of history.
3. To be like God is to be like Jesus — Christ-like. Jesus spent His entire earthly existence reliant on the Father and seeking to do the will of the Father.

B. Stewardship is an invitation. God is the Creator and Giver of all gifts. As caretakers, "the stewards," care for God's gifts.

1. A good steward is always asking, "What would God have me do?"
2. Those who give of themselves to the building of God's kingdom, to the life and mission of the Church, are "disciples of Jesus." Being a disciple of Jesus means that we respond to the call of Jesus to follow His examples and teachings. His way of life becomes our way of life.
3. Stewardship constitutes a way of life that is both privileged and challenging. Becoming a disciple of Jesus leads naturally to a life of stewardship and results in intense joy.

NOTES...

NOTES...

4. As good stewards, one takes on the mission of Jesus by placing their resources of time, talent, and treasure at the disposal of God. The gifts that one receives are not to be used solely for personal benefit; rather they are to be used for God's glory. All are invited to share a portion of the gifts they receive in the building of God's kingdom through our community of faith, starting with family — the domestic church — the parish, the diocese, and the universal Church. Participation in the life of the parish and diocese is necessary for spiritual growth, since it brings each person shares in the mission of Jesus.
5. Sharing gifts with others is giving back to God rather than giving away. All that one has is on loan from God.

III. The U.S. Bishops' pastoral letter on stewardship.

A. The American Bishops communicated this understanding of stewardship in their 1993 pastoral letter *Stewardship: A Disciple's Response*. "The life of a Christian steward models the life of Jesus. It is challenging and even difficult, in many respects, yet intense joy comes to those who take the risk to live as Christian stewards." There is a fundamental obligation that originates from the Sacrament of Baptism. The U.S. Bishops point out that Jesus' self-emptying is unique. It is within the power of disciples and a duty that they imitate Christ in self-emptying love.

B. The U.S. Bishops' Pastoral Letter poses the question, "Who is a Christian steward?" They provide four characteristics that describe a Christian steward.

1. The first characteristic of a Christian steward is one who lives with gratitude. A Christian steward is "one who receives God's gifts gratefully." Gratitude acknowledges God as the Giver of all gifts. A profound sense of gratitude to God provides a true perspective of reliance on God — children of God and Disciples of Christ.
2. The second characteristic of a Christian steward is one who lives with accountability. A good steward is "one who cherishes and tends God's gifts in a responsible and accountable manner." A true disciple knows that he or she will be held accountable for how all God's gifts have been managed or used.
3. The third characteristic of a good steward is one who lives with generosity. The Bishops describe a Christian steward as "one who generously shares God's gifts with others out of a profound sense of justice and love." Generosity may be the most powerful attribute of Christian stewards because it impels them to live outside of themselves — often in ways that seem to contradict their own interests.
4. The fourth characteristic of a Christian steward is one who gives back to the Lord with increase. Jesus' parable about the stewards makes it clear that God wants the gifts that have been given to be developed — not just for one's own sake, but also for the common good and the building of the Kingdom. A Christian steward is called to be productive and to make a profound difference in the world. Stewardship promotes a way of life that is both privileged and challenging. A stewardship way of life is one that identifies the givers as Disciples of Christ. Stewardship is a way of life synonymous with being "Christian."

C. The U.S. Bishops underline three convictions in their Pastoral Letter:

1. First, each baptized Christian is called to be disciple of Christ. This calling is challenging, it's difficult, and it requires a daily struggle. It cannot be done. God's grace is needed. This comes through prayer.

2. Second, all are called to a change of heart through an entire way of life. It is not just tithing. It is not just giving ten percent of ones earnings; rather, it is giving a proportionate amount and then being held accountable for what we do with the other proportion. This change of heart — conversion — requires all to be involved with the mission of Jesus. It is not just giving a percentage of time; it is be involved completely in the mission of Jesus. People simply cannot spend time on a worthy parish project and then not be accountable with how they spend relaxation or entertainment time. The Christian steward recognizes that each breath is a gift from God.
3. Third, God calls all persons to look at who they are and what they do with the gift of life. The question must be asked, "What do I own, and what owns me?" At the time of death a person will ask, "Am I leaving my treasure or going to it?"

D. The Bishops talk about a number of destructive "isms": materialism, relativism, hedonism, individualism, consumerism; all of these exert a power influence on our society and make it more difficult for us to grow as disciples and good Christian stewards as we struggle to live out our lives according to God's will.

1. The Bishops see themselves, and us, as Catholic citizens of a wealthy, powerful nation facing many questions about its identity and role in the waning years of a troubled era. We are members of a community of faith blessed with many human and material resources, yet often uncertain about how to sustain and use them.
2. A Christian steward has a deep understanding, an insight of a certain way of seeing life and all that life holds. This insight is a grace in which we can see God present and active in the works of creation, not only at the beginning of time, but moment-to-moment, throughout our lives in the here and now. This outlook on life is the outlook of a Christian steward. The words that the Christian steward longs to hear are "Come, you who are blessed by my Father. Inherit the kingdom prepared for you from the foundation of the world" (Mt 25:34).

IV. A disciple's response.

A. A stewardship way of life is a set of values, a spirit that affects one's entire life. A good steward knows that life is beyond living with this constant urge of desire whenever they see what they don't have. Eternal fate is determined by the millions of mundane, daily decisions that one makes through the course of one's life.

B. There should be a definite difference between how a disciple lives and how their non-believing neighbor lives — especially in this materialistic world. The disciple's lifestyle should persuade their neighbor to want to draw nearer to Christ, because their focus is on God's people and God's kingdom, not things. Jesus speaks of hearts being where ones treasure is. Christians invest in other things beside homes, cars, food, entertainment, and all of the stuff that is vulnerable to rust, moth, and theft.

C. Stewardship is counter-cultural. In an affluent society, many are addicted to money, material things, machines, clothes, entertainment, and all that distracts from one's relationship with God.

1. A steward's efforts are focused on God. Similar to Jesus' challenging words that anyone who "wishes to come after me must deny himself, take up his cross, and follow me" (Mt 16:24), a steward allows for his or her ego to die, deprives

NOTES...

NOTES...

the self of immediate self-satisfaction, renounces the things of this world as mine, and recognizes all to be God's, to be used for God's glory, not for the glory of the self.

D. Stewardship is trusting God the Father to the extent that we trust as Jesus trusts, and live as Jesus lives. Jesus said many times that He came to do God's will, that He must be about the Father's work. Should we also base our lives on pleasing the Father? Jesus said He is the Truth. The Christian steward considers what Jesus would have me do in every circumstance of life knowing that God provides.

FOCUS QUESTIONS

1. How would you describe a spirituality of stewardship?
2. What trends in contempory culture prevent people from engaging in a life of stewardship?
3. If you were to do a presentation in your parish on the topic of stewardship, what would be the five most important points you would make?

Concluding prayers
Intercessions
Closing prayer
Hymn (optional)

RESOURCES

Catechism of the Catholic Church, 828,948, 2013-2015, 2683
Lumen gentium (Dogmatic Constitution on the Church), Vatican II
Stewardship: A Disciple's Response, United States Conference of Catholic Bishops
Essentials of the Faith, McBride, chap. 24

Session Forty-one

Catholic Spirituality

LEARNING OBJECTIVE

To present a clear understanding of the essential components of authentic Catholic spirituality.

Hymn: "The King of Love My Shepherd Is"

Invitation to prayer – silent prayer

Oration:

Lord God,
Shepherd of our souls,
you give us Christ,
the fullness of your revelation.
Help us to live by his gospel
through the holy life of Mother Church.

We ask this through our Lord Jesus Christ, your Son,
who lives and reigns with you and the Holy Spirit,
one God, for ever and ever.

Scripture reading: John 10:7-11

So Jesus said again, "Amen, amen, I say to you, I am the gate for the sheep. All who came [before me] are thieves and robbers, but the sheep did not listen to them. I am the gate. Whoever enters through me will be saved, and will come in and go out and find pasture. A thief comes only to steal and slaughter and destroy; I came so that they might have life and have it more abundantly. I am the good shepherd. A good shepherd lays down his life for the sheep."

TEACHING TO BE PRESENTED

I. The true nature of Roman Catholic spirituality.

The term "spirituality" is familiar in contemporary culture. Psychology and many aspects of the New Age Movement have broadened the scope and interpretation of spirituality. Because of these movements, it is important to be clear as to what "Catholic spirituality" truly is. Within the rich tradition of Catholicism, spirituality is the way a person responds to the call to holiness through the life of grace. Spirituality is a growing union with God through a personal relationship with Christ. This invitation to discipleship always involves conversion, a change of heart. Catholic Spirituality is a call to renounce sin, uniting ourselves to the Lord's preeminent victory over

NOTES...

sin and death, His Paschal Mystery. This call is intensely personal and it simultaneously bring us into communion with Christ's Bride, the Church. Through Baptism and the other sacraments, most especially the Eucharist, we are linked ever more deeply to Christ our Savior and to those redeemed by the Blood of His Cross. Catholic spirituality is based upon a "foundational spirituality" which involves the life of faith and prayer, a growing relationship with the Blessed Trinity, the sacraments, a love for Christ's Mystical Body the Church, and the transformation through grace to the witness of a life of holiness and the practice of faith, hope, and love.

II. The life of faith.

A. To believe is to live in a relationship of communion with God. Faith is a gift from God. Faith allows the certitude that the heart can find belonging in another — in God. God reveals Himself as "steadfast love" desirous of union with each created person. God at the same time gives His creatures free will. To believe in God is a decision that each person can choose or decide not to make. The Paschal Mystery of Christ is the great reality of death to self, giving rise to new life. Thus, to truly find the self, one must die to the self. Our hearts yearn for God, and life's fulfillment is never found in self-absorption but rather in transcending the self to be for another — for God.

B. The life of faith is a decision of the mind and heart. One cannot choose what one does not know. Accepting the message of Jesus as handed down through the teachings of the Church informs the mind. Through the will the heart chooses the truths of Christ. A person of faith entrusts the self to a relationship of love with Christ. Faith nurtures in the heart the conviction that it can find fulfillment in God alone. Faith must always be growing, strengthening one's center in God through Jesus and the Holy Spirit.

C. The act of faith is challenged in many ways. In a culture that is advocating the self and self-fulfillment as the ultimate goal of life, a "dying to self" approach does not appeal to the modern media audience. The life of faith has its own challenges.

1. The natural desire is to want to see what is so precious in life. God is not visible to the believer. This is a natural frustration. One must not be discouraged by the doubts this might provoke.
2. Catholics are called to believe in the Tradition of the Church. Faith, by its very nature, can cause doubt, darkness, and questions. This is a challenge to the believer. God cannot be seen with the human eye. However, faith provides its own certitude. Faith is more than feelings. It is a decision to accept the teachings of the Church. The life of faith is never static. As in any relationship, it is either growing or declining.
3. It is totally acceptable to question aspects of faith. This leads to deeper understanding when the questions are pursued. To question the issues of faith is not a betrayal to the One who is total Love. As long as the questions are asked with humility, faith seeking understanding will lead to enlightenment. Because the love of God is unfathomable in this life, a fullness of understanding is not to be expected. Each new insight leads to deeper commitment. Only in eternity will one have the vision that brings total certainty. In the meantime, faith is a romance with God to be lived in this life with joy and trust.
4. Questioning faith in a state of arrogance will not lead to peace. Anger that is improperly channeled will not lead to the "conversion of heart" leading to a deeper quest for the love abiding in God alone. One of the great tragedies of the life of faith is the barrier of anger misdirected.

5. The life of faith leads us to trust in God's merciful love. Scripture speaks of God's desire to extend His mercy. Despite the manifestations of evil in the contemporary world, hope is always God's gift because of His mercy.

NOTES...

III. The life of prayer.

Prayer is the engagement of the mind and heart as one seeks union with God. It is the life of grace transforming a person to become strengthened in their personal relationship with Christ. It is their participation in the life of the Trinity, God the Father, Son, and Holy Spirit. The fruits of this engagement are transformation into the likeness of Christ. People can expect a fulfilled life when they truly commit themselves to a life of prayer.

A. God deals with persons individually. Each person must discern what God is asking of them. A married couple raising a family will plan how they will integrate prayer into their family life. The most important aspect is how they will fulfill God's will for them. God's will for a person who entirely devotes their life to prayer in a monastic setting is different from an elderly couple living their retirement, awaiting entrance into eternal life. Praying the rosary and visiting the Parish Church for ten minutes a day to visit the Blessed Sacrament may be the prayer life of the elderly. For each varied circumstance, God will grace them according to their fidelity. A person who prays for fifteen minutes a day and a person in monastic life may both come to a profound union with God. Each person must discern what God is asking of him or her in prayer. God is the one who gives grace. As the giver of life, God is intimately involved in a personal relationship with those committed to faith and prayer.

B. The Life of Prayer has many expressions: Adoration, Praise, Thanksgiving, Petition. All people must familiarize themselves with the fundamentals of the life of prayer. All paths lead to contemplation with God. This is the highest form of prayer. Whatever their life's circumstances, if they are faithful to communion with God, they will find joy and peace in union with God. The life of prayer is the greatest challenge of the human heart, but fidelity will lead to the greatest fulfillment of the human spirit.

IV. The sacramental life.

Christians are initiated into the life of Christ through the Sacrament of Baptism. The Catholic Tradition is the only religion that traces its origins back to Christ without any deviations. All other denominations are sects. A sect is a group that has strayed from the original Church of the founder. Catholicism can trace its origins directly back to the person of Christ. Christ instituted the seven sacraments.

A. According to the *Catechism of the Catholic Church* the seven "sacraments are 'of the Church' in the double sense that they are 'by her' and 'for her.' They are 'by the Church,' for she is the sacrament of Christ's action at work in her through the mission of the Holy Spirit. They are 'for the Church' in the sense that 'the sacraments make the Church' (St. Augustine, *De civ. Dei*, 22, 17: PL 41, 779; cf. St. Thomas Aquinas, *STh* III, 64, 2 *ad* 3), since they manifest and communicate to men, above all in the Eucharist, the mystery of communion with the God who is love, One in three persons" (CCC 1118).

B. The Catholic Church possesses the fullness of Christ's life through the seven sacraments. No other sect has this fullness. "'Since all the faithful form one body, the good of each is communicated to the others.... We must therefore believe that

NOTES...

there exists a communion of goods in the Church. But the most important member is Christ, since he is the head.... Therefore, the riches of Christ are communicated to all the members, through the sacraments' (St. Thomas Aquinas, *Symb.*, 10). 'As this Church is governed by one and the same Spirit, all the goods she has received necessarily become a common fund' (*Roman Catechism* I, 10, 24)" (CCC 947).

V. **Loving the Church.**

A. A common comment among poorly informed Catholics is "I love your Jesus but not your Church." A common criticism directed to many contemporary Catholics is that they have a cafeteria mentality. They think they can pick and choose what they want to believe. This mentality has caused serious discrepancies in the formation of and witness to people choosing to live a Catholic life.

B. The perfection of the calling and belonging to the Catholic Church is charity. This goal of holiness "'governs, shapes, and perfects all the means of sanctification' (LG 42)" (CCC 826).

1. To choose Catholicism means to accept in faith all components of what it means to be Catholic.
2. The Church is made up of people in need of redemption. The Church embraces sinners. All members of the Church, including her ministers, must acknowledge that they are sinners (cf. 1 Jn 1: 8-10). In everyone, the weeds of sin will still be mixed with the good wheat of the Gospel until the end of time (cf. Mt 13:24-30).
3. Hence the Church gathers sinners already caught up in Christ's salvation but still on the way to holiness:

   "The Church is therefore holy, though having sinners in her midst, because she herself has no other life but the life of grace. If they live her life, her members are sanctified; if they move away from her life, they fall into sins and disorders that prevent the radiation of her sanctity (cf. 1 Jn 1:8-10). This is why she suffers and does penance for these offences, of which she has the power to free her children through the blood of Christ and the gift of the Holy Spirit" (CPG #19).

4. Learn to love the Church as Christ does. Christ has chosen the Church to be His mystical body. He sacrificed His life for His Bride, the Church.

C. The Church as Mystery of Christ.

1. The Church as Mystery of Christ cannot be defined. It can only be viewed in light of the "Mystery of Christ." In order to exist in culture, the Church, like every other institution, must have a structure to maintain effective and stable functioning in society. The Church has a hierarchy. Often people confuse the need for a structure within the Church as the essence of Church. Every human organization needs a structure.
2. As a mystery of God's love, the Church is the Bride of Christ, the Mystical Body, the proclaimer of the Good News of Christ. The Church has great concern for society, and in her history the world has benefited from her concern for the common good of all people. People who see the Church from the perspective of Christ come to love the Church. Christ, through his Bride, the Church, calls all to union. Life is about redemption and the journey to eternity, forever with God. In this life, each person has the capacity to choose good or evil. The Church leads all people to goodness and love.

VI. Ecclesial movements within the Church.

NOTES...

A. Catholicism has a rich diversity of expressions. This is good, as long as these expressions stay faithful to life in the Church.

1. The Holy Spirit brings unity to diversity.
2. Each Catholic is called to live a foundational spirituality which includes the life of faith, prayer, and sacraments within the Church.

B. Catholic life is lived in a parish. Parishes make up a diocese guided by a teacher and shepherd, namely the bishop, who is appointed by the Pope.

C. There are also many ecclesial communities in the Church. For some members of the Church, belonging to one of these groups helps them in their journey to God. Not all people, however, feel called to belong to such a group.

1. Each person is called to life in a parish, and an ecclesial community is not a substitute for this.
2. Some contemporary ecclesial communities are:
   - Communion and Liberation
   - The Charismatic Movement
   - Focolare
   - Opus Dei
   - The Neocatechumenal Way

   There are also many others.
3. Each of these movements has a *charism*, or a gift of service to others. For example, Opus Dei is meant to focus in a special way on finding God in work and daily life. The Neocatechumenal Way emphasizes a renewed living of baptismal promises.
4. These movements in no way give an added guarantee to eternal salvation in Christ, but many people find them to be a positive experience in their journey.
5. God looks into the heart of each person and awaits the "yes" of faith, the growing union through sacramental life, and the witness of a life transformed by charity.
   a. Whether or not one is a member of an ecclesial group, the important reality is to respect how God draws each person to himself through the life of the parish church.
   b. True humility in imitation of Christ eliminates any form of elitism.

D. The Catholic Church provides a rich and profound spirituality for each and every person. The challenge is to accept the call to holiness and to be faithful to its journey.

VII. New Age spirituality.

A. In our contemporary world, confusion exists regarding spirituality. Sometimes psychology is considered spirituality. A greater challenge that has arisen is called "New Age" spirituality. In the last number of decades, technology and the vast arenas of communication have enticed people with trends that appeal to either the poorly informed or those who have lost faith in the centrality of the Incarnation of Christ and belief in the Blessed Trinity. New Age spirituality appeals to those seeking the divine in their lives.

B. In 2003 the Pontifical Council for Culture presented the Church with a Christian reflection on the "New Age" called *Jesus Christ, The Bearer of the Water of Life: A Christian Reflection on the "New Age."* This document identifies that much of what

NOTES...

is being called New Age is really not new. Rather, it is a return to ancient gnostic ideas that existed in the Second and Third centuries.

C. In looking at some of the central themes of the New Age, the 2003 document states:

> *New Age* is not, properly speaking, a religion, but it is interested in what is called "divine." The essence of *New Age* is the loose association of the various activities, ideas, and people who might be attracted to the term. So there is no single articulation of anything like the doctrines of mainstream religions. Despite this, and despite the immense variety within *New Age*, there are some common points:
> - the cosmos is seen as an organic whole
> - it is animated by an Energy, which is also identified as the divine Soul or Spirit
> - much credence is given to the mediation of various spiritual entities
> - humans are capable of ascending to invisible higher spheres, and of controlling their own lives beyond death
> - there is held to be a "perennial knowledge" which pre-dates and is superior to all religions and cultures
> - people follow enlightened masters.

D. New Age spirituality is complex. Because of its wide permeation within contemporary culture, it is necessary for people to be very discerning.

E. Catholic Spirituality is founded upon Jesus Christ, the human and divine person sent by God, as the fullness of His Revelation. Through the Holy Spirit, the third person of the Blessed Trinity, Catholic Spirituality brings new life to each person destined to eternal beatitude with God.

FOCUS QUESTIONS

1. Explain why the life of faith and prayer are essential to Catholic Spirituality.
2. What would you say to people who believe they can have a relationship with Jesus without the Church?
3. How can a Catholic know whether or not they are involved in the *New Age Movement*?

Concluding prayers
Intercessions
Closing prayer
Hymn (optional)

RESOURCES

Catechism of the Catholic Church, 826, 947, 1118
Dives in misericordia (The Mercy of God), John Paul II
Jesus Christ, The Bearer of the Water of Life: A Christian Reflection on the "New Age." Pontifical Council for Culture, Pontifical Council for Interreligious Dialogue
Lumen gentium (Dogmatic Constitution on the Church), Vatican II
Solemni Hac Liturgia (Credo of the People of God: Solemn Profession of Faith), Paul VI
Ecclesiam suam (Paths of the Church), Paul VI

Session Forty-two

Being an Active Parishioner

Spiritual and Corporal Works of Mercy

LEARNING OBJECTIVE

To understand the pastoral care of one's particular parish and the need to share that role through ministry, prayer, and other works of charity based on the concerns of the community.

Hymn: "We Are Many Parts"

Invitation to prayer — silent prayer

Oration:

God our Father,
in all churches scattered throughout the world
you show forth the one, holy, catholic and apostolic Church.
Through the gospel and the eucharist
bring your people together in the Holy Spirit
and guide us in your love.
Make us a sign of your love for all people,
and help us to show forth
the living presence of Christ in the world,
who lives and reigns with you and the Holy Spirit,
one God, for ever and ever.

Opening Prayer
Mass for the Local Church (E)

Scripture reading: Philippians 2:1-5

If there is any encouragement in Christ, any solace in love, any participation in the Spirit, any compassion and mercy, complete my joy by being of the same mind, with the same love, united in heart, thinking one thing. Do nothing out of selfishness or out of vainglory; rather, humbly regard others as more important than yourselves, each looking out not for his own interests, but [also] everyone for those of others.

Have among yourselves the same attitude that is also yours in Christ Jesus.

NOTES...

TEACHING TO BE PRESENTED

I. The parish community.

A. The nature of parish.

1. "'A *parish* is a definite community of the Christian faithful established on a stable basis within a particular church' (CIC, can. 515 § 1)" (CCC 2179).
2. A pastor (or shepherd) is given charge over the parish by the authority of the diocesan bishop (CCC 2179).

B. Faith formation through parish life.

1. The parish initiates Catholics into the ordinary expression of liturgical life. It gathers them together in the celebration of Sunday Mass. It offers an opportunity to share at the Eucharistic table even on a daily basis. Ample times are planned and announced for regular reception of the sacrament of Penance. Parish missions also enhance the spiritual development of Catholics and bring the parish together as a faith-filled community (CCC 2179).
2. The parish teaches an understanding of the Word of God and the doctrine of the Church. Of particular concern are programs in preparation for the sacraments (i.e. RCIA, RCIC, Baptism preparation, First Penance preparation, First Holy Communion preparation, Confirmation preparation, marriage preparation).
3. The parish cares about the religious education of young people. Although this responsibility falls chiefly on parents, the parish facilitates solid classroom opportunities for catechesis. Care is always taken in the preparation of catechists who love the Church and desire to impart solid and love-filled knowledge to young Catholics. Parish elementary schools and diocesan high schools should be seen as true gifts to the community and a source of grace for the Catholic community.
4. Parishes should provide opportunities for the continuing education of adults in the faith. Bible studies and other catechetical formation programs are vital to a parish.

C. A life of service through parish activity.

1. The parish practices charity through good works in the community. The pastor sees to it that the sick, the elderly, and the dying are regularly visited and their sacramental needs are fulfilled. Collections of money, food, and clothing for the poor are visible signs that the parish is truly alive in the spirit of social justice.
2. The parish must remain a visible sign of welcome to all people, especially those whom the world might reject. Each parish must stand as a haven of peace, a home for the poor, and a place where prejudice and discrimination are not tolerated. Those with physical disabilities should feel welcome in the parish church. Care should be taken to assist those with specific needs (i.e. providing access for people with disabilities and assistance for the hearing impaired).
3. The pastoral council is a team of dedicated parishioners who advise the pastor concerning the spiritual needs of the parish. Such a body provides an important link between the priest and his people.
4. Care should be taken to explain to parishioners the true meaning of tithing. Many parishes have instituted "sacrificial giving" programs to help people understand the good that a parish can do through proper administration and responsible stewardship. Care should also be taken to properly explain the

importance of the annual Bishop's Appeal and the necessary help which it provides for the financial development and outreach for all of the needs of the diocese. Each pastor selects certain men and women to advise him in the financial matters of the parish.

5. Those who are to be initiated into the Catholic faith must be made aware of their obligation to be active parishioners. They should feel truly welcomed into the parish community and should know that the entire parish supports them in prayer through their spiritual journey and discernment process.
6. It is imperative that new Catholics are introduced to the members of the parish staff. Such an opportunity to meet workers in every field of parish life might best be incorporated into this particular evening of reflection.

NOTES...

II. The corporal and spiritual works of mercy.

A. Corporal works of mercy.

1. Feed the hungry.
2. Give drink to the thirsty.
3. Clothe the naked.
4. Visit those in prison.
5. Shelter the homeless.
6. Visit the sick.
7. Bury the dead.

B. Spiritual works of mercy.

1. Admonish the sinner.
2. Instruct the ignorant.
3. Counsel the doubtful.
4. Comfort the sorrowful.
5. Bear wrongs patiently.
6. Forgive all injuries.
7. Pray for the living and the dead.

C. The Church traditionally lists obligations by which Christians have to physically and spiritually help those in need. A great deal of these works of mercy have already been covered in the sections on the Ten Commandments. The works of mercy should be applied to daily living and the viable life of any parish community (CCC 2447).

III. The precepts of the Church.

A. The precepts of the Church are moral obligations nourished by liturgical prayer. These precepts are "meant to guarantee to the faithful the very necessary minimum in the spirit of prayer and moral effort, in the growth in love of God and neighbor" (CCC 2041).

1. The first precept: attending Mass on Sundays and Holy Days of Obligation.
2. The second precept: confessing sins at least once a year.
3. The third precept: receiving Holy Communion at least during the Easter season.
4. The fourth precept: observing the prescribed days of fasting and abstinence.
5. The fifth precept: helping to provide for the needs of the Church.

B. Parishioners have the obligation of assisting the parish in regards to its material needs.

1. Monetarily, one gives according to one's means.

NOTES...

2. Volunteering through the giving of time and talents is another way of fulfilling this obligation (CCC 2043).

FOCUS QUESTIONS

1. Why is it important to be a member of a parish?
2. What is the relationship of the spiritual works of mercy and virtue?
3. Canon Law tells us that we only need to confess serious sins. The precepts of the Church oblige us to confess our sins once a year. What is the wisdom of this precept?

Concluding prayers
Intercessions
Closing prayer
Hymn (optional)

RESOURCES

Catechism of the Catholic Church, 2179, 2447, 2041-2043

Index of Hymns

Hymns are found in *Worship* unless otherwise indicated.

Session One: "On Eagle's Wings," *Gather,* p. 261
Session Two: "The King of Love My Shepherd Is," p. 609
Session Three: "Faith of Our Fathers," p. 571
Session Four: "Holy, Holy, Holy! Lord God Almighty," p. 485
Session Five: "Sing Praise to Our Creator," *People's Mass Book,* p. 43
Session Six: "Praise to the Lord, the Almighty," p. 547
Session Seven: "Turn to Me," *Glory and Praise, Volume I,* p. 57
Session Eight: "O Come, O Come, Emmanuel," p. 357
Session Nine: "Let All Mortal Flesh Keep Silence," p. 523
Session Ten: "Sing of Mary, Pure and Lowly", p. 404
Session Eleven: "The Cry of the Poor," *Gather,* p. 26
Session Twelve: "O Sacred Head Surrounded," p. 434
Session Thirteen: "Crown Him with Many Crowns," p. 496
Session Fourteen: "Come, Holy Ghost," p. 482
Session Fifteen: "O Christ the Great Foundation," p. 618
Session Sixteen: "We Remember," *Gather,* p. 417
Session Seventeen: "For All the Saints," p. 705
Session Eighteen: "Jerusalem, My Happy Home," p. 690
Session Nineteen: "Earthen Vessels," *Glory and Praise, Volume I,* p. 17
Session Twenty: "Grant to Us, O Lord, a Heart Renewed," *Christian Prayer Book,* Hymn 90, p. 605
Session Twenty-one: "Praise God From Whom All Blessings Flow," *Glory and Praise,* p. 682
Session Twenty-two: "You Are Near," *Glory and Praise,* Volume I, p. 59
Session Twenty-three: "Amazing Grace," p. 583
Session Twenty-four: "What Wondrous Love Is This," p. 600
Session Twenty-five: "Praise, My Soul, the King of Heaven," p. 530
Session Twenty-six: "At the Lamb's High Feast We Sing," p. 459
Session Twenty-seven: "At That First Eucharist," p. 733
Session Twenty-eight: "Gift of Finest Wheat," p. 736
Session Twenty-nine: "O Christ, the Healer," p. 747
Session Thirty: "When Love Is Found," p. 745
Session Thirty-one: "Alleluia! Sing to Jesus," p. 737
Session Thirty-two: "All People That On Earth Do Dwell," p. 669
Session Thirty-three: "Go Make of All Disciples," p. 628
Session Thirty-four: "Gather Us In," p. 665
Session Thirty-five: "To Jesus Christ Our Sovereign King," p. 497
Session Thirty-six: "Anthem," *Gather,* p. 298
Session Thirty-seven: "The Church's One Foundation," p. 618
Session Thirty-eight: "One Bread, One Body," *Glory and Praise,* p. 499
Session Thirty-nine: "Where Charity and Love Prevail," *Glory and Praise,* p. 644
Session Forty: "Will You Let Me Be Your Servant," *Gather,* p. 476

NOTES...

Session Forty-one: "The King of Love My Shepherd Is," p. 609
Session Forty-two: "We Are Many Parts," *Gather*, p. 310

Deiss, Lucien. *Biblical Hymns and Psalms, Volume I.* Cincinnati, OH: World Library, 1965.
Gather. Chicago, IL: GIA Publications, 1988.
Glory and Praise, Volume I. Phoenix, AZ: North American Liturgy Resources, 1977.
Glory and Praise, Second Edition. NE Hassalo, Portland: OCP Publications, 2001.
People's Mass Book. Cincinnati, OH: World Library Publications, 1970-1971.
Worship. Chicago, IL: GIA Publications, 1986.

Bibliography

CCC — *Catechism of the Catholic Church, Second Edition.* Washington, DC: United States Catholic Conference, 1997 (Libreria Editrice Vaticana).

Codex Iuris Canonici (Code of Canon Law). Washington, DC: Canon Law Society of America, 1983.

Biblical Basis for the Catholic Faith, The. Salza, John, Huntington, IN: Our Sunday Visitor, 2005.

Dictionary of the Bible. McKenzie, S.J., John L., New York, NY: Touchstone Book - Published by Simon & Schuster, 1995.

Dictionary of Biblical Theology. Leon-Dufour, Xavier. Ijamsville, Maryland: Word Among Us Press, 1988.

Encyclopedia of Catholic Devotions and Practices. Ball, Ann, Huntington, IN: Our Sunday Visitor, 2002.

Essentials of the Faith Updated: A Guide to the Catechism of the Catholic Church. McBride, O.Praem., Alfred, Huntington, IN: Our Sunday Visitor, 2002.

How to Read the New Testament. Charpentier, Etienne, New York, NY: The Crossroad Publishing Company, 2000.

How to Read the Old Testament. Charpentier, Etienne, New York, NY: The Crossroad Publishing Company, 1982.

New Catholic Answer Bible, The. Thigpen, Paul, editor, Huntington, IN: Our Sunday Visitor, 2005.

Our Sunday Visitor's Encyclopedia of Catholic Doctrine. Shaw, Russell, editor, Huntington, IN: Our Sunday Visitor, 1997.

Our Sunday Visitor's Encyclopedia of Saints. Bunson, Matthew; Bunson, Margaret; Bunson, Stephen; Huntington, IN: Our Sunday Visitor, 2003.

OSV's Encyclopedia of Catholic History Revised. Bunson, Matthew, Huntington, IN: Our Sunday Visitor, 2004.

Separated Brethren, Revised: A Review of Protestant, Anglican, Eastern Orthodox, & Other Religions in the United States. Whalen, William J., Huntington, IN: Our Sunday Visitor, 2002.

Vatican Council II: The Conciliar and Post Conciliar Documents, New Revised Edition, Volume 1. Flannery, Austin, O.P., editor, Northport, NY: Costello Publishing Company, 1992.

Vatican Council II: More Post Conciliar Documents, Volume 2. Flannery, Austin, O.P., editor, Northport, NY: Costello Publishing Company, 1982.

NOTES...

Where We Got the Bible: Our Debt to the Catholic Church. Graham, Henry G., Rockford, IL: TAN Books & Publishers, 1977.

Documents of Vatican Council II

SC — *Sacrosanctum concilium* (Constitution on the Sacred Liturgy). December 4, 1963.

LG — *Lumen gentium* (Dogmatic Constitution on the Church). November 21, 1964.

UR — *Unitatis redintegratio* (Decree on Ecumenism). November 21, 1964.

MF — *Mysterium Fidei* (Mystery of Faith). September 3, 1965.

CD — *Christus dominus* (Decree on the Pastoral Office of Bishops in the Church). October 28, 1965.

NA — *Nostra aetate* (Declaration on the Relation of the Church to Non-Christian Religions). October 28, 1965.

DV — *Dei verbum* (Dogmatic Constitution on Divine Revelation). November 8, 1965.

AGD — *Ad gentes divinitus* (Decree on the Church's Missionary Activity). December 7, 1965.

GS — *Gaudium et spes* (Pastoral Constitution on the Church in the Modern World). December 7, 1965.

United States Bishops

GDC — *General Directory for Catechesis.* Washington, DC: United States Catholic Conference, 1999. Congregation for the Clergy.

Sowing Seeds: Notes and Comments on the General Directory for Catechesis. Washington, DC: United States Catholic Conference, 2000. Department of Education, United States Catholic Conference.

National Directory for Catechesis. Washington, DC: United States Conference of Catholic Bishops Publishing, May 1, 2005.

Adult Catechesis in the Christian Community. Washington, DC: Office for Publishing and Promotion Services, United States Catholic Conference, 1990. International Council for Catechesis.

Our Hearts Were Burning Within Us. Washington, DC: United States Catholic Conference, 1999. United States Conference of Catholic Bishops.

Nurturing Adult Faith: A Manual for Parish Leaders. Washington, DC: National Conference for Catechetical Leadership, 2003.

General Instruction of the Roman Missal. Washington, DC: United States Conference of Catholic Bishops Publishing, 2003.

Stewardship: A Disciple's Response. Washington, DC: United States Conference of Catholic Bishops Publishing, 1993.

Economic Justice All. Washington, DC: United States Conference of Catholic Bishops Publishing, 1986.

Called to Global Solidarity. Washington, DC: Office of Social Development and World Peace, United States Conference of Catholic Bishops, 1997.

Sharing Catholic Social Teaching: Challenges and Directions. Washington, DC: Office of Social Development and World Peace, United States Conference of Catholic Bishops, 1998.

Living the Gospel of Life: A Challenge to American Catholics. Washington, DC: Secretariat for Pro-Life Activities, United States Conference of Catholic Bishops, 1998.

Catholic Perspective on Crime and Criminal Justice. 2001.

Everyday Christianity: To Hunger and Thirst for Justice. 2001.

Faithful Citizenship: A Catholic Call of Political Responsibility. Washington, DC: United States Conference of Catholic Bishops, 2003.

By Pope John Paul II

RH — *Redemptor hominis* (The Redeemer of Man). March 4, 1979.

CT — *Catechesi tradendae* (Catechesis in our Time). October 16, 1979.

DM — *Dives in misericordia* (The Mercy of God). November 30, 1980.

LE — *Laborem Exercens* (On Human Work). September 14, 1981.

FC — *Familiaris Consortio* (The Role of the Christian Family in the Modern World). November 22, 1981).

APR — *Aperite portas Redemptori* (Open the Doors to the Redeemer). January 6, 1983.

SD — *Salvifici doloris* (On the Christian Meaning of Human Suffering). February 11, 1984.

RD — *Redemptionis donum* (Apostolic Exhortation of His Holiness John Paul II to Men and Women Religious). March 25, 1984.

To the Youth of the World. March 31, 1985.

DeV — *Dominum et Vivificantem* (The Holy Spirit in the Life of the Church and the World). May 18, 1986.

RMat — *Redemptoris Mater* (Mother of the Redeemer). March 25, 1987.

MD — *Mulieris Dignitatem* (On the Dignity and Vocation of Women). August 15, 1988.

CL — *Christifideles laici* (Lay Members of Christ's Faithful People). December 30, 1988.

VS — *Veritatis Splendor* (The Splendor of Truth). August 6, 1993.

OS — *Ordinatio Sacerdotalis* (On Reserving Priestly Ordination to Men Alone). April 22, 1994.

EV — *Evangelium vitae* (The Gospel of Life). March 25, 1995.

UUS — *Ut unum sint* (On Commitment to Ecumenism). May 25, 1995.

The Genius of Women. June 29, 1995.

NOTES...

NOTES...

EE — *Ecclesia de Eucharistia* (On the Eucharist in Its Relationship to the Church). April 17, 2003.

MND — *Mane Nobiscum Domine* (Stay With Us, Lord). October 7, 2004.

By Pope Paul VI

Sacerdotalis caelibatus (On the celibacy of the priest). June 24, 1967.

ES — *Ecclesiam suam* (Paths of the Church). August 6, 1964.

ID — *Indulgentiarum doctrina* (On Indulgences). January 1, 1967.

CPG — *Solemni Hac Liturgia* (Credo of the People of God: Solemn Profession of Faith). June 30, 1968.

HV — *Humanae vitae* (On the regulation of birth). July 29, 1968.

DCN — *Divinae consortium naturae* (On the Sacrament of Confirmation). August 15, 1971.

MC — *Marialis cultus* (For the Right Ordering and Development of Devotion to the Blessed Virgin Mary). February 2, 1974.

PP — *Populorum progressio* (On the Development of Peoples). March 26, 1976.

By Pope John XXIII

MM — *Mater et Magistra* (On Christianity and social progress). May 15, 1961.

PT — *Pacem in terris* (Peace on Earth). April 11, 1963.

By Pope Pius XII

HG — *Humani generis* (Concerning some false opinions threatening to undermine the foundations of Catholic doctrine). August 12, 1950.

By Pope Leo XIII

RN — *Rerum Novarum* (On the condition of the working class). May 15, 1891

Other Documents

Jesus Christ, The Bearer of the Water of Life: A Christian Reflection on the "New Age." Pontifical Council for Culture, Pontifical Council for Interreligious Dialogue.

Catholic Traditions in the Home and Classroom: 365 Days to Celebrate a Catholic Year. Ball, Ann. Huntington, IN: Our Sunday Visitor, 2005.

Compendium of the Social Doctrine of the Church. Pontifical Council for Justice and Peace, Rome. October 25, 2004.

Gifts of the Spirit: Multiple Intelligences in Religious Education. Nuzzi, Ronald. Washington, DC: National Catholic Educational Association, 1999.

Holy Communion and Worship of the Eucharist Outside Mass. Sacred Congregation for Divine Worship, 1973.

Contributors

Most Reverend John M. D'Arcy
Bishop of Fort Wayne-South Bend

Sister M. Jane Carew
Director of Catechesis
Diocese of Fort Wayne-South Bend

Margaret Hanlon
Theology Teacher

Victoria Schwab
Theology Teacher

Paul Thigpen
Editor, *The Catholic Answer*

Harry Verhiley
Director of Development
Diocese of Fort Wayne-South Bend

NOTES...

NOTES...

NOTES...